GUERRILLA
GARDENING

GUERRILLA GARDENING

GARDENING

A Manualfesto

David Tracey

NEW SOCIETY PUBLISHERS
CITY OF KAWARTHA LAKES

Cataloging in Publication Data:
A catalog record for this publication is available
from the National Library of Canada.

Cover design by Diane McIntosh. Images: iStock.
Interior photos: David Tracey unless otherwise specified.
Back cover photo: Maya McKechneay.

Printed in Canada.
First printing March 2007.

New Society Publishers acknowledges the support of the Government of Canada
through the Book Publishing Industry Development Program (BPIDP)
for our publishing activities.

Paperback ISBN: 978-0-86571-583-7

Inquiries regarding requests to reprint all or part of *Guerrilla Gardening*
should be addressed to New Society Publishers at the address below.

To order directly from the publishers,
please call toll-free (North America) 1-800-567-6772,
or order online at www.newsociety.com

Any other inquiries can be directed by mail to:

New Society Publishers
P.O. Box 189, Gabriola Island, BC V0R 1X0, Canada
(250) 247-9757

New Society Publishers' mission is to publish books that contribute in fundamental ways to building an ecologically sustainable and just society, and to do so with
the least possible impact on the environment, in a manner that models this vision.
We are committed to doing this not just through education, but through action.
We are acting on our commitment to the world's remaining ancient forests by
phasing out our paper supply from ancient forests worldwide. This book is one
step toward ending global deforestation and climate change. It is printed on acid-
free paper that is 100% old growth forest-free (100% post-consumer recycled),
processed chlorine free, and printed with vegetable-based, low-VOC inks. For further information, or to browse our full list of books and purchase securely, visit
our website at: www.newsociety.com

NEW SOCIETY PUBLISHERS   www.newsociety.com

For every
planter, weeder, grafter, or reaper
who lept the fence to share

*All my relations**

*Traditional blessing among Indiginous Peoples
that has also leapt the fence.

Contents

Introduction 1

  Ever onward 3
  You rule 4
  School's out 7
  Right of way 8
  Now fear this 13
  City of no return 14
  How to use this book 16
  Are you the one? 17

1 The Big Idea (Or What to Say
   If You're Stopped) 19

  A brief history 19
  Lock down, plant up .21
  By the people, for the people 22
  Yippie Park 24
  Green Guerrillas 24
  If I can do it... Donald Loggins 34
  Power Plant — Nasturtium (*Tropaeolum majus*) 35

2 Where to Start (You DO Live Here
   So Why Aren't You Home By Now?) 37

  Think eco-citizen 39
  The forest not the trees 44
  Nature on holiday 45
  Wilderness is within 46
  Cities are alive 46
  Starting-out spaces 47
  A tale of two cities 48
  Use it or lose it 50
  Grow up 50
  Get back 53

Park this 53
Green roofs are the new black 54
Bed time 55
All roads lead to home 56
You said it — Robert Sarti 57
If I can do it... Robert Klose 58
Power Plant — Poppy (*Papaver somniferum*) 59

**3 What to Use (Don't Reinvent the Wheel,
Borrow Someone's Car)** **61**
Coolest tools 61
Dig this 63
More for less 67
Fund-raising fun 67
Dirt-cheap dirt 69
Black gold 71
Garden goods 72
Real free trade 73
Seeds of death 73
Free rain 74
Digging for treasure 76
You said it — Loren Rieseberg 76
If I can do it... Bev Wagar 78
Power Plant — Sunflower (*Helianthus annuus*) 80

4 Growing Basics (The Root End Goes Down) **81**
Think like a plant 82
The dirt on dirt 85
Fertilizers and all that crap 86
No mono 89
Pests or friends 90
Why natives rule 91
Easy edible landscaping 92
Seed bombs 93
You said it — David Tarrant 95
If I can do it... Al Pasternak 97
Power Plant — Potato (*Solanum tuberosum*) 98

**5 Naturescaping 101 (There's Always
Somebody Home in a Habitat)** **101**
Land claims 103
Designing for diversity 104

Will chirp for food 107
Room to grow 108
Don't be a buggist 109
No slugsidized housing 111
You said it — Terry Taylor 112
If I can do it... Susan Kurbis 116
Power Plant — Apple (*Malus domestica*) 118

6 Get Off the Grass (Make It a Meadow) 121

Good crop, bad crop 122
Kick your grass 125
Fields of dreams 126
From the ground up 128
You said it — Bill Stephen 129
If I can do it... Mark Yardas 132
Power Plant — Lavender (*Lavendula species*) 134

7 Grow Your Own Community Garden (It Takes a Village to Raise a Turnip) 137

Garden grail 138
Choose the right place 139
Choose the right people 143
Call to order 144
How to ward off developers (and their offspring) 145
Link it or lose it 147
What have you done for me lately? 147
Grow your own 149
Q&A — Muggs Sigurgeirson 150
If I can do it... Les King 153
Power Plant — Sweet pea (*Lathyrus odoratus*) 154

8 When to Work Within (The Art of Aikido Politics) 157

The care and feeding of city officials 159
Push or pull 162
You're blocking 164
Oh bother 164
Q&A — Alan Duncan 166
If I can do it... Tom Wuest 171
Power Plant — Scarlet runner bean (*Phaseolus
coccineus*) 173

9 Start Spreading the News (Information
   Is Just Fertilizer With Better PR) 175

Mass media and how to move it 176
What's the news? 179
Right on time 181
I'm busted 182
Alternative media options 184
Signs that work, signs that don't 185
Q&A — Peter Gibson 186
Power Plant — Jerusalem artichoke (*Helianthus
   tuberosus*) 193
If I can do it... Matthew Green .194
Power Plant — Blueberry (*Vaccinium species*) 196

Conclusion: Where to Go From Here
   (Make Your City the Salvation of the World) . .199

Living *la vida local* 200
Go team go 200
You are the culture 201
Live in the city of your dreams 202
Get up and grow 203
Q&A — Jim Diers 205
If I can do it... Amy Twigge 207

Bibliography 211
Notes 215
Index 219
About the Author .227

Introduction

Have you ever been walking down some gray and dreary street, feeling gray and dreary yourself, when you spotted a flower growing out of the pavement and it changed your whole day?

Me neither. But it could happen if more people became guerrilla gardeners. That's the hope of this book.

It's meant to be two things: 1) a manual for people using plants to reclaim public space for the public good, and 2) a manifesto inspiring you to join them. So it's a manualfesto. Not quite a call to arms, but something better: a case for shovels (long-handled to save your back, although trowels are great for clandestine work).

You could also consider it a guidebook to urban adventure. Guerrilla gardening is exciting, tiring, heartening, enlightening and more. You'll feel a warm glow of achievement at growing beauty out of urban blight. Blisters and sore muscles too, but the pain will be sweetened by knowing it comes from a body rediscovering ancient rhythms of work on the land. But let's not stop there. The more lasting changes, and the real blossoming, may happen within.

Guerrilla gardening offers a way to see your city in a different light. You may redefine your role as a citizen as you discover new ground on which to make a stand. Start by shedding that urban exoskeleton of cynicism and dread. Continue by merging into a larger movement of all things living. No longer a passive consumer, you become what has never been needed more: an active citizen engaged in your environment.

Guided by an eco-based code of ethics, armed with a determination to make the landscape itself a declaration of interdepend-

If you throw back your shoulders and look up into the sky, you will see what else is yours.

— Alfred Carl Hottes

ence, watch what happens when you move to the pulse of the planet. You have environmental insights and political epiphanies. You begin to reshape your days to reflect a more natural world view. You learn how to merge with the cycles, seasons and flows. Your hands get dirty and your back gets sore and you love it, because you know it means you're truly alive. Count on all this to not only sharpen the significance of your everyday routines but — stay with me here — to put you on the right side of history in the most important battle of our time: the struggle to determine how we'll all live together in the cities of the future.

Phew.

Got all that?

Good. Because now comes the fair warning.

Guerrilla gardening is not for everyone. You should know this from the start. It's not all sunshine and daisies. The title may sound romantic, but the work can be grueling. Sites may, by definition, be uninviting. Growing conditions are often harsh. Routine chores can be a logistical grind.

You say fence, we say link in the global struggle for urban salad liberation.

No matter how hard you try and how many hurdles you leap, it may still not be enough. Some of your campaigns will end in defeat. The emotional high you reach on one project — say in turning a chain link fence into a living salad — will only make the drop seem that much steeper on your next when the Man (or the Man's saggy-uniformed security guy) rips out your entire field of zinnias.

Ever onward

It's never fun to lose, especially when the loss involves not just some seedlings but the brilliant future they once contained. Yet that must not deter you. A guerrilla gardener cannot dwell. You must forget that the odds are always against you and defeat forever a few boot-stomps away. Remind yourself instead that every garden is a gamble, then repeat your vow to keep growing.

What else can go wrong?

Oh, right. You might get arrested.

It would be unusual. But since you may be, strictly speaking, planting on property which at least in some literal sense you don't exactly *own*, legal implications are possible. No point denying it. There are laws on these things. They could be used against you. You could go to jail.

So let's be honest. If you feel for whatever reason that you're not up to the mission, put this book down, back slowly away and return to your comfortable life. No one will fault you. On the contrary. You know your limits better than anyone. You understand the importance of staying within a comfort zone when making key life choices. So do what you must. Thank you for coming. And good luck.

Still with us?

Good. Because that warning was just a ruse to get the naysayers out of the room. The reality is that while you may get questioned or even stopped, it's unlikely you would ever be charged. Unless you wanted to be, of course, to make a case or because you feel a jail cell makes the best backdrop for a political declaration.

It turns out the declining crime rate all over North America has yet to reach the point where police squads must busy themselves with vegetables. And even if you were by some mean quirk brought in and then charged, a conviction would still be unex-

The force that through the green fuse drives the flower Drives my green age

— Dylan Thomas

pected. Who would rule against you? There are 90 million gardeners in North America. You need just one of them on your jury or in the judge's chair. Gardeners are a tribe. They understand each other. They commiserate. Weather, slugs, powdery mildew? They know, and how terrible. Cops who don't even grow their own tomatoes? Tsk-tsk.

Even so, if the prospect of a mug shot and a rap sheet is still making you nervous (implausible as it may be), you needn't worry. There's plenty to be done in guerrilla gardening that is entirely legal. That part is up to you.

You rule

In fact, every part is up to you. Guerrilla gardening is autonomy in green. You don't have to join a club or pay any dues or accept any codes. You even get to define it for yourself. I call it "gardening public space with or without permission." But as definitions go, I have to admit, that's pretty thin.

The gardening part is easy enough, if we can agree it means "tending a defined space for the cultivation or appreciation of natural things, usually plants but not necessarily if you include weird art like those giant blue tubes representing pencils or something."

Woody Guthrie's most famous song "This Land Is Your Land" was written in 1940 but that's probably not the version you learned in school. The milder form was tame enough to become an election campaign song for George Bush Senior, backed by the sound of Woody spinning in his grave. The original, penned in response to Irving Berlin's feel-good "God Bless America," featured Woody's radical critique of a society divided by poverty and greed. This verse could be the guerrilla gardener's theme song:

As I went walking, I saw a sign there,
And on the sign, it said "No Trespassing."
But on the other side, it didn't say nothing,
That side was made for you and me.[3]

The harder question is: what public space? In a time of growing gated communities and video surveillance, when a soccer stadium can make 1,000 fans take off their *pants* to avoid upsetting a corporate sponsor,[1] what does "public space" even mean anymore?

One traditional definition uses the right of access. Public space is where everyone is allowed to go, to do whatever they want, so long as it's legal. I can wear an offensive t-shirt and hand out political leaflets in my local park, but probably not in my local shopping mall if the mall owner has different standards.

A problem with this distinction for guerrilla gardeners is that it's based not on how life really works (ecology) but on the law. And what good is a lawyer when both the park and the mall's planter boxes may need our help?

So let's use "public space" here in its widest sense to mean all the places we as a society share environmentally. This can include private land even if the only access is visual. It would follow that cities, those grand experiments in social living, have a lot of public spaces: parks, streets, lots, fields, industrial sites and more…the firehouse lawn, the gas station shrubbery, the bank building's parking lot.

Whatever the title deeds say, we as a society created these places the way the Mayans built the pyramids at Chichén Itzá. Our shared

Build it and they will come, eventually, to pick the fruit in this community orchard in East Vancouver.

environment is defined by both the natural and built spaces around us. Together they make up our urban ecosystem. Because everything in an ecosystem is linked, these places affect the city and those living in it in countless physical, mental, spiritual and other ways. So enhancing these public spaces with guerrilla gardening can be seen as a public right. Maybe even a public duty. But don't let me go too far.

The "with or without permission" clause in my definition was added only to emphasize the all-inclusive nature of the pursuit. Let no one try to tell you your project doesn't count because it's on the wrong type of property or because you had the gumption to ask the land owner first. You may be surprised to learn how many will say yes.

With guerrilla gardeners always free to choose their own level of commitment and all acting on their own initiatives, how can we define success? The proof is in the planting. Does it look better? Function better ecologically? Make birds and butterflies happy? If the answers are no, *what* are you planting? Never mind that for now. Will your next operation do better? The only definition of failure should lie in giving up.

Because guerrilla gardening is such a life-affirming activity, I'm tempted to declare at least one condition for inclusion: non-violence. But who am I to say? I once asked the Dalai Lama whether violence could ever be justified. I expected the Nobel Peace Prize winner to issue a standard denial; I just needed the quote. Instead he said it wasn't that easy, because there may be times when violence is necessary. "What counts for any action are your motivation and the results," he explained. Note that for him,

Working the good earth with your bare hands is as fun as fingerpainting, but washing up later can be a chore. No matter how hard you scrub, you never seem to get clean. Next time, before you go out, rub plenty of lotion into your hands. It'll help keep your skin from absorbing tiny particles of soil.

To keep your fingernails dirt-free, scratch a bar of soap. The soap easily washes out later, but in the meatime it prevents soil from collecting beneath your fingernails.

motivation involves compassion even for one's enemies and results may be judged best after generations. So where does that leave the rest of us? Wondering, as usual. In the meantime I recommend not blowing up stuff while you work on your better nature, and keep on planting as part of the practice.

School's out

By this point you may be wondering whether you have what it takes to become a guerrilla gardener.

Perhaps I can answer by describing my own introduction to the urban wild life. I went on my first mission when I was 11 years old. In fact, I led it.

This was in the build-up to Earth Day, which we had learned about all week in school. By Friday I was brimming with it. I knew what side I was on. Pollution was the enemy. I even knew where the enemy was: an empty city lot I walked by every day on the way to school.

That weekend I enlisted two pals to help pick up and carry out all the garbage. We also pulled out weeds by the armload. Then we got flower seeds from somewhere (I hope we didn't steal them) and planted what we believed would be the revival of a ratty patch of land leading to the triumph of ecology all over town.

I don't remember the flowers ever blooming. In retrospect, watering might have helped. But that wasn't the most important thing. Our little band of three — at least for a time — was a part of things. We were engaged. That empty lot, too creepy to play in with its towering weeds and broken glass, could intimidate us no longer. We were making it ours. But not just ours. We were making it everybody's. For two idyllic days we hummed with the fervor of the righteous as we hauled and dug and sweat. It really is a shame about that water.

Some good must have come out of the experience. I went on to become a community-based ecologist. Eventually. The high school years were a bit of a lapse. My strongest connection to the landscape then involved a loathing of our suburban lawn which my father, apparently even less enamored, ordered me to cut every weekend.

Things picked up in university where I studied politics and environmental studies. One of my nicknames (which fortunately

Landscape is personal and tribal history made visible.

— YI-FU TUAN

didn't last) was "Nature Boy." It may have had something to do with not wearing shoes. Or maybe the semester I lived in the forest behind campus, where I learned a valuable lesson. All other things being equal, it's good to have friends with hot showers.

By and by I graduated and, with no other prospects, went into journalism. This seemed to suit me when I got a newspaper job in Japan. At least I enjoyed it, getting paid to write not only about the concrete onslaught of Tokyo but also on things such as the Penan nomads' anti-logging campaign in Borneo and the native gardening trend in Australia.

More recently I began to wonder about doing more than reporting on the environment. I decided I wanted to shape it too. After all, it isn't some big external unapproachable thing out there — it's all around, far, near and inside us too. It seemed prudent to know how, so I went back to school to get a Master's degree in Landscape Architecture. I combined taking courses with previous experience in tree planting and orchard management to become a certified arborist. I helped launch an engaged ecology group that teaches citizens to plant and care for the urban forest. And I continued to do volunteer work on community greening campaigns.

> *I'm old enough to remember the 1950s, when public connoted good and private was considered suspect, greedy, untrustworthy. But then I saw it turn around, from public as bad schools, inefficient government, and slums to private as a transcendent force in society, the hope of Fortune 500.*
>
> — Lewis Lapham

Right of way

One day a neighborhood group asked for advice on a project. It involved an enthusiastic crowd of keeners, some prize heritage apple trees, and a scheme to plant them through guerrilla gardening. I didn't think they should do it.

The idea was certainly intriguing. The group had received dozens of donated apple trees, bare-root and ready for planting. They had found a supply of free shipping crates that would work as planter boxes. The only problem: no room to start a community orchard. The obvious choice, the local community garden, had no extra space. Beside the garden, however, and separating it from the park next door, was a short, potholed, troublesome street the residents had been trying to get closed for years. It was hardly a city conduit, with T-stops at either end, but its remoteness did make it popular with johns bringing in prostitutes, garden thieves with trucks who steal in bulk and illegal campers. The group's suggestion? Put the trees right *on* the street.

No sooner was the idea mentioned than the room came alive. People loved it. Everyone started talking at once. If brilliant ideas produced floating light bulbs we would have needed sunglasses. Finally I couldn't help cutting through the giddiness to ask: "But what will the city say?"

"Who cares?" Followed by laughter and genial hoots of derision at the notion of the city having anything pertinent to contribute.

"Yes, well, maybe," I went on, feeling like the hand-wringing sidekick in an adventure film, written in to moan about everything that can go wrong. "The thing is, planting that many trees would take a while. Someone would probably see you."

"They might." Shrugs. "So?"

"So…they would stop you."

"They might *try*."

Where to grow? The answer from the plant world is: everywhere.

"Oh. Well…what if the city didn't notice, not then, but they do later? It's still their street. They'll come and take the trees out."

"Not if we sit in front of the bulldozers." Cheers this time, and laughter, and calls of "Now you're talking," and "Right on."

Such civic passion is not unusual, especially in committee rooms and far from the looming bulldozer blade, but this group was from the neighborhood that had stopped the city from building a highway through downtown Vancouver in the 1970s. This was an era of urban planners all over North America driven by the vision of happy people in the suburbs streaking to and from their jobs in gleaming downtown towers via big, wide cars on big, wide freeways. The planners got their wish, wrecking cities all over the continent as one urban core after another turned into a wasteland of commercial highrises and cars but few people, especially after dark.

Too few cities were spared the gutting effects of the well-intended renovations. In Vancouver the plans went off the rails when, after replacing a few blocks of turn-of-the-century houses with apartment buildings that Brezhnev would have loved, the planners ran into determined opposition. The highway scheme was shelved, and today Vancouver runs a thriving cottage industry hosting urban planners from around the world who come to learn how to nurture a livable city.

Even with this caliber of citizen, I felt a clutch of misgivings about the enterprise. "What if a city crew comes when no one's around, takes out all the trees and sends you a bill?"

"We don't pay."

"We've been after them for years about that street," another added, "and we've never had any response."

People started talking all at once about public meetings, potholes, drugs, thieves and prostitutes. It grew into a heated agreement.

"I shouldn't have to explain used condoms to kindergarteners," said one teacher.

I nodded over and again, familiar with the arguments and the anger at city inaction. I knew that apple trees in planter boxes would do well and beautify that street. They went on the side of the street, as it turned out, so they wouldn't be blocking traffic. And

Think of how your space will look, but also how the world will look *from* your space. Is there a spot where the view is really special? It might make a good place for a bench, or a bend in the path that encourages a pause. The best view may not necessarily be the most sweeping one. In fact, showing off everything at once can sometimes make a spectacular sight get too familiar too soon. Think of framing a picture.

maybe it could be the first step toward reclaiming the neighborhood. One big park certainly did sound better than the status quo.

"Okay, I'm in," I said, silently congratulating myself on knowing at least when it was time to shut up and learn.

There are two categories of guerrilla gardening operation. The first involves undercover work. Often performed at night, when outdoor workers are absent and potential witnesses in bed, the project is executed quickly and quietly. Get in, do the job, and get out before anyone has time to think about why all those eager people aren't employed during the daytime like other landscapers. You plant and run, perhaps literally if you hear sirens.

Freedom lies in being bold.

— ROBERT FROST

In the other type of operation you work by day. You don't skulk or hide behind dark hoodies or bandana masks. You wear work clothes and work gloves. If you happen to have a safety vest, or any kind of occupational vest, wear it. A worker's vest is like a backstage pass. If anyone stares, you offer the slack-jawed nod of the hourly wage earner and resume digging. People see what they expect to see, even when the evidence is against it. Act as if you belong and everyone will assume you do.

So it was that, not long after the meeting, 20 or so people looking like any other group from the community garden appeared on the site. Work parties are normally held on Sunday, but this was Tuesday, a regular day for city employees. We had just unloaded 30 crates from a semi-trailer and begun filling them with compost and wood chips when a car appeared, bearing the emblem of the city's Engineering Department. Just our luck — an emissary from the largest, best-funded and most powerful department in the city.

The first rule of guerrilla gardening should be "Get Away With It," I thought ruefully at that moment when it seemed we were hooped before we'd planted a single tree.

"Keep moving," someone muttered from the side of his mouth, chain gang-style. I stole a glance up from the wheelbarrow I was pushing. The others were staring at their boots.

"Don't anyone say anything," someone hissed as the car drew nearer.

"I'll do the talking," an older member of the group announced, to my relief, but even he looked like a poster for criminal contrition as his eyes darted in every direction but at the driver. "Whatever happens," he whispered, "you guys keep shoveling."

Won't that be hard with handcuffs, I wondered as the car rolled almost to a stop before us, the driver turning to look. Not much older than a teenager, perhaps a junior engineer, he seemed distinctly bored. A guy on a morning break, looking for a quiet spot to sip his coffee. Nodding vaguely in our direction, he rolled past and was gone. We hadn't even registered.

With the sudden reprieve, we laughed and joked about who had been the most nervous. We also quickened the pace. One visit like that was a lucky pass. Who knew what category of municipal employee might show up next?

Ten minutes later we all did when a police patrol car turned in and cruised up the street toward us.

We cursed bitterly. Junior must have called them. The Man doesn't get his own hands dirty, no. He has the whole jack-booted apparatus of the State to do his thuggery.

But this cop barely slowed down, didn't bother to glance. We clearly weren't his table either. Later a fire truck drove by with the same heartwarming lack of concern. No one from the city was

Access denied…except to individuals with hands and feet.

interested in our planting project. In our vests and work gloves we looked as if we knew what we were doing. No hoodies, no masks.

By mid-afternoon the trees were planted, staked and watered. Later that spring, the first blossoms appeared. And at least one small section of a formerly unloved street was now a part of the urban citizens' revolution to green the city and save the world.

The lesson: guerrilla gardening worked. And it worked in spite of me. So if you're still wondering whether you're up to the task, remember my example and do not follow it. Be bold. Courage can feed itself, if you take off the leash and let it run.

Now fear this

For the vital question of why you might want to put yourself through episodes such as this, consider a few statistics I gleaned in a few scary minutes of net searching:

- One-third of the world's amphibian species may soon disappear. No one knows why.
- The earth is in its warmest period in recorded history, with at least some of the hot air coming from dolts yelling at Al Gore.
- Marine mammals are dying in the Pacific, and we do know why. Their brains are rotting from pollution.
- Almost one third of North America's 645 native bird species are in decline.
- Half the world's rainforests have been destroyed within the last century. Every minute (the time it takes you to read this paragraph, if you go over it a few times) another 95 acres get razed.

Also the chemicals in breast milk. Asthma in urban areas. Dwindling sperm counts. More cancers of everything.

Let's stop there. This book is not about gloom and doom. It's about how we fight back. I wish I could say it's ultimately about how the truth will out, love will reign and environmental grooviness spread over the land like honey over toast, but that would take more optimism than I have to muster. Of course I try to look on the bright side, if only because it's a more successful strategy for getting things done, but as humans we've got an awful spotty record to have to build on. Cities have never quite worked before. No urban center has ever lasted. What is the history of civilization? The story of one failed city after another.

Foods high in antioxidants are believed to slow the effects of aging. The theory hasn't been proved. But the idea is that antioxidants counter the damaging effects of "free radicals" in the blood. And you thought "free radicals" were a good thing. Here, according to research reported in the *Journal of Agricultural Food Chemistry,* are the 20 most antioxidant-rich foods. How many can you grow in a guerrilla garden?

1. Red beans
2. Wild blueberries
3. Red kidney beans
4. Pinto beans
5. Cultivated blueberries
6. Cranberries
7. Artichokes
8. Blackberries
9. Prunes
10. Raspberries
11. Strawberries
12. Red delicious apples
13. Granny Smith apples
14. Pecans
15. Sweet cherries
16. Black plums
17. Russet potatoes
18. Black beans
19. Plums
20. Gala apples[4]

City of no return

But let's put that in perspective. Hominids have been around for three or four million years. During that time we got pretty good at hunting and gathering. As *Homo sapiens* we've mostly been farmers for the past 10,000 years, and if you ignore the cruel fact of recurrent famines, we've done all right there too. But now we've evolved again, this time into something quite different. According to the United Nations, more than half the people on earth now live in cities.[2] And with a million more people moving into cities every week, it's obvious there's no going back. We are an urban species, a planet of city people. It's an arrangement never attempted before on a scale so grand. Cities may not have worked so far, but that's not a helpful excuse because this time we have no other choice.

Like some people, I've had a love-hate relationship with most of the urban areas I've been in. Typical for an edge species thriving in the interface between ecosystems, I'm drawn by all the rich opportunities the complexity of cities presents. I'm happy to join in the frothy mix of cultures. But I'm also as affected as anyone by the onslaughts of visual blight, pollution, noise, crime and social degradation.

In studying landscape architecture I learned to see public space as a design problem — and "problem" is the right word. How did we let it get this bad? The influence of profit-making corporations on every part of our lives is so vast we've almost stopped noticing. Every big city in North America has more private security guards than public police officers. Shutting yourself off from society no longer marks you as eccentric, it just means you can afford to live in a gated community. In one neighborhood mentioned in this morning's newspaper, residents — evidently proud of the fact — put up a public sign announcing 24 hours per day of recorded video surveillance.

We don't have to live this way. Many people don't realize yet that we are far from powerless. We are as strong as we choose to be. In spite of near-total government capitulation to corporate dominion, we are the ones who create the greatest living achievement of humankind, the city. (Yes, I did mean to write "greatest" and also "living.") We are the civic designers and social engineers and urban planners who invent these collective masterpieces through the

The first thing I tell people to do is plant a garden.

— Thomas Pawlick
author of *The End of Food*

daily decisions we make on where and how we live, work, shop and play.

I decided to write *Guerrilla Gardening: A Manualfesto* to join the growing campaign to help cities bloom. By combining what I've learned through reporting from urban areas on six continents with what I studied about urban ecology and tried firsthand as a community planter and activist, I hope to make the case that:

1. Cities are too important to leave to people who don't care.
2. Gardening is easy, although sometimes tricky when you don't have permission.
3. The planet can be saved by committed gardeners because
4. We are planting the seeds of a brighter future and
5. Our time has come.

Meet me at my office,
third tree from the left.

How to use this book

I called this book a manualfesto to mean a how-to guide with
why-for inspiration for anyone interested in planting beyond
their own property. It contains the most helpful information on
the topic I could find, some from personal experience but more
from asking those who know more than I ever will.

Included are first-person "If I can do it…" accounts of guerrilla gardeners describing what did and didn't work. More of the
former, fortunately, although we certainly needn't avoid the latter
because mistakes are good opportunities to learn. Also included
are interviews with various experts in first-person excerpted and
longer Q&A formats. Each chapter also has a short "Power Plant"
section describing some proven winners you might want to try.

You could read the book from start to finish in the given order,
but that's up to you. No one's watching. If you prefer, turn straight

These things will sell for thousands once Pottery Barn catches on.

to the chapters most applicable to your situation. Or you could flip around at random. Added throughout are plenty of boxes, info bars, fun facts, growing tips, design suggestions and interesting or perhaps even inspirational quotes. These were chosen to make the reading experience a pleasure as well as an education. They're also meant to help those with diminished attention spans stay focused (but not you…you even read inside parentheses). The idea is to take either the lesson or the spirit of what you find in here and apply it to your own campaign furthering the green insurgency.

Are you the one?

Wait, let me answer for you. The answer is yes.

The rest of the book is an elaboration on this idea, with what I hope is enough detail to prove it.

If you opened the book because you wanted to improve the environment — stick around, we're just getting started.

If you're still unsure, but curious enough to wonder whether you fit in, Chapter One might help by providing an overview of where guerrilla gardening is from and where it may be heading.

Let's say you read that, and you're keen. What next? Chapter Two explains how to find a spot to start, beginning with advice on using an ecological approach in evaluating city spaces.

Now that you have a site, what are going to do with it? Chapter Three discusses the things you'll need to begin creating your opus on the land.

This, for some, is where it starts to get scary. Not the silly legal stuff, but the stricter laws of nature. What to do with the fact that you're a black thumb squashing every plant to have come under your care? Worry no more. Chapter Four explains the basic laws of gardening in non-technical and easy to understand terms. It's meant to reassure you that you can indeed grow things. Or maybe you still can't, but why do you think nurseries have end-of-season sales?

Once you've learned to see your city as a living thing, you're bound to wonder where all the rest of its creatures are. Chapter Five is all about creating spaces for urban dwellers beyond the human realm — of which there are millions. If only they could buy books too.

What's the biggest crop plant in North America? If you answered "lawn grass," you probably grew up in the suburbs. And you'd be right. Biggest and dumbest, we might have said, for huge amounts of effort, money, resources, poisons and angst go into those curiously drab, even aseptic, spreads of green. Chapter Six explains how to turn a lawn into a meadow, or (if that seems ambitious) at least into something more interesting.

Chapter Seven takes you to the peak of guerrilla gardening, the dream site, the spot you plant and tend so impressively that they let you keep it...also known as a community garden. This is where you learn how to start one and, just as importantly, how to keep one.

In any creative campaign it can sometimes help to suddenly turn the tables. Chapter Eight makes the case that you should not be bound by any limits, including the ones that say you must be contrary. Most ecological restoration work is done through official channels. This route isn't for all guerrilla gardeners (and you should be warned the meetings alone can be deadly), but if you do well here you can make a lasting impact.

Chapter Nine describes what you can do when you're not out pulling weeds and planting seeds. It explains how to pass the message of urban greening on. Ideas, after all, are seeds that may bloom into something grand.

What? Not be out planting things? The conclusion winds up by contesting the very idea. It includes some hopeful thoughts for the future along with a final exhortation to stop reading books, grab your tools and get out the door. There's a world out there that needs help. And you, green-spirited soldier, are the one to help it.

CHAPTER ONE

The Big Idea

(Or What to Say If You're Stopped)

The first thing to say, if it's the police and you think you're going to be arrested (the handcuffs are a clue), is…nothing. Any justification now may only be used against you later. But as we've seen, it's more likely whatever police you do meet will be on routine patrol and simply curious to know why you're digging holes after midnight. In this case, you may as well come clean. Tell them what you're doing.

And what, they may ask, is guerrilla gardening?

Try this: "It's a volunteer campaign to improve the environment. Will you join us?"

Later when you're all sitting down together as chums, sharing coffee and deep-fried sugary treats, you can explain how guerrilla gardening began and why it matters today more than ever.

A brief history

We will never know the name of the world's first guerrilla gardener. We don't even know which era of history to search for that original freethinker, someone who may have looked over one shoulder, then the other, then dropped a seed or bean into an unauthorized patch of land before hurrying away in anticipatory glee.

We do know agriculture developed in separate parts of the world beginning roughly 10,000 years ago. In the Fertile Crescent, including present-day Iraq, early settled societies grew wheat, barley, peas and lentils. In what is now China and Thailand rice, millet and hemp were cultivated. In the Americas corn, beans and potatoes became staple crops. It may be true that the skill of cultivating plants arose from the need to feed growing settlements, to stave off the ever-present terror of starvation. But who's to say

Hope can neither be affirmed nor denied. Hope is like a path in the countryside: originally, there was no path — yet as people are walking all the time in the same spot, a way appears.

— Lu Xun

What is a city, but the people?

— SHAKESPEARE in "Corialanus"

it didn't happen the other way around? Our affinity for raising food may have risen from the joy of gardening itself, developed as a leisure activity by people secure enough to experiment. Once it was seen to produce more food — no doubt doubling the joy of its practitioners — settlements and eventually cities may have emerged to reap the abundance.

Whether from joy or fear or a mixture of both, the great change occurred. Long before we settled down to tilling fields, however, we were already plant people. Our general knowledge of botany today — in terms of what it has to offer in food, medicine, clothing, building materials and more — would mark us as the tribal idiots if we ever went back in time. It's reasonable to assume that plants were part of the power structure of any locality. The chief or queen or ruling council may well have had a favorite plot or tree or berry patch to which others were forbidden access. Who wouldn't want a currant bush of one's own? And because the history of human development can be read as one kind of authority being challenged after another, it's just as likely someone sharp would have quietly picked a few berries or seeds to spread in a more accessible area, say, just outside the kitchen.

To go back even further for evidence that guerrilla gardening is in our genes, consider Eve and Adam. They harvested the one plant in all existence they were told to leave alone. Admittedly, this tale paints them more as thieves than gardeners, but if "gardening" had yet to be called as such, it was as close as they could come. What do you think happened to the seeds of that apple?

But beyond any tribal myths, the history of guerrilla gardening would be a book in itself. It would encompass politics, property, sociology, horticulture — and much else. What wouldn't fit? Growing things is nurturing life itself, the ownership part being just one variable.

Among the first groups the history might explore would be the Rom, or Roma — known also as Gypsies, though not kindly as that term can be considered pejorative. The Roma are believed to have first trekked out of Northwest India more than 1,000 years ago, and they have been on the road ever since. On traveling routes they planted seedling potatoes at favored stopping places, knowing they would be back at harvest time to reap a crop grown on someone else's land.

Lock down, plant up

One could mine history and speculation to turn up a host of rene-gade growers, but the off-limits nature of the task makes practi-tioners reluctant to speak or write of their exploits. Perhaps the most moving examples of people driven to garden away from home involve prisoners. There is a poignant tradition of those in captivity fostering growth out of the soil to which they are con-fined. We know the desire to sow and tend and reap is a human urge, but to see how it is carried out amid the most oppressive conditions imaginable is truly amazing.

Near the end of World War II, American POWs in Germany's Stalag XVIIB prison camp asked permission to grow vegetables. With food supplies dwindling everywhere, they told their captors the gardens were needed to supplement the meager diet. Probably they were. The authorities allowed seeds and small gardening tools into the camp. How happy this made the gardeners among them will have to be imagined, since accounts of the exploit were written by prisoners digging escape tunnels under the camp, who now had a safe place to dispose of extra soil. You might want to keep this tale in storage for the next time someone complains about local authorities. Sure, they may act like Nazis, you can say, but at least they're not *actual* Nazis.

Gardening in captivity also features in the lives of the two most heroic figures of our age: Nelson Mandela and the present Dalai Lama. Mandela, imprisoned for 27 years by South Africa's apart-heid government, writes endearingly of the plot he was eventually allowed to tend in the stark prison yard on Robben Island. Since visiting the place called "Hell-hole Robben Island" and seeing its dusty yard with the narrow strip along one wall where Mandela managed to eke out a few vegetables, I've never considered any growing space too narrow. The Dalai Lama lives in a different type of captivity, residing in India in a condition of self-imposed exile since China invaded his country in 1959. He lives in a bungalow in Dharamsala where his hobbies include tending a garden about the size a typical North American suburbanite might get to grips with on weekends. One of the things that these two remarkable men have in common is a recognition of the centrality of gardening. They have used it as a natural conduit for some of their extraordi-nary determination, patience and love.

Worse yet, there are those who would abandon the tangible world altogether in favor of a virtual reality assembled in computer networks — memory palaces dislodged from the earth and inhabited by electronic speculation. We intend to remain unabashedly earthbound, ready to spend our limited days imagining palpable places, places that people can reach on their feet and fill with their presence.

— DONLYN LYNDON and CHARLES MOORE in *Chambers for a Memory Palace*

Guerrilla gardening isn't just gardening. There's room for talent of all types. If you're keen to help a cause but not sure where you fit in, try asking yourself a few key questions.

What's your passion? What traits do you admire in other people? What would a tiring but fulfilling day have been spent doing?

Look for matches that fit your own abilities. These don't have to be things you're good at already, so long as you're eager enough to learn. Can you transplant perennials? Organize meetings? Collect seeds? Write communiqués? Install irrigation? Raise funds? Inspire volunteers?

Everybody is good at something, they just may not know it yet. Happiness is also famously difficult to define, but I think that one secret to being happy is finding out what you love and pursuing it with vigor. Maybe happiness is just a by-product of fulfilling your duty to yourself.

The present day has no shortage of desperate places that can summon the instinct for gardening. Boston lawyer Sabin Willet described in the *Washington Post* what he'd learned from one of his clients held by mistake in the US concentration camp at Guantanamo Bay. He has been in legal limbo since the US admitted he was never an enemy combatant, but Saudi Arabia refuses to take him back. Using plastic dinner spoons, prisoners plant seeds they've sequestered from meals. They've managed to start watermelon, peppers and garlic, says Willet, who adds:

> Maybe the History of Guantanamo will have a few uplifting footnotes. America denied them seeds and trowels and they created life anyway. We tried to withhold beauty, but from the grim earth of Guantanamo they scratched a few square meters of garden — with spoons. Guantanamo is ugly, but man's instinct for beauty lives deep down things.[1]

By the people, for the people

Modern history's best known guerrilla gardening campaign, although it may not have used the term, is the struggle for People's Park in Berkeley, California, in the spring of 1969. The 2.8-acre city lot of character homes and hippies was bought by the University of California for a parking lot and playing fields near campus.

People's Park in Berkeley, California, was won at a terrible cost: one died and scores were injured.

The site was cleared for construction, but when funding withered it was left an empty, muddy mess. The locals decided it would better serve the area as a park. So they made it one. Hundreds answered the call one Sunday to plant trees and grass and flowers. There was a live band, free food and even a permanent Free Box set up where anyone could donate clothes or other things for the needy to pick up at will. The newly-crowned People's Park lived up to its name, at least for a few heady weeks.

Then California Governor Ronald Reagan, eager to challenge the radicals ruining the state, ordered authorities to take back the land. Park users were ordered out, the trees and flowers were pulled up, and a perimeter fence was erected to keep anyone from planting anything else. Such heavy manners in a place like Berkeley in a time like 1969 would have a predictable response. The *San Francisco Chronicle* reported Reagan saying: "If there has to be a bloodbath, then let's get it over with." When a crowd of thousands marched toward the site, police shot them. One man — not a demonstrator — was killed, another was permanently blinded, and hundreds were sent to the hospital.

More demonstrations over more years eventually secured the land as a park. Squabbles continue today over the ultimate plans for the site. Twice the Free Box has been destroyed mysteriously, but the legacy of People's Park endures. Crystallized in the rallying

The largest use of public space in most big cities is for cars. There are 6,374 miles of streets in New York City.

We're playing those mind games together
Pushing the barriers, planting seeds
Playing the mind guerrilla
— JOHN LENNON in "Mind Games"

Handing out flowers before the fatal demonstration.

call used at the time, "Let a Thousand Parks Bloom," it would go on to inspire campaigns thousands of miles away.

Yippie Park

One such inspiration was the "All Seasons Park" created by Yippie guerrilla gardeners in Vancouver in 1971. The site on prime waterfront land downtown is at the entrance to Stanley Park, the city's justifiably famous main attraction. The Four Seasons Hotel chain had bought the land to develop a resort complex which would have blocked public view of the park to all but its wealthy customers. And who should come to the rescue but Yippies, the counterculture alternative to the usual alternative, the more puritanical traditional left. Yippies scheduled a demonstration to oppose the project which included suddenly rushing onto the site at a pre-arranged signal and — it really is a fabulous location — they decided to stay. They put up tents, planted trees and flowers and food crops and generally made it a freak fixture on the downtown scene. The name they chose, "All Seasons Park," turned out to be prescient when the occupation lasted more than a year. It ended only when a wealthy philanthropist stepped in to buy the land as a donation. And today many of Stanley Park's seven million annual visitors pass through "Devonian Park" entirely unaware of the role guerrilla gardening played in its preservation.

Green Guerrillas

The first use of guerrilla gardening as a term probably came from New York. As this is the world's big city (name me another where you can buy a Kurdish T-shirt and get a Mongolian throat-singing lesson right on the street from the same Zimbabwean chemical engineer), it's an apt birthplace for the campaign, as well as an ongoing inspiration. The Green Guerrillas are now an established urban agricultural support group helping thousands of neighbors create and run community gardens, but when it started in 1973 it was a small handful of locals hoping to reclaim a single empty lot.

Much of the credit goes to Liz Christy, a Lower East Side artist with a big heart and a green thumb. Near her home was an empty lot on the corner of Bowery and Houston Streets, the kind of garbage-filled space you can walk by for years without really noticing. One day she watched as a child was about to climb into

A garden is an attempt to establish meaning by giving form to nature.

— ROBERT B. RILEY

DESIGN TIP

Nature is still the best teacher when it comes to many garden styles, even some formal ones. Take your design inspiration from places in the wild you love. Learn to treat plants not as individual specimens to fill in holes, but as part of a grander theme. Mimic how nature places its species selections. Sometimes they're in clusters, other times in long graceful curves. Plants in straight lines, rows or tight wiggles have their purpose, but it may merely be to call attention to their planter.

an abandoned refrigerator with the door still attached. Horrified, she got the child out and berated the mother, only to be told back that if she cared so much about garbage why didn't she do something about it? So Christy got some friends together to help clean the place up. The garden they then planted turned out to be the spark that lit the fire for what would grow to be hundreds of similar projects. The original site was renamed the Liz Christy Garden after Liz died of cancer at 39. Her ashes were spread over the garden grounds because, as all good growers know, there's no such thing as death, just more stages of life between spells as compost. And who would deny that Liz Christy lives on in the hundreds of community gardens throughout New York and beyond that thrive today thanks to the dedicated work of her and her crew?

Guerrilla gardening today is riding a popular wave. It's spreading to places around the world through events big and small, some more successful than others, but all part of a grand work in progress. One prominent recent attempt was staged by Reclaim the Streets, a London group behind the "mass guerrilla gardening action" in the heart of the city on May Day 2000. So long as Britain can produce groups which describe themselves this way: "A direct action network for global and local social-ecological revolution(s) to transcend hierarchical and authoritarian society (capitalism included), and still be home in time for tea…" — well, there will always be an England.

Activists were invited to the event outside Parliament by "Resistance is Fertile" flyers which read, "Come prepared and ready to get your hands dirty. Bring with you everything you need to make a Guerrilla Garden: a sapling, vegetable seedlings, flowers, herbs. Subvert the packaging of the Capital: turn designer trainers into plant pots, traffic cones into hanging baskets… Start planting now."

Liz Christy at the site she helped bloom.

Below: If I can make it there, I can make it anywhere. A New York City lot before and after it became the Liz Christy Community Garden.

Parliament Square evidently survived the green brigades. Since the event has not become an annual tradition, we can surmise its success was limited. Reclaim the Streets has since "grown up and left home," according to their website.[2] But other groups in England have taken up the flag, including one managed by a resourceful advertising industry chap who hosts a website inviting enthusiasts to check in with reports of planting projects from around the world (guerrillagardening.org).

If the above reads as somewhat scant in terms of history, it does help to make a point. Guerrilla gardeners should be less interested in the legacy than in adding to it. If you can imagine still sitting with your police officer pals, who have eaten their donuts and finished their coffee, and are now waiting for the rest of your promised explanation, tell them: the best stories have yet to be written.

Among the reasons why:

Guerrilla gardening is fun

How did environmental politics get so earnest and dull? Has there ever been a rallying call more numbing than "sustainability"? Who decided that anyone working on environmental issues must

---

SIX EXCRUCIATING RHYMES FROM THE "GREEN GUERRILLA SONG"

1. Well the green guerrilla gang said, Just for a lark
   Let's go and plant off the beaten park
2. So they saved all the seeds from the veggies that they ate
   And dried them in the sun on an old paper plate. Recycle.
3. There were pomegranates, custard apples, pawpaws and pineapples
   Grapes in the gum trees and birds in the elderberries.
4. And it bloomed like a jungle in the smog city sun
   But when they started harvesting a copper said, Come
5. The judge frowned down saying, Growing food for free
   Is going to ruin the economy. Ruin. The. Economy.
6. Lots of red cabbage, long radish, nuts from macadamia
   And something from Tasmania.
   Subversion from Tasmania!
   Permaculture! Manic mulcher!

appear grimmer than the consequences involved? If every worth-while cause gets the dynamic visionaries it deserves, what's with Al Gore?

Guerrilla gardening takes its style cues from the garden, which is to say, life itself. That makes it messy, funny, tragic, random, happy, sad and…what else? Whatever works for you. But if it isn't at least fun, at least some of the time, why do it?

To give a personal example: on Labor Day weekend Vancouver used to host a professional car race. For three days the streets would fill with the high octane roar and whine of race cars and the town was inundated with advertising for all things drinking and driving. This was the Molson Indy. Conceiving a counter-event to promote the bicycle, activists staged a critical mass ride for near-naked participants, and called it the Wholesome Undie. I mention this not just to highlight the potential connection between guerrilla gardening and political wit, but because my daughter laughs every time I say "Wholesome Undie." If you have small children, you can try this at home.

Yes, the earth is in drastic shape, and OK, we're all going to die, but no, we will not in the meantime be driven into becoming dour,

The experience of being in a place where the forces are resolved together at once is completely restful and whole. It is like sitting under an oak tree: things in nature resolve all the forces acting on them together; they are, in that sense, whole and balanced.

— CHRISTOPHER ALEXANDER

From the Australian-made "Songs of a Green Guerrilla," described as "an inspiring album of songs about life, the environment, permaculture and the power of change — all original music written and performed by Robyn Francis, supported by local musicians."[4]

I'm going to go out on a limb here and say I don't believe this will ever become a generational anthem. And I hope I didn't sound snarky when I called the rhymes excruciating. That was unfair, and I apologize. It's the music that's excruciating. Imagine a cheesy new wave '80s band backing vocals that could be a Down Under Deborah Harry in the middle of a seizure.

It's kind of catchy though.

Who needs plants? Leonard Knight poured thousands of gallons of paint and a lot of love into the creation of Salvation Mountain at Slab City, California.

hand-wringing, finger-wagging scolds. We will have fun and we will save the planet at the same time. Why? As pursuits they go well together.

Guerrilla gardening is fundamental

Agriculture is a fundamental human skill, easily recovered if lost, I believe, so deep is it in our genes. For this reason it is also a fundamental human right. Whether or not you own property — an alien concept in all but the most recent slice of human history — you have a birthright to continue in nurturing seeds into plants.

You may not have actualized this skill yet, judging by the last eight houseplants you've killed, but don't be discouraged. Plant cultivation is in your DNA. Gardening is one of those ancient attractions, like walking or staring into the campfire, that can hypnotize. So trust me, you do have what it takes. The only techniques needed are basic and easily learned, either with the help of a half decent book (ahem) or on your own through trial and error.

As for those houseplants? They're weird, not you. Well, maybe you are too, but that's still OK, though I do wonder what you did to that rubber tree. Those things are practically indestructible.

Guerrilla gardening is radical

Radical: "Of or to a root or origin."

Sometimes pruning is enough to fix a problem plant. Other times the problem is too big, and you have to get right to the root or origin. Maybe even replace the whole thing.

For us this means we should be as radical as the situation requires. A grape vine obstructing a pathway can be pruned back. As for the transformation in social consciousness required to create the shining eco-city of the future, we're talking about more than a few snips and cuts. But you have to start somewhere. Every act of guerrilla gardening is a local tactic that also addresses a global crisis.

Guerrilla gardening is your right

Or it's not, depending on how you define your rights. But if they include being able to take an active role in preserving and improving your shared environment, you've got a strong case. Then it just comes down to the details.

Some say it goes beyond a right to become a duty. Again there's a case to be made, but it may not be helpful to make it in a way that puts people on the defensive. Many will be doing their part already, and it may have nothing to do with leather gloves and rubber boots. The battle for a just and healthy world is fought on many fronts. Whichever way you contribute, try to offer others the encouragement and space they need to find their own path. The work of guerrilla gardening is heavy enough without having to carry the pressure of someone else's expectations. It's always better not to coerce but convince by example.

Naturally, if anyone asks, you're free to expound. The reason you're doing this, you might say, is not just to make one patch of the neighborhood more pleasant to look at, but because you believe the entire city is worth the effort. And because you decided that, rather than wait for the world you want your children to grow up in to just appear, it was better to start making it yourself.

If your society is a working democracy, all the adults in it share responsibility for the legacy it creates. We know already we're going to leave a worldwide disaster, from the empty rainforests to the patented mutant crops. Basically, we've got a lot of 'splaining to do. Sure, we can try to claim non-culpability. We didn't tell the logging companies to raze the forest or ask Monsanto to design a freakish canola plant that requires Monsanto chemicals. But try that excuse on the next eight-year-old you meet who's just beginning to learn about the environment. Now imagine being able to explain what you've been doing to try to make things better.

Not that you have to justify anything, including your own life. With or without your help, eight-year-olds will grow into sullen teens soon enough. Guerrilla gardening should never feel like a duty. It is, in fact, a privilege.

Guerrilla gardening is creative

We live in an age when style, taste, culture, opinions and a lot more are increasingly dictated to us. Defenders of the status quo, seeing no culprits, demand to know by whom you imagine you're being proselytized? But the question should not be by whom, but by *what*. An estimated $500 billion is spent each year on advertising telling us what to buy, wear, eat, drink, drive, watch, think and feel. We're so inured to corporations influencing our decisions that we hardly notice they're there. They're cultural oxygen, invisible and ever-

The first law of a work of art, either on canvas or on the earth, is to be whole.

— EDWARD ANDRE

Then Vancouver Mayor Tom Campbell wasn't pleased when Yippies took over land downtown to create a park.

"It's a sad weekend in Vancouver's history," he said. The young people "showed a complete disregard for authority. This is a breakdown of society. And this is what is happening across Canada. How much property rights does anyone have left? And really, what have they accomplished? I think it's vandalism. If they want to be creative, I'll give them lots of bushland they can go out and be creative with."[5]

> *For observing nature, the*
> *best pace is a snail's pace.*
>
> — EDWIN WAY TEALE

The whole global warming thing has never seemed more perilous, but it's not like we should be surprised. French mathematician and physicist Jean Baptiste Fourier wrote in 1824 about the harmful effects of transforming carbon in the earth into carbon dioxide in the air by burning fuel. He thought it might lead to a blanket of heat-trapping gas that would warm the planet like a greenhouse. And Swedish chemist Svante Arrhenius calculated way back in 1896 what might happen if we "evaporate our coal mines into the air."

It took until the late 1980s, when temperatures were soaring, for these ideas to receive mainstream scientific support.

present. When we are reminded, we rarely make the connection that their purpose is not to enhance our lives but to make money for shareholders.

The techniques described in this book are a fraction of what can be done. Good ideas feed off each other, morphing into something entirely new. Feel free to take any of the tips you find here and tweak, shift, reshape or invert into something better. But don't forget to share what you've done to keep the process organic and alive.

The lesson here is that we create the future. Not the corporations, not the advertisers, not the marketers, not the profiteers. They need us, not the other way around. We're the fish that fill the sea, and we're free to swim in whatever direction we choose. Together we have the knowledge, skill and energy to generate our own ideas about the ideal city and to put those ideas into action in actual places. A shovel is a powerful tool.

Guerrilla gardening is diverse

Let a hundred flowers bloom, Chairman Mao famously said, and let a hundred schools of thought contend. When this credo welcoming dissent didn't produce the response expected, Mao criticized those too timid to speak. Now the letters arrived by the millions, a wall of democracy was established for posters and the country rang with the air of new-found intellectual freedom. Until Mao decided it was too threatening and launched a campaign of retribution against his critics that would lead eventually to the death of millions. That could never happen to us as guerrilla gardeners, because we have no leaders. The idea behind the movement is as simple and unstoppable as a plant poking up through a crack in the pavement. We're made up not of rulers and subjects but of every part of society itself. We are diverse.

The pursuit of gardening cuts across the usual social divisions of class, ethnicity, age and everything else. Kids, grandmothers, your new neighbors from Tunisia, the banker down the street anxious to relax — everyone gets it. You can't typecast a typical gardener because there isn't one. This is the great potential of the guerrilla gardening movement.

Why is diversity good? For one thing it's more interesting, which might be enough, but that's not the main reason. Diversity is good because it's the natural way of the world. We know from tending plants how monocultures are violations of the normal way life sorts itself out. Unlike a healthy ecosystem, a monoculture tends to be weak, susceptible to disease, greedy for certain nutrients and perhaps boring besides.

Guerrilla gardening thrives on differences. Different gardeners, different styles, different attitudes, different tactics — all leading to same result: a healthier environment and a better city.

Guerrilla gardening is ethical

Even if you are on the right track, it doesn't mean you get to run whatever train you like. Remember, you're part of an ecosystem too. That means you share a responsibility for the web of life that supports you and everything else.

So don't plant things that aren't going to fit. The best/worst example is an exotic (meaning foreign) invasive species. These are plants that take advantage of the local conditions to dominate. They spread rapidly to crowd out everything else. Check with experts in your area before you introduce any plants that could become invasive. Every state and province keeps a list. Local naturalist or ecological groups will be happy to help.

Another ethical reminder: don't steal plants. You may not believe in karma, but anyone who has ever had their garden robbed will tell you that a plant thief is a creep. You don't want the burden of looking in the mirror each morning to find a creep staring back. If you steal someone's plant, you're not just taking the roots and stems and leaves but the hours of care that went into it and the hours of enjoyment that might still be to come from it. Are there times when stealing is justified? Say, robbing from the rich to give to the rest? Here you're walking a more slippery ethical slope than I can help you navigate. At a minimum, I would say unless you have the gonadal fortitude to tell the owner face-to-face why your cause is so great that it justifies thievery, figure out another way to get your plants.

Finally, and this may be more about aesthetics than ethics (although there is some overlap), don't impose your bad taste on the public if it's really bad. Yes, garden trends change and preferences vary and nobody can presume to judge for another, but some things just shouldn't be done. How will you know? Ask a

---

Butterflies are dying. A massive study of studies — research into six surveys conducted over 40 years involving 15 million records of butterflies, birds and plants — found 71 percent of the butterfly species in the United Kingdom in decline.

The Natural Environment Research Council which reported the result said it raises speculation the world is heading for a "sixth mass extinction." The fifth mass extinction happened 65 million years ago and killed off all the dinosaurs.[6]

Depressing? Yes.

Debilitating? No. Not if you create a garden with plants that will attract, feed and help butterflies do whatever they have to do to make more butterflies.

DESIGN TIP

Planting a new garden means taking on more than just the ground. You've got at least three layers of space to consider: trees for the upper canopy, shrubs for the middle layer, and smaller plants or groundcovers for the bottom. Look at a natural setting for ideas on how to fit things together in the vertical realm.

friend. Better yet, ask someone who's not a friend. Oh, but you have an artistic statement that simply must be made? Public land may not be the best medium for you to educate the philistines. Perhaps a museum or a gallery or a local coffeeshop. Oh, but they don't get your stuff? Keep practicing then. But not in the garden.

Guerrilla gardening is political

Every plant is political. You could go a long time ignoring the fact, and most people do, but it won't work in the long run. The depoliticizing of our daily lives in much of Western society has led us sheep-like to the present crisis.

Every bit of land you see around you, from the lawn across the street to the street itself to the schoolyard at the end, is used according to a decision made by someone. The decision may not have involved you at the time, but you're involved now because it makes a difference in the kind of world you live in and react to every day. If land matters, so too do all the things that may or may not grow on it.

Remember after 9/11 when we were told that our lives would soon be back to normal if we just kept going out and buying stuff? No. Your purpose in life is not shopping for trinkets. You were not born to maintain the status quo in a world where, on that same awful day, 35,600 children died of starvation.

When you're a guerrilla gardener, you're an active participant in the living environment. You're no longer content to merely react to what happens to the spaces around you. You're a player, which means *you* help determine how those spaces get used. And when you're in tune like this, every plant counts.

Guerrilla gardening is ecological

Naturally, but how will you know? In most cases it will be obvious. A healthy ecosystem tends to be a delightful place to be in. It feels alive. Walk from a parking lot into a meadow. Go from a city park's baseball diamond lawn to a city park's mixed forest. That feeling you get? Of being at home? That's the one.

When in doubt, the best yardstick is biodiversity. Does your project enhance the number and variety of living things at the site? Consider yourself an eco-soldier, and march on.

Guerrilla gardening is organic

Organic is like "nature," a word that can mean almost anything. I use it here in two ways. One is to describe a gardening style free of synthetic fertilizers and pesticides. The other refers to the movement itself as a natural, living, growing phenomenon.

Yes, you could break this rule in the garden. You could apply some Monsanto-spawned death juice, like one of my neighbors, who once provided a perfect photo-op by standing in the middle of a front yard consisting entirely of rocks and spraying Roundup on the sole dandelion plant with the temerity to emerge. Sadly, I didn't have my camera at the time. But I urge you to forgo the death juice. Go organic. You'll feel better. So will the millions of living things on the tiny space you were tempted to zap. Yes, millions. I didn't count them, but other people did, the kind who wear white lab coats. They insist there are more living things in a teaspoon of soil than there are people on the planet. Even if they're off by an order of magnitude or two, that's still a lot of things living in the soil. Do you really want to lace it with poison?

Guerrilla gardening is life-affirming

When we work like galley slaves on the land not just for ourselves but for unseen others it confirms our role as a positive force for good. This puts us in sync with the rest of the living world.

"Life from its beginning more than three billion years ago did not take over the planet by combat," said Austrian physicist Fritjof Capra, "but by networking."[3]

Welcome to the club.

Guerrilla gardening is fun

Oh, I said that already? No matter, in comedy they call it a "callback." It's good to hear it again and again until it's ingrained, because you'll want to have it like a mantra when you're outside and cold and wet and you've been digging for hours, only to discover that slugs have consumed every last leaf of the lettuce seedlings you were about to transplant.

Note that the word "fun" is open to interpretation and can include squashing all the slugs you can find. Humor is famously elusive of definition.

In guerrilla warfare, more than in any other type of military effort, the psychological activities should be simultaneous with the military ones, in order to achieve the objectives desired.

— CIA Manual: Psychological Operations in Guerrilla Warfare

What's a garden?
- An earthly rendition of paradise.
- An archetype of the relationship between people and their environment.
- A place where physical work, mental reasoning and spiritual appreciation are synthesized in the soil.
- A hands-on opportunity to connect with nature.
- A chance to manipulate the second most important living things on earth, plants.
- Or a chance for plants to manipulate us.

Rookie gardeners sometimes wonder, when the first sprouts pop up, whether they're from the seeds they planted or weeds. It's not easy to tell the difference when everything is tiny and green. If you think you might not recognize your intended crop, plant the seeds in a shape you're sure to notice. A straight planting line (beside a shovel handle or beneath a string tied between two stakes) is easy enough, but you don't have to restrain your creative desires. A zig zag or letter or any other shape you know you'll be able to spot later will do the trick. Any sprouts that fit your chosen shape are allowed to stay. All others get the hoe.

IF I CAN DO IT...   Donald Loggins, Green Guerrilla

"We didn't worry about the legal issues. Well, sometimes we did when we tossed seed grenades."

Resilience is the sharpest tool in the guerrilla gardener's shed. Take the case of the Green Guerrillas in New York City. Not only were they working without a template in 1973, they were challenging popular notions of land use in one of the world's most intensely populated urban areas.

That they remain to this day is a testament to the indefatigable spirit of both guerrilla gardeners and New Yorkers. The Green Guerrillas now serve as a resource center for thousands of community gardeners. Original member Donald Loggins still works with the group. He talks about the growth of guerrilla gardening out of that single Bowery lot.

The Green Guerrillas were started in 1973 by Liz Christy as an urban greening movement. Up until then no one thought of guerrilla gardening.

At the start there were about ten of us. As the gardens looked better, more people joined. First from the Bowery area, then from the East Village, Harlem, Brooklyn and other areas. It was not so much out of gardening desires, it was more to improve the neighborhood. At the time no one wanted the land. The area was full of drug dealers. Buildings were empty. It was seen as a campaign for people power. It was about community empowerment.

One or two landlords got upset and put up fences, so we came up with the seed grenades. In the end it made their fenced-in property look better. They actually did work to get the plants started, if you used the right seeds. Morning glories worked best.

We didn't worry about the legal issues. Well, sometimes we did when we tossed seed grenades. But the city owned most of the land and didn't care. The Bronx was burning at the time so a few people making things greener was not an issue for the city.

We faced some opposition. After about a year, in 1974, the city wanted to bulldoze the first garden. Liz called up the media, a film crew was sent out, and the city backed down.

What can people learn from our experience? They should know it takes a lot of work. But it's fun. It's worth it. I would say, try to avoid getting too businesslike. Just make a decision and do it, don't keep talking about it.

The future for us is about keeping what we've got. After many lawsuits we got the city to convert most of the gardens to official park land. With the price of real estate in New York City today, no one will see vacant land open up for gardens. We have preserved our ground. So now we tend the gardens we saved.

POWER PLANT — Nasturtium (*Tropaeolum majus*)

Small garden, big dreams, and you want both flowers *and* food? Nasturtiums are the perfect crossover plant. They're not a compromise in either category.

The prolific tangles of green are smattered with brilliant orange, yellow or red saucers, making a rambunctious beauty that adds exuberance to almost any kind of growing space. And both leaves and flowers are delicious, adding a spicy tang to salads in particular. The leaves are said to have ten times more vitamin C than lettuce, although that may say more about lettuce ("water you have to chew") than anything. I've also read the seeds can be dried and ground in a pepper mill as with black pepper, or pickled as a substitute for capers, and may one day try.

Nasturtiums are native to South and Central America. They'll grow almost anywhere sunny, and will bloom extravagantly even in poor soil, so long as it's not soggy. Sow in spring when it's warm, or start earlier indoors with seeds in small cups. They're reliable enough to make an excellent choice for kids growing their very first plant.

Did you know: Monet used to purposely let nasturtiums sprawl across the footpaths in his garden at Giverny.

Nasturtium — Tropaeolum majus
Credit: From William Woodville's "Medical Botany," published in London in 1794, illustration by John Sowerby. (All botanical engravings supplied from the collection of Richard Jeffrey.)

CHAPTER TWO

Where to Start

(You DO Live Here So
Why Aren't You Home By Now?)

Blockbucks, Starbuster, MacTaco King. Where are we? Could be almost anywhere. Cincinnati? Milan? Dalian? Cities are looking more alike every year. The feeling of being home, in a special place, where you belong *because* it's a special place, has never been harder to muster. Just a generation ago, your identity was largely based on where you were from. Now we live in a small world, supposedly the global village, but what kind of village encourages isolation, alienation, disembodiment and waywardness? No wonder one of the highest compliments we can give a person today, because it happens so rarely, is to call him or her "grounded."

I'm not exactly complaining. I know I'm lucky to have grown up in a time and place that let me travel. I never felt pressure to stay on the farm, or run the family business or keep Pottersville from swallowing my home town. (Partly because we had no farm or family business and Potter gets thrashed by Jimmy Stewart every Christmas anyway.)

The flip side is that I can't even name my home town. As the family of an air force major, we tended to move to wherever the Canadian military was most needed. (Insert your own joke about the Canadian military here…my favorite involves the navy operating fewer submarines than the pirate attraction in an Edmonton mall.) Raised as a semi-nomad, I'd always been curious to see how real nomads live. The ones I eventually met seemed no less content or fulfilled than city people. So if you want to move, I say… move. Let the peoples of the world mingle and unite. If you want to marry outside your clan, marry outside your clan. Blends are

The revolution is not an apple that falls when it is ripe. You have to make it fall.

— Che Guevara

the best anyway. When I was a boy some of the schools I attended were as white as Wonder Bread. Today my children sit in class with kids from countries I can't even pronounce. Who do you suppose is learning more about how the real world works?

But there is at least one thing we lose in the post-modern, rootless, go-anywhere way of life: a sense of caring for something that seems like home. You need to observe at least a few growing seasons to work not just on the land but *with* it. Poet Gary Snyder explains,

> To say "we must dig in" or "here we must draw our line" is a far more universal application than growing your own food or living in the country. One of the key problems in American society now, it seems to me, is people's lack of commitment to any given place — which, again, is totally unnatural and outside history. Neighborhoods are allowed to deteriorate, landscapes are allowed to be strip-mined, because there

More than a sidewalk, it's a guerrilla gardener's treat for the rest of the city near Hastings Street in Vancouver.

is nobody who will live there and take responsibility; they'll just move on.[1]

Think eco-citizen

So how to reconcile the need to preserve and use local knowledge with the modern appeal of global mobility?

You're never going to convince people who see better opportunities over the horizon not to move. Particularly young people. Nor should you try. But you may be able to get them to see the whole earth as their home.

I know, I know, this sounds too simple, or maybe too long-haired and hippie-ish. As if I'm pushing spaceship earth, the Gaia principle, the mother provider and all that. Even if I am, it may not be in the patchouli way you're thinking. I mean instead to suggest that ecology is the best tool you can use if you hope to understand where you are — and you can carry it with you. Of course local knowledge is indispensable (which is why you'll often

Think your place is too built-up to plant in? Tokyo, the world's biggest city, looks completely covered from above. Down on the street level, however, opportunities abound.

Trying something is the first step toward failure.

— HOMER SIMPSON

learn more about a new place from elders than from academics). And of course Gary Snyder is right, but people are going to move, especially when they're young. Our ancestors did. Why do you think our legs are the most powerful muscles we have? We're built to walk all day. So until you do settle into a place where you can make your stand, why not develop some eco-awareness skills that work everywhere? Then you can be an effective guerrilla gardener no matter where you end up.

It begins with land you're on, for whatever reason, right now, where you can start making connections.

Water is life. On some level it's the answer to everything. Remember in the film "All the President's Men" when Woodward and Bernstein kept themselves on the track of the crooks by repeating, "Follow the money"? You will not go wrong in the natural world if you do the same by remembering "Follow the water."

Unless you're up for a real challenge, in starting out you may want to avoid places with plant-unfriendly features such as:

Shade. Fewer than five hours a day of sun will make it difficult to grow things well, at least for most vegetables and fruit. There are other plants you can grow, however — think of a woodland understory — so it may not mean the site is a write-off.

Compacted soil. Former parking lots or sites where heavy machinery has been used may have soil packed so tightly there's little room for water or oxygen to move freely. Anything you try to plant here is probably going to struggle, unless you can either break up the soil or mound up something lighter on top.

No topsoil. Construction sites are often scraped clean of topsoil as a first step. This may be set aside and returned after construction if planting is part of the plan, but if not, and you try on what's remaining, your plants could have a rough time trying to survive the nutrient-poor subsoil.

Depressions. Low-lying pockets where water collects or frost settles can be hard on many species. Look into plants which can handle wet feet, or dig a little more and turn the area into a pond.

You're in a watershed. In other words, an area of land that drains into a common body of water such as the ocean, a lake or river. You and the grand web of life supporting you share in the physical features of that watershed. They may look and feel markedly different from those of another watershed even if it happens to be close by on the map. To know your watershed is to begin to know just where you stand on the earth.

How do you find out about your watershed? Watch the elements. Rain happens, and then what? It has to go somewhere. It may be obvious (i.e., you're on the side of a mountain above a lake), or you could get a topographical map of your area and figure it out by the elevations. Water finds its own level and gravity always wins, so that level is going to be downhill. Alternatively you can probably locate your watershed with a few minutes of net searching. The US Environmental Protection Agency has a site dedicated to the task called Surf Your Watershed (epa.gov/surf/). Or your local naturalist club or research librarian should be able to help.

Find out your source of drinking water. It could come from rain or snow falling a surprisingly long distance away. Another

Apples grow fine along a fence or even as a fence.

If fences make good neighbors, planting something to beautify an ugly barrier should earn you friends for life. The following are a few suggestions for things that will grow happily along or up a fence:

- Fruit trees such as apple, pear, peach or plum on dwarf root stock (trained into an attractive espalier, they can become the fence itself)
- Grapes (prune hard in winter to direct the next year's growth to where you want it)
- Hawthorne (may add security through occasional thorns)
- Holly (sharp leaves stay evergreen and discourage climbers)
- Morning glory (keep in pots to prevent an annoying persistent spread…or not)
- Pole beans (offer to split the crop as a neighborly gesture)
- Clematis (choose from scads of varieties for flower colors, bloom times, etc.)
- Climbing rose (get one with a fragrance to improve the scent too)

potential surprise could come from a basic reading of your sewer system, only this time in learning how close by the result gets dispatched, especially if what you flush is delivered not far beyond your favorite beach. Dismaying, perhaps, but this is information, and information is good. Particularly here because it's helping you see your city less as a place of street patterns or property districts and more as a natural part of the planet. It means you're learning to recognize the larger flow of things.

Next you might want to understand the air. Where does your weather come from? Your local TV weather buffoon is generally a reliable source, but pay more attention to the maps than the happy chatter. Notice which way the air flows come and go. Because TV encourages viewing with only bovine interest, we tend to retain little from the weather forecast other than whether tomorrow will bring rain, but you can astound your neighbors with what you learn about the larger patterns by applying it the next time you're outdoors and change is in the air. Point to the sky and explain where those clouds are coming from and where they're going and why, then see if their jaws don't slacken in amazement. If they ask why you know all this stuff, tell them you're just trying to understand the world as a budding bioregionalist connected to the splendor of life all around you.

Of course, where all this leads is up to you. Most gardeners go no deeper into understanding their own biological region than to find out what plant hardiness zone they're in. If you don't know your zone, someone at the local garden center will tell you (maybe not the new guy sweeping up but certainly the woman who orders the plants). The US Department of Agriculture system is the one most commonly used, but there are others. Typically based on the lowest winter temperature for the area, the zone system warns you away from plants likely to freeze to death in your yard come February. Some gardeners place more faith in these broad restrictions than they do in their own children. But you needn't be bound to what are after all just guidelines. Others dispute the zone concept itself for ignoring local microclimatic factors (wind blocks, land depressions, etc.) and things such as humidity, length of the growing season and so on. And then there are the "zone denial" gardeners who delight in proving the experts wrong. Beyond all this, there's the bizarre weather everywhere these days, making the

DESIGN TIP

One way to prevent an empty city space from being taken over for something unwanted (how about another $5 latte place?) is to use it. A space used is a space claimed, even if that use is for a guerrilla garden and the claim is dubious. Developers looking for places to buy and flip for fast profit prefer sites that are not controversial. If you can make a place look loved and cared for, you increase its chances of continuing as a community amenity. Every city has beautiful public spaces that were off-limits until someone came up with a bright idea for what to do with them.

whole thing a crap shoot anyway and possibly rewarding the foolish or bold for making plant choices everyone else thinks are daft. So if you're considering an early run on the local pineapple crop for Michigan, start planting now.

Finally there's the land itself. We'll get a little deeper into soil in Chapter Four, but it would not hurt you at this point to understand a broad view of what your topsoil might be and how it got there. For example, I have a neighbor living just outside Vancouver in the lowlands formed by the delta of the mighty Fraser River. His yard is a rich, loamy treasure of nutrients from hundreds of miles away brought in by the river. My neighborhood at a higher elevation didn't get the same influx of sediments. Our soils are typically mixtures of clay, sand and glacial till left behind when the last Ice Age retreated 11,000 years ago.

What good does knowing this do? In my friend's case, it means his gardening chores are that much easier. He doesn't bother with soil conditioning or fertilizer regimes or making sure he gets the right micronutrients into the mix. Pretty much any plant he decides to plop into the ground is going to do well. But in my case, it

It is difficult to design a space that will not attract people. What is remarkable is how often this has been accomplished.

— WILLIAM WHYTE

Sure it's a watery planet, but 97 percent of that water is salty and no help to us when we're thirsty. Two percent of what's left is trapped in polar ice or deep in underground aquifers, again no help. Less than one percent of the earth's water is available for drinking, washing, irrigation and so on. But mostly for irrigation: 70 percent of the fresh water we use goes on crops. The world's water problem lies not in getting enough to drink; it's getting enough to pour onto farms.

One simple way to save water: take showers instead of baths. Unless you're the type to stay under the spray singing the entire first act of *Die Walküre,* a shower uses half the water of a typical bath.

Another tip: fix those leaks. An estimated one in five toilets has a leak. How bad can they be? I just met an auditor who traced a $700 spike in a water bill to a leaky toilet. Get that dripping tap taken care of, too. People in drought-stricken countries would be shocked to learn how much drinking water we waste every year through leaks alone.

means I have to look more carefully at the particular conditions of the patch I'm planting. If they're found wanting (as they often are), I know I'll need to add organic material to the soil to ensure the plants get all they need to grow.

The forest not the trees

This subheading could have been, "The relationships not the objects." Gardeners tend to focus too much on the plant at hand. It's an unfortunate remnant of our transformation into city people. We've lost a fundamental knowledge that was general in the rural days. These days who knows when the next new moon is due? How many outside a few fishermen, boaters and surfers know there are two low and two high tides each day?

Your guerrilla garden plot is about more than your plot. It's part of a larger process. Nature is always on the move. This flow is called life. If your project can preserve or enhance a vital part of the flow, it adds to life and inspires more of the same. This means your project is a success.

Sometimes it can be powerful enough just to point out there *are* connections. An example is the painted salmon found on many of the gutters and storm drains in the Pacific Northwest. They're easy to make, using a simple fish-shaped stencil and a spray of paint, but the result is an evocative reminder that we're citizens of Salmon Nation where everything that runs down those drains

You get zero miles to the gallon but the back seat is a make-out spot.

means something, and possibly something drastic for living creatures lower in the watershed.

Nature on holiday

Our fundamental ideas on city living in North America are in transition. A century or so ago cities were seen as pestilent. US politician Thomas Jefferson grew increasingly fond of the farm through his years in Washington, and held the agrarian ideal up as the pinnacle of healthy living, while English writer Charles Dickens described the effects of urban pollution on its weakest victims — the poor — in ways that could almost make you taste the soot. But cities are coming back. That old pejorative term from the Industrial Era — the "Big Smoke" — has largely fallen from use, although it curiously lingers on for a few places, whether deserved or not. Toronto? You keep trying.

Cities are nature too: downtown Vancouver seen over the forest of Stanley Park.

Our new and growing appreciation recognizes cities as more than crowded cesspools. We're learning they can be as healthy as we design them to be. Along with that understanding comes the knowledge that we don't need to parcel out nature-based experiences through rare visits to wilderness areas somewhere "out there." More people are realizing that nature is everywhere, including in the city.

And it goes deeper still. Because we're also starting to understand that nature is not only a factor in how a city works but is a part of us as well.

Wilderness is within

We are the wild. Our bodies, minds and spirits have developed through millions of years of evolution to survive in the outdoors.

Look at what we can do immediately after coming into the world. Not much. Babies are basically sacks of blubber when it comes to survival skills, but they can do two things remarkably well: suckle (which is obviously important) and grab cylindrical objects, which is not. Let an infant grab your finger to see how strong this grip can be. I suspect the explanation lies in the generations we spent growing up in trees. The ability to hold on to a small branch might have been the difference between life and a fatal fall.

The late human ecologist Paul Shepard defined "wilderness" as the place where "wildness" is found, and went on to say it's ingrained in who we are. Like crows and foxes and other edge species, we can survive in domesticated areas but we're really hard-wired to thrive in the wild. Some critics scoffed that Shepard expected us to climb back into the trees. But his point was not that we need to return to the Pleistocene; in fact we couldn't because we never left. It's in our brains, and in our wild, undomesticated DNA.

Cities are alive

This notion is exciting but hardly new. Jane Jacobs probably said it best back in the 1960s. Still it hasn't caught on, or we would never accept the poisoning of our own homes the way we do. At least we seem now to be on the verge of accepting the reality that city people can't go on stealing the way they do, taking in too many resources, spewing out too much waste, fouling their own nests and those beyond in the process.

The new urban ideal — the ecological city — will be increasingly recognized as the high point of human design, even as cities continue to be the battlegrounds for sane and healthy development. But we can't lose this one, because it's all we have. If we are going to save the planet from environmental Armageddon, it will have to happen first at home, beginning with the way we live. This involves, as the ecological footprint people tell us, a rethinking of our lifestyles. We have to figure out an appropriate way to live on the earth that doesn't ruin it for millions of others or for future generations. For our part this can all start with the reclaiming of public spaces by the public for the public. So yes, our cities are gardens, but at the moment they're being tended by lunatics and greedheads. Guerrilla gardening is a way to begin taking back control.

Is it public or private? A few stone steps inviting people into a space can make the question irrelevant.

Starting-out spaces

So where should you plant?

The easy answer is: everywhere. You are limited only by your imagination when it comes to finding places to do guerrilla gardening.

Don't think first in terms of where you *can* do it. Take the wider view. Find all the places where you *must* do it simply because they need it so badly.

Consider empty lots, the narrow strips beside and between streets, back alleys, unused fields, parks, lawns and parking lots. But not just there. Keep an eye out also for industrial areas, the strip beside railways, school grounds, public utilities, under bridges, and the planter boxes around gas stations and strip malls.

Even in the most heavily developed parts of a city there will be ample opportunities for guerrilla gardening. In fact, these areas probably need it more than the rest. Don't believe your city isn't appropriate because it's too built up or all the good sites have been taken. Unless you're living in a toxic wasteland too dangerous to plant anything in (in which case my professional advice is…*run*), your city has more planting spots than you will ever be able to reach. It's ready to support a lush jungle, if given the chance. One study cited by landscape architect Michael Hough found that

Venice, a considerably built-out urban place, has 147 types of plants within its city limits.[2]

A tale of two cities

Hough argues in the classic design guidebook *City Form and Natural Process* that urban areas tend to support two types of landscapes. One is the "pedigree" landscape of lawns, flowerbeds, trees, fountains and so on — the types of planned places that have long been the province of professional designers and engineers. These need continual inputs of energy, engineering and horticultural technology for their survival.

The second type is the fortuitous landscape of naturalized urban life found commonly in the forgotten places of the city. Here he mentions the back alleys of immigrant neighborhoods as well

> *One is poetically and spiritually drawn to make little gestures.*
>
> — GARY SNYDER

Guerrilla gardeners might learn a few things from the Urban Explorers, starting with their delightfully subversive disdain for the normal conventions on trespassing. On the other hand, the places they like to explore tend to be dark, dank, manmade structures far removed from the normal walks of life. Which sounds adventurous all right, but how badly do you want to know what the inside of your city's storm drain system really looks like?

The following terms are taken from the Urban Explorers website (infiltration.org), from which you can also buy the "Access All Areas" guide book and read a tribute to Ninjalicious, a late and much-missed pioneer.

back breaker: (adj.) long, low tunnel in a drain
ball buster: (adj.) round concrete pipe drain with wide section of water
buildering: (n.,v.) climbing buildings, with or without tools and support devices
burn: (v.) ruin for others through lack of subtlety (i.e. "some guys burned the new tunnels by tagging everywhere, now they're kept locked")
CIHY: (n.,v.) short for "can I help you?"; query often directed at infiltrators

as pavement cracks, rooftops, industrial sites and more…and he finds these places curiously *more* alive.

These two contrasting landscapes, the pedigree and the natural and cultural vernacular, symbolize the inherent conflicts of environmental values. The first has little connection with the dynamics of natural process. Yet it has a high value in the public mind as an expression of care, aesthetic value and civic spirit. The second represents the vitality of altered but none the less functioning natural and social processes at work in the city. Yet it is regarded as a derelict wasteland in need of rehabilitation, the unredeemed blight on the urban landscape, the disorderly shambles of the poorer parts of town. If we make the not unreasonable assumption

Perhaps a garden is best considered as a precise point of connection between a human and the earth — a psychic umbilical to the earth's spirit. I know mine is just that for me.

— ROBERT THAYER

credibility prop: (n.) an item such as a clipboard or briefcase, carried or used by an infiltrator to reduce suspicion
creeper: (n.) one who infiltrates
expo: (n.) from expedition; a mission attempted by a group of people
infiltration: (n.,v.) going places you're not supposed to go in general; covers urban exploration as well as simply dropping in to conventions uninvited and the like
seccers: (n.) short for security guards
shrinker: (n.) drain that gets smaller as you head upstream
social engineering: (n.,v.) from hacker jargon; dealing with people such as employees and security guards in a manner that allows you to get past them or obtain information from them
urban adventure: (n.) very much like urban exploration, but with the focus on experiences rather than sight-seeing
urban exploration: (n.) the investigation of manmade structures not designed for public consumption, from mechanical rooms to stormwater drains to rooftops; usually such areas are off-limits

All some plants need is a helping hand, or line, to help fill the vertical space.

that diversity is ecologically and socially necessary to the health and quality of urban life, then we must question the current values that have determined the image of nature in cities.[3]

So which of the two landscape types should guerrilla gardeners think of planting first?

If you answered "both" you're absolutely right.

Use it or lose it

An empty city lot makes a classic guerrilla gardening site, and a good place for a dramatic entry into the campaign. If we agree that a city is a shared experience, something we all create together, what kind of anti-social message is made by someone who buys a prominent space in a crowded district and leaves it to collect litter?

Often these lots will be fenced. An industrial row of chain link may be an apt expression of an owner's commitment to the neighborhood. And what is a fence but a red flag to the bullish determination of the guerrilla gardener? Wire cutters are not expensive. They're even cheaper to rent for an afternoon. A few snips along one pole and some power-bending is all it takes to open a walk-in entrance.

Or you could find the owner to ask for permission to garden the site. Some will be supportive and may even contribute the cost of clean topsoil and plants. They may have never shown an affinity to help the neighborhood in which they've invested before, but perhaps only because nobody ever asked.

Grow up

Trees are the largest, hardiest, most attractive and most important plants in any urban area. Seeing your city as an urban forest can help shift your perceptions as you discover new sites to garden. Where you once saw subdivisions and lots and streetsides, now you will notice clearings, copses, *allées*, orchards, mixed deciduous and conifer stands, and everywhere a wondrous variety of trees. As well as areas that need trees.

Simply observing how trees grow can expand your abilities as a garden creator. You'll learn to see a garden site not simply as the ground but also the space above it. This is interesting even in winter when most greenery is gone because the bare architecture of the wood is even more evident.

Once planted, most trees need no help to look good and will generally suffer when someone tries to reshape them into something they're not. But that doesn't mean they can't be used in creative ways. On my street the neighbors planted a clematis vine at the base of an English hawthorn. The hawthorn looks fine in flower every June but awful every July when an incurable fungal disease robs it of its leaves. Just when the hawthorn is looking particularly forlorn, to the rescue comes the intensely purple twining flowers of the clematis spiraling up the trunk and into the bare branches.

Vines can be used elsewhere to good effect in creating a towering impression. You don't need an ailing or dead tree for support. How about a utility pole? A wrap of string or tape will help get the growth off to a proper spiraling start.

Perhaps you're tired of looking at an ugly wall. Boston ivy (*Parthenocissus tricuspidata*) is a formidable three-leafed beauty that climbs better and sticks faster than the related five-leafed Virginia creeper (*Parthenocissus quinquefolia*). These vines are not evergreen, but the fall colors are fantastic and even the winter growth is interesting in its own ropey way.

If you're looking for height but have a shady spot, you might try a climbing hydrangea (*Hydrangea anomala* subs. *Petiolaris*). It may take a long time (even years) to settle in, but once it decides it likes a place the upright growth can be dramatic. An established climbing hydrangea can be a traffic-stopper with a mass of white blooms looking like an improbable waterfall. Wouldn't that rusting industrial tower near the railroad tracks look better covered in blossoms? Or the walls of that abandoned factory you have to see everyday on the drive home?

Another champion climber that can work well in the shade is the akebia vine (*Akebia quinata*). You should know that this one is not shy. Plant it, water it and watch out. I once put one in an unlikely courtyard spot with limited sun and sandy soil, and wondered if it would live. The next time I checked it was on the third floor balcony. In places with mild winters akebia vine leaves even stay green, although they may look a bit scraggly. Other bonuses

Finding growing space means more than looking for bare patches of earth. The vertical plane is filled with areas that can hold plants. Even a concrete wall can be turned into a garden site if it has enough cracks and gaps to allow roots to spread.

Groundcovers such as alyssum or stonecrop should do well in walls once you get them established. So will most drought-tolerant herbs such as thyme and oregano. Whatever you try, make sure the gaps you're planting in have enough space to hold soil without it washing away (chicken wire crammed into the opening can help). The same planting mix you use for your containers will do.

The hardest part may be keeping the wall moist while the seeds germinate. Tiny pockets of soil dry out quickly. You might have better luck with established plants.

Gardens don't need ground, as seen on top of a four-story building in the Roppongi district of Tokyo.

are small but fragrant flowers in mid-spring and a weird, fleshy fruit that's as sweet as you'd like although too rife with seeds to make a meal.

Get back

In some residential block designs, the back lanes are designated as the working sites for deliveries, garbage collection, electrical hook-ups, sheds, extra cars, compost piles or whatever else the neighbors aren't supposed to see. Plant people know these can make more interesting places to walk along than the manicured turf and prim shrubs of the front lawns. Some ignored back lanes can be bursting with almost forgotten growth. I once lived in a house that came with a back lane passage filled with a big hedge of hazelnuts. How it got there was a mystery, but I suspected squirrels — those guerrilla gardeners of the animal world — because every fall I would see them raiding the hedge before scurrying off with the loot. Following one of the pirates one day revealed hiding places and more hazelnut shrubs growing in spots all down the lane, something no respectable neighbor would have permitted on their front lawn.

Let the squirrels be an inspiration. If they can get away with planting things in forsaken places, so can we. Hazelnuts are actually a pretty good choice. You have to be sharp to beat the critters to the nuts, though.

Park this

Every city has plenty of vast parking lots, narrow parking strips, lanes reserved for parking and isolated parking spaces. We honor idle automobiles as if they were visiting royalty by offering them our finest urban locations. These places are generally designed by engineers or landscape architects in the most efficient way possible to cram the maximum amount of cars into the minimum amount of space. I don't know anyone who gets enthused by the task. In most projects, the parking lot is seen as the necessary evil, the annoying thing you have to include before getting to the interesting parts of the design.

What's there is there, but that doesn't mean you can't make it better. Often these spaces come with a few non-paved sections to accommodate a mitigating shrub or two. Typically they hold the

A garden is like those pernicious machineries which catch a man's coat-skirt or his hand, and draw in his arm, his leg, and his whole body to irresistible destruction

— Ralph Waldo Emerson

most uninspired plants in existence: limp, dirty, sad little bushes chosen from the catalogue of hardy and dull specimens.

Help these places out. A robust tree in a place like that might do everyone a world of good. Planting it would be a gamble, since anything but a tree of considerable size at installation might fall victim to the next maintenance visit by the weed whacker. Still, you could try. Look for trees that volunteer in the toughest spots in your area. In my region, the smooth sumac (*Rhus glabra*) is a renegade that will move into the grungiest areas with no more than broken pavement for soil, but it's also a tropical and frilly looking thing with a gorgeous flame of fall colors. (Note that sumac is considered invasive in some regions.)

Parking areas may also make good candidates for annual flowers. Simple, easy to plant either as seeds or seedlings, their generous blooms may help save their lives when the wrecking crews do show up. No one enjoys pulling up flowers unless they're putting in something better.

What if your targeted parking sprawl has not a single planting spot? If it's a barren sea of concrete or asphalt from end to end? I don't know what to say as I've never rented a concrete saw for a nominal fee at one of the many construction tool rental places around town, then cut a rectangle into the surface, then used crowbars, shovels, picks or sledgehammers to break everything up and lift out all the material in between. Then I've never dug down to loosen up the compacted soil beneath and add some organic material such as compost to ready it for planting with seeds or established plants… I wonder how it would work though.

Green roofs are the new black

Although they're rapidly gaining *caché* as the new enviro-feature on the block, green roofs are not exactly new. Sod roofs were a fixture in Viking settlements centuries ago.

Look down from a high spot on almost any big city and you'll probably see a vast expanse of unused grey, the kind of wasted space that makes a guerrilla gardener drool. But while the current trend in green roofs may open up some avenues for guerrilla gardeners, this is not as ripe a target as it may appear at a glance.

Access is one problem. It's not too hard to stop people from entering your building, let alone getting on top of it. Even if you

Getting others to join you in your guerrilla gardening campaign can be as important a task as planting or pruning. If you keep your group small in the beginning it'll be easier to find like-minded folks with whom you're apt to get along.

Know yourself well enough to understand what type of people you're most likely to work well with. How important is it to keep things fun? Are you willing to work through an obstacle even if it means screwing up the regular schedule? How will you respond if others join the group with different opinions on how to get things done?

If you structure your group properly in the beginning, with everyone at least clear on what you're doing and why, you might save yourself a lot of strife later on down the line.

can get up there easily enough, will it be easy to work on? Will there be a water source? Then there's the question of whether the structure has been constructed to handle the weight of a large garden. Most existing buildings haven't. A big load of soil, water and plants could be too heavy for the roof to bear.

A few containers, however, would be fine. If the roof is flat, it's been designed to hold at least the weight of snow or pooling water, both of which are considerable. All this talk of water might serve as a warning, though, that rooftop conditions can be hot, dry, windy and harsh. You may want to do some research on what plants are likely to do well. Some rooftop garden designers stick to species that need little in the way of irrigation once established. Sedums are currently in vogue in some green roof circles, although it might take the general public more time to develop a similar fondness (I haven't yet). Or you could try something like lavender. It looks good, smells wonderful and can endure a dry spell. You'll probably still need to water occasionally. Glazed pots are better than regular clay types in keeping the soil from drying out.

Bed time

At some point in your search for spaces it may come to you that your city is teeming with sites that have already been designed, built and filled with shrubs, but the ones put in there look so grim and tortured that something must be done to free these absurd balls of bio-domination. Often these sorry embellishments of government buildings, banks, strip malls and dentists' offices may even be overlooked to the point of now holding no more than dirt. Whatever well-meaning decisions may have been made when these places were designed, they've often been left to deteriorate into unloved, hard-bitten excuses for living spaces. They're ripe for intervention.

Your imagination is required here. So is your cunning. The problem is, these planting beds may still be tended by a professional landscaping service. Let us now spare a moment of sympathy for the poor plant monkey hired to do the soul-killing job of keeping all but the designated dreariest of species out of these wretched confinements.

Regular maintenance means that despite your best efforts to grow a tasty bean crop over a granite block bearing a corporate

DESIGN TIP

Think of how people will not only *see* but *be* in your space. Will the experience be comforting? Stimulating? Unsettling? Geographer Jay Appleton described the "prospect-refuge" aspect of landscape preferences. Based on what mattered to our ancestors in the African savannah, he said, even today we tend to feel most comfortable in a spot offering prospect, such as a wide view over the surroundings which just might include predators (like lions), as well as refuge such as trees offering a place to escape.

Whether you accept the theory or not, it may be worth considering when figuring out where to locate a bench within your garden site. Few will sit long on a bench with its back exposed to a busy place. (Not that this stops designers who have not read Appleton from putting benches there.) Move the bench to a small hill with its back against the trunk of a spreading tree and people will linger comfortably.

logo, or to improve the petroleum-filled air around a gas station with some night-blooming jasmine, your plants may only get yanked on the next routine visit.

The best advice here is to do the recon right to pick your places and times carefully. Some locations may have slipped off the schedule and budget for care, their parched weeds an invitation to act. Others may be visited only once or twice a season, making them likely prospects for alterations that not only go undetected but could even be helped next time the crew does show up. Still others that are in more prominent locations or managed by more wealthy institutions may be more regularly tended, yet are still too enticing as prospects to just give up. In that case you may accept that your plants are going to be removed, but deem the site worth changing nonetheless because of the number of people who will see the result, although for a limited time.

All roads lead to home

When a group of Portland residents decided they needed a public space for gatherings, they didn't just ask the city to build them one. They made it themselves, getting permission from a property owner to use an empty lot and creating out of recycled materials a structure that let them store pillows and books and games to use for weekly potluck parties.

News of the project spread. The structure was broken down to lend out to other neighborhoods. The concept evolved beyond a search for more empty lots. Working out the math that most public space is devoted to streets, and that most streets are devoted to cars, some of the forward thinkers of Portland decided to break the monopoly by turning intersections into community gathering spots. In one neighborhood, the crossway became the focus for a community Tea Station where free tea was made available 24 hours a day. A Produce Station was set up where anyone could give away or receive free food.

Portland authorities, initially against the whole idea, eventually saw the writing on the wall. City Council passed an ordinance allowing citizens to convert certain intersections into public squares.

Yes, you may try this at home, perhaps starting with a visit to the City Repair website where you'll find the inspiring story of how they made it work: cityrepair.org/ir.html.

In a world increasingly concerned with the problems of a deteriorating environment, be they energy, pollution, vanishing plants, animals or productive landscapes, there is a marked propensity to bypass the environment most people live in — the city itself.

— Michael Hough

I talked to dozens of guerrilla gardeners in researching this book, meeting people who had a wealth of growing experiences, but none could beat this: Robert Sarti got involved in guerrilla gardening back in 1971. That was during his Yippie days and the All Seasons Park protest in Vancouver described earlier.

He went on from there to a career in journalism and another career on the side in activism, leading frequent battles with city officials over environmental issues including a campaign to get more parks into low-income areas.

Yippie enthusiast Robert Sarti

On plants as political tools: The motivation for the All Seasons Park protest was about politics, not gardening, but the gardening fit right into it. When you plant seeds you're saying that you're going to be around to wait for them to come up. It can be a shot across the bow, a way of saying, We're here and it's not just a one-day thing. Starting a garden is a very important act. Very resonant. It shows you have a commitment to the future because that's what gardening is. The same thing happened in Berkeley at People's Park. People planted things there to establish stewardship, to demonstrate caretaking of the land. These were pre-steps to a conscious guerrilla gardening movement, but they show these feelings are really deep and they're inherent in everybody. Putting down roots is a powerful term which refers both to gardening and you having a stake in the land you're on.

On how to begin: Start off with a row or something. Unless it's land in contention, most people aren't even going to notice. If that works and nobody does anything, you can expand it. The owner, if it's an empty lot, usually isn't going to care. For a city-owned lot, if you want to try going through the authorities, get a group of people, go to City Hall or the Park Board and say, We would like to take a chunk of this. The worst that can happen is someone will tell you not to do it. And there's a high prospect of success. People should be encouraged. Do it just for the fun of it. Or go to an empty lot and throw flower seeds down. Watch that for a year and you'll think, Oh I'm making an impact here, and the next year maybe you can do more. Using gardens as a political statement can be very, very powerful.

On the history of the activity: Now we call it guerrilla gardening but people have been doing this a long time. People grew victory gardens from the time of the war. My partner's father used to grow potatoes out on the parking strip beside the sidewalk. Guerrilla gardening has always been there.

IF I CAN DO IT... — Robert Klose, Professor Renegade

"I work at night when there's no one around. I want it to have that sense of nobody knowing who did this."

Robert Klose is a biology professor at Maine's University College of Bangor. He's also a gifted essayist, an author and a guerrilla gardener.

Klose lives in Orono, Maine, in a working class neighborhood he says is ignored by the rest of the city (or at least by the beautification crews who keep to the wealthier districts). Near his home was a space he wrote about in a much-reprinted essay for the *Christian Science Monitor* which had, "a rail line, and between it and the sidewalk a gravel, refuse-strewn buffer, perhaps eight feet wide. Across the road was a cement plant, also with its buffer. Not a tree, not a bush, not a daisy. Even the wildflowers seemed to reject this place."[4] An ideal spot, he explained later, for someone to sneak out and plant.

> I looked at that site in front of the cement plant for a couple of years wondering what would happen if I just put a small tree in there. Any company with the kind of mindset that would leave the site untouched all that time could not possibly care. Or if they did care, they would care enough to leave what I planted alone.
>
> I went looking for rescues, which is what I call saplings that aren't going to make it. I found a wild cherry tree in the forest that was in the shade of several other bigger ones, so I used that. I planted it one night, and they let it stay.
>
> Of course, this is like a tattoo: you get one and then you have to get another. I went looking for more plants. Everything I use is free. I don't buy plants. I usually look for hardy ones that I call aristocrats because they can take care of themselves.
>
> I work at night when there's no one around. I want it to have that sense of nobody knowing who did this. If they saw me, teenagers or whatever, they might think, Oh those were just put in there by the guy down the street — let's pull them up. But when they just appear like that, people may think a higher power has put them there. Or maybe an aggressive trucker with big muscles from the cement plant.

I have long believed that the garden is a better symbol of peace than the dove.

— IAN L. McHARG

There's a small house nearby, a solitary, blue, ramshackle thing. It's a rental, when they can find tenants, who are typically poor and never stay for long. Nobody has ever seemed to care much for the place, to go by the small front yard which never had a thing growing in it. That is until I started my planting campaign. I noticed one day, after I had planted a lilac across the street, they planted a lilac on their lawn. It was scraggly but obviously put in with care because it was staked and mulched. A few days later I planted some more things, and then so did they. If you can make something beautiful, as beautiful as possible, people will take a vested interest and they'll work to keep it that way.

I suppose I could have just stuck with my own lawn. But I look at the bigger picture. This is my neighborhood. This is where I live. It might reflect the travels I'd made through Europe. You see people there adopt public places, like the ladies scrubbing down the cobblestones. Why? Just because it makes the village more attractive for everybody. In the United States you do things like this and invariably someone accuses you of being a communist. Bike lanes, public transportation, co-ops — someone always thinks it's communism. On my campus, I just succeeded in getting bike racks put in. Can you believe it? At the faculty meeting last year I didn't say, "Who will help me?" I said, "Who will object?" It's much easier for people just to keep their hands down. So I took that as unanimous approval and I went and got the bike racks. Someone once it said it's easier to ask for forgiveness than to ask for permission.

What would I say to a judge if I got caught doing this? Hmm. I've been in hot spots before and the words have always come to me. At the time. I suppose I would say, I acknowledge that I planted wrongly on land that wasn't mine. I could argue that the land was not posted with a No Planting sign, but I'm not going to make that argument. I would argue, Your Honor, that I didn't harm the land. I improved the land. Not only did I improve it for the owners, but I improved it for the public good. If that's a crime, then I am guilty.

> The "control of nature" is a phrase conceived in arrogance, born of the Neanderthal age of biology and philosophy, when it was supposed that nature exists for the convenience of man.
>
> — RACHEL CARSON in *Silent Spring*

POWER PLANT   Poppy (*Papaver somniferum*)

It's the "flower of joy" according to some of the earliest records of its cultivation in Mesapotamia as far back as 3400 B.C.E. Grown today in North America mostly for its beauty and tasty seeds, the opium poppy elsewhere

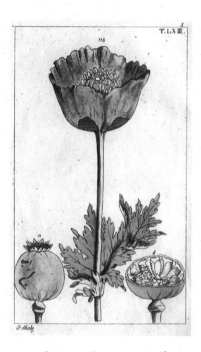

Poppy — Papaver somniferum
*Credit: Gottlieb Tobias Wilhelm
"Unterhaltungen aus der Natur-
geschichte" (Encyclopedia of Natural
History), published in Vienna from
1810, illustration by J. Schaly.*

has earned a reputation as a magical plant. And why not? No other flower has held such a sway over humanity: propping up governments, making some people rich, enslaving others, providing invaluable medicines for centuries and even leading to an international war.

The opium poppy (sometimes called the common poppy or poppyseed poppy in an attempt to placate the nervous) comes in a variety of color and style choices including single or double blooms, plain or cut-edge petals. All are large and striking enough to draw a passerby in for a closer look. The same genus includes other worthy species such as the papery and pastel-colored Iceland poppy (*Papaver nudicaule*) and the self-seeding Flanders Field poppy (*Papaver rhoeas*) famous for its poetically-inspired war memorial connection.

Planting requirements vary according to the species, but poppies are not considered difficult and will grow in most ordinary soils with full sun. They don't like being transplanted, though, so scatter the seeds in spring wherever you want them to grow, or in the fall if your winters are mild. To prolong the bloom of those brought indoors, sear the cut end of the stem with a flame or boiling water. This is supposed to prevent the milky sap from blocking the uptake of water.

But what about the law? Aren't poppies technically illegal even though the seeds can bought in leading nursery catalogs (and also found on that bagel you had this morning)? Nobody seems entirely sure — in the current climate with the US government War on Terror, Drugs and other Nouns — how far the arm of this law might reach. You're certainly unlikely to be arrested for growing a pretty garden. But beyond that? Some gardening experts insist that scoring the seed pod and processing the gooey extract into anything potent enough to make a difference requires a field's supply of plants, the growing conditions of an Afghani valley, and an Afghani alchemist or two hovering over the stove. It's also been said a few pods crushed and steeped in hot water can make a vaguely euphoric tea. I wouldn't know in either case.

Did you know: The word "heroin" was coined by in 1895 by its inventor, the Bayer Company.

CHAPTER THREE

What to Use

(Don't Reinvent the Wheel, Borrow Someone's Car)

We have too much stuff. I mean "we" in the collective sense of Western society. Unless you've embarked on a personal campaign to cut back, Mahatma, you're probably included. Our living spaces and storage areas are crowded with useless manufactured "goods." Once a year we realize how ridiculous it is to shelter crate-loads of inanimate objects with no apparent purpose in our lives, and so we have a yard sale. But it doesn't work. Because the neighbors have a yard sale too, and for some reason, maybe because we're as fascinated by trinkets as any Pacific island cargo cult, we end up buying and storing as much crap as we sell.

This chapter is about all the things you need to be a guerrilla gardener. The short answer is: not much.

The longer answer is: keep reading. But it's still not much.

Even my kids know the basics of this rule through learning the Three Rs at school: Reuse, recycle, and one more I forgot. But those two are probably enough. Especially reuse. We should take that one seriously.

Little things lead to bigger things — that's what seeds are all about.

— PETE SEEGER

Coolest tools

Technology has produced some pretty amazing things recently, but when it comes to what we use to personally dig holes, move earth, hack weeds and so on, we're not much further ahead than in the Iron Age. New twists get tried all the time. Like that twisty three-pronged fork in the TV commercials, they may even get popular for a spell, but the people I know who bought one and gushed about it at the time were back to their usual shovels and hoes in a couple of months.

Egg cartons make good trays for starting seeds of things such as annual flowers and lettuce. The pressed paper type will hold up long enough for the seeds to germinate, but break down easily once in the ground so you needn't disturb the delicate roots when transplanting.

Start by poking a hole in the bottom of each cup with a nail. Cut off the carton lid and put it under the cups to collect the water that drips through. Fill the cups with sterile seed-starting mix. Place two or three seeds in each cup and cover with a little more mix. Wrap the whole thing in a plastic bag to retain moisture and store it in a warm place.

When the seeds germinate, remove the plastic bag and move the carton to a bright windowsill. After about two weeks, snip off (don't pull out) the one or two extra plants so that each cup has just one plant. If you like, an organic liquid fertilizer can be used when watering, but only at ¼ to ⅓ strength. After about four to six weeks, harden off the plants by putting them in a sheltered spot outside for a week. When it's time to plant out, separate each cup and break up the walls before burying.

Tool selection is obviously limited to your budget, which is why finding well-made used equipment can be your best move. If you are buying new, resist the temptation to snag the cheapest thing in the store. It's true, the prices can be surprisingly low for some tools, and tempting for that fact alone. I know I'm always reluctant to pay anything more than I have to. But with tools (unlike, say, with clothes or restaurant meals) you're usually going to get what you pay for, and a $12 hoe that bends or breaks or is a pain to use is no bargain. If you accept this reasoning but still find yourself in the store aisle leaning toward the bargain-rate dubious stuff, try some simple math. Divide the cost of the tool by the number of years you might expect to use it. A $12 hoe that lasts a year costs $12 per year. After that you'll need to buy another, if you're still interested after the physiotherapy. A $60 hoe that lasts 60 years costs $1 a year, and then you get to give it to your grandchildren. If you can't afford quality tools, you're better off saving up until you can or else pooling your money together with friends to share. The bottom line isn't just the cost, but what you get for it. If it's important work, it's important to do it properly. A gardening tool should be a joy to pick up and use.

The list of equipment you might want when starting out could be long. Yes it would be grand to have a solid round-point shovel, a sharp-edged border spade, a wide-bladed scooping shovel and a decent selection of trowels. Also a fork and a pry bar and a weeding hoe or two, along with a bow rake and a lawn rake if you're going to be working on grass. Toss in some bypass secateurs (pruners) and shears and loppers and a foldable saw. Don't forget a big carry bag or drop sheet tarp to handle trimmings and, oh yes, a wheelbarrow to carry everything.

Grand it would be, but not all necessary. You can often improvise with things on hand, especially if you're a group and some of the members have garages full of stuff. But you do need a good shovel. Maybe a trowel, too. But at least get the shovel.

Some garden celebrity experts who may or may not be in cahoots with the manufacturers will insist you need more than one shovel. How many? Oh, three or four should do: a round-pointed one for digging holes, a wide-faced type for scooping and moving things, something with a straight edge for cutting clean holes and edges, one with a deep, narrow blade for transplanting and bulb planting and so on. Long-handled shovels are recommended because they let you work with a straight back (an ache-saver), but a shorter type with a D-ring handle can be useful in a tight place in the bushes or down a deep hole. It can get more involved if you let the pedants insist that no one digs holes with a shovel, because that's what a spade does, while the former is more properly employed in shoveling or casting soil. What*ever*. I'm going to assume you aren't out to create an arsenal (at least not yet) and also that you, like me, are comfortable not calling a spade a spade when it's easier to call all those things shovels.

Dig this

So which shovel will it be? Individual preferences will of course vary. Gardeners can get particular about their favorites and will tout them the way some talk up a favorite beer or musical group. Generally if it works for you and does the job, you've got the right tool. If picking it up gives you a pulse of pleasure and a heightened sense of anticipation, along with a compelling desire to tighten your grip and bend your knees and plunge it through the earth's crust at once, you've got the right tool worth bragging about.

If you aren't sure yet what that might be, you won't go wrong buying a classic "round-tipped" pointed shovel with a fairly wide blade that makes both digging and tossing dirt effective in a single tool. Look for a blade forged from a single piece of cast steel — that's the kind made by pouring molten steel into a mold. Cheaper models use thinner sheets of steel stamped into the final shape. For one thing, these aren't durable, which you're likely to discover at an inconvenient time. For another, because the stability they do have depends on the curved face, they have an annoying tendency to let clay or wet soil stick to the back, making you work harder with each lift.

You can tell a lot by how the blade fits onto the handle. This is called the "tang." They say if you use a new word in a sentence three times it will be yours, so here's one opportunity: when the garden store employee shows you the cheapest shovel on the shelf, say: "Do you have one with a longer tang?" The best shovels have tangs extending well up the handle, and include custom fitting or a bolt for a solid seal.

Even if you are on the right track, you will get run over if you just sit there.

— JOHN RAY

DESIGN TIP

Rocks make great garden features, suggesting an elemental connection to the foundations of the earth. At least the right rocks, placed properly, do. A big stone partially buried to resemble a natural protrusion will appear more formidable than a bunch of smaller rocks scattered as if by accident about the ground.

Placing rocks properly is an art. Don't just drop them onto the first place you reach because they're heavy. Examine each specimen carefully to determine which way it's inclined to lie, whether horizontally, vertically or diagonally. Place groups of stones in combinations that please the eye — three together look better than two, but not if you space them equally apart.

Be glad of a few days of peace in this garden where the nightingales sing. When the singing has been silenced the beauty of my garden will be gone, too.

— KHUSHAL KHAN KHATTAK,
17th-century Afghan poet

Now look closely at the blade edge. A narrow angle is best for digging a straight-edged hole. But you'll get more use out of a wide-angled type good for digging the more common saucer-shaped hole.

Wooden handles remain the most popular. And why not? Wood is light, flexible, feels good in the hand and might well outlast you. There are newer versions of shovels with fiberglass handles that are said to be pretty good too. I don't think I'll buy one. It doesn't seem worth it, on an environmental scale, to replace a renewable resource like ash trees with all the gunk that goes into making fiberglass. Besides, it feels right to combine wood and skin and soil the same way our grandparents and their grandparents did. Although you should watch it on the skin. Gloves are always a

Who you calling trash? The following suggestions are meant to inspire even more ideas on how to breathe new life into old objects (and reduce the amount we send to the landfill).

Before	After
Large cable spool	Picnic table, work bench
Broken concrete, used brick	Pathway, patio
Railroad tie	Raised bed (non-food)
Used tire	Container, swing
Driftwood	Garden fence
Plastic pail	Container, storage
Plastic gallon jug	Scoop, watering can, cloche
Loading pallets	Compost bin, fencing
Oak barrel	Container, mini-pond
Egg carton	Seedling flat
Bathtub	Container, water storage
Metal bed frame	Trellis, gate
Old piping	Fencepost
Scrap lumber	Sign, cold frame, raised bed
Carpet scraps	Mulching, weather stripping
Milk crate, wooden crate	Seating, storage
Old window screen	Food dryer
Old glass window	Cold frame, greenhouse
Hockey stick	Stake
Old trash can	Container, compost bin

good idea when working in repetitive motion. Again, it's worth it to spend a little extra for a quality pair that fits properly and feels good to tug on. That way you're more likely to use them and actually get some work done.

One last thing to buy along with your shovel: a file to keep it sharp. Many gardeners never file their shovels, and never wonder why it takes so long to dig a hole. The difference between a well-honed tool and the average dull one can be startling. Your hardware store will set you up with the right file. If you want to sound as if you know what you're talking about, ask for a 10-inch bastard cut mill file. No, I don't know why it's called a bastard cut either. I do know, however, that sharpening a shovel is fairly easy if you hold it in a secure position (a vice is handy if you have one), place the file on the edge of the shovel at the same angle it's been sharpened to already, then push (don't pull) repeatedly until you get a smooth, clean, shiny edge. And now that you know the importance of a sharp tool, you'll glare appropriately when someone borrowing your shovel drags it along the pavement or tries to break rocks with the pointy tip.

I said you could get by with a single shovel and I meant it, but there is one more tool that's highly recommended. It is a specialist's item, but that's what guerrilla gardeners are. Some times we must be mobile, versatile and discreet all at once. There are situations (waiting in a bank line, asking a cop for directions) when a shovel could be considered conspicuous. This is when you will be glad you have a trowel.

A trowel is a mini-shovel, and a good one is a wonder. It is a tool made to encourage earth-related intimacy. It will bring you as near as possible to the hands-in-soil joy of nurturing growing spaces without actually using your fingers to scrape and dig. A trowel can dig holes, kill weeds, divide perennials, save seedlings, transfer soil and perform many more of your routine garden chores, although things do take longer when you work in small steps.

Trowels come in an astonishing range of shapes and configurations — even more than shovels. The garden tool industry has managed to pack a lot of options in those few short inches of metal and wood (or more likely, plastic). You can buy them with serrated edges to cut through roots, scooped blades to act as

Do you live in a neighborhood with a talented gardener? Does this garden include some gorgeous perennials that you just know would look great in some other part of town, say in one of your guerrilla gardening plots?

Many perennials fare better after being divided as it encourages new growth. If the plant you're admiring is a candidate, watch your neighbor carefully when the weather starts to warm in late winter or early spring. At the first sign of activity in the garden, you must pounce.

First, praise the plant. Next, praise the planter. Then inquire innocently whether there will be any extra portion left behind after the plant is divided. And if so, might you suggest one use for it? Why, yes, now that you mention it, the plastic bag you happen to have in your back pocket would make a good carrying device.

carrying devices, and sectioned baffles to hold seeds. Perhaps the most important consideration for a guerrilla gardener is the size. You want one small enough to take anywhere (try fitting it into your daypack or briefcase or pocket) yet strong enough to do a tough job without bending or breaking. Portability is key because you'll feel better when you can walk the city streets knowing you're prepared to handle any impromptu project that might come up. Whether it's a volunteer maple seedling in need of rescue or a handful of sunflower seeds that belong in the soil beside a school fence rather than in the garbage can, trowels can turn inspiration into reality. If you see a good one, buy it (they're rarely expensive). I've gone through a number of them but am still searching for the perfect one. When you do find a favorite, take care to hang on to it. Like sunglasses, they're small and likely to disappear.

A weed is a poor creature whose virtue has not yet been discovered.

— RALPH WALDO EMERSON

You can too, with some recycled materials and a few flower seeds.

More for less

How can you get the goods you need for free or cheap?

Ask.

The combined garages of a typical suburban neighborhood in North America hold enough shovels to dig another Grand Canyon. Many of them have not touched soil in years, and will remain that way for more years to come until you or your group show up with a brochure announcing your community-minded intentions and requesting donations of under-used gardening tools and supplies.

Some of the things you get offered may not be worth the trouble. A rusty hoe with a wonky attachment probably belongs in the city dump. But look carefully. A little sanding and sharpening and tightening could bring it back to life, or if not that, the handle might still be usable when attached to another tool.

You could also try your city landscaping department. They typically buy sturdier stuff. When the budget calls for new supplies, they may be happy to have you cart away their old shovels and hoses and more.

Fund-raising fun

A lot of people cringe at the idea of asking for money, but that's partly because they forget an important point: you're not begging, you're helping people do what they really want to do, even if they don't quite know it yet.

Potential funders are everywhere, although few organizations will open the door to anything but a group. It doesn't cost much to get your squad registered as a non-profit society. That opens up your prospects to a variety of funding sources, including corporations with staff hired to do nothing but figure out how to give money to people like you.

Naturally, it's not that easy. You may not be the first group to show up with a good idea on how to improve the environment. The traditional financial fishing holes have been crowded for a long time. You should feel encouraged to try nonetheless, as applying is free. Anything that helps your application stand out while still meeting all the funding guidelines can be good — although perhaps not the fact that you're a guerrilla organization. Think carefully about your group name if you are planning to go for

Hybrid seeds are developed to maximize certain traits borrowed from their parent species. This can be a good thing. If we can grow vegetables outside their normal range, we're happy. One disadvantage is that hybrid plants typically benefit from the vigor of the first generation after the cross, but after that all bets are off. They may still produce seeds, but (as I've discovered after an entire season nurturing hot peppers) the plants that grow from them may be infertile and thus produce no fruit. Or if they do produce fruit, it may be something unexpected.

If you're in an experimental mood, go head on. You might come up with something interesting or valuable. But if you're keen on getting precisely what you want, plant and collect the seeds from known varieties such as heirlooms and leave the tinkering to someone else.

Now if you will take any flower you please and look it carefully all over and turn it about, and smell it and feel it and try and find out all its little secrets; not of flower only but of leaf, bud, and stem as well, you will discover many wonderful things. This is how to make friends with plants, and very good friends you will find them to the end of your lives.

— Gertrude Jekyll
in *Children and Gardens*

official funding. Smash the Capitalist Urban Machine? Catchy, but you might have better luck in institutional funding circles with something like the Neighborhood Improvement Council of Environmentalists.

Of course not many guerrilla gardeners will ever get as far as official funding or even think to try. So what to do when you still need at least some money for materials and things and you just don't have it?

Time to get the creative juices flowing. Tap into sources you haven't seen tapped before. Ask friends for ideas, maybe from places where they work, shop, play or volunteer. Is there an event/party/show you can stage that will give everyone an excuse to have fun and drop a few bucks? Local artists and musicians often have the least money but are the most generous with their work and time. Local businesses aren't necessarily run by profiteering swine; they may well be owned by people just like you. Which could mean they don't have much money either, but they might have something to chip in, perhaps sandwiches and drinks, or space for a fundraiser party, or help in printing up flyers, or at least a discount

Aphids are fascinating creatures. Ants must think so too. They farm aphids like cows, herding them onto their favorite plants where there is emerging foliage, stroking them to extract their sweet honeydew and fighting off any insect predators that might try to rustle them away.

The trouble with aphids is how they suck the sap right out of the leaves of your tender crop. To keep them out of your prized fruit tree, you may have to discourage the ants that bring them up the trunk by using a sticky substance like Tanglefoot. Tape plastic wrap or foam in an 8" band around the trunk and slather the sticky stuff on it. Try not to get any on you because it's like the world's stickiest booger that will not let go of your finger (not that *you* would know what that's like).

Garden books often recommend ladybugs (ladybird beetles) as an anti-aphid strategy, but this idea may be more quaint than useful. Ladybugs are kind of pricey for a bug (I'm told they must be collected in the wild since no one has yet set up a lady-on things you were going to buy anyway. It never hurts to ask. Even if you get turned down this time, you might start a relationship you'll both find rewarding for years to come.

Dirt-cheap dirt

Some of the spaces you attempt to garden will come with soil that's all but unworkable. True, anyone can transform a compacted, clay or rocky wasteland into a fertile site — or at least anyone can with a small army. Garden books often describe techniques such as "double digging," an odd exercise in which you attempt to enhance bad soil by unearthing the even worse subsoil. Maybe it does work, but it's always looked to me like a chore. Exhaust yourself on one project and you're less likely to take up another. So when it comes to poor ground, consider simply growing above the mess by introducing fresh soil.

Where to get it? Try the internet to find your area's free or recycled goods, starting with Craigslist.org. Somebody always seems to be offering free topsoil from their building projects in my city, and maybe yours too.

Shade happens. Rather than avoid it, pick plants that don't need or want all that much sun. The choices are vast. Here are a few:

Annuals — begonias, foxglove, impatiens

Perennials — bleeding heart, ferns, phlox, hosta

Trees/Shrubs — azalea, blueberry, fuschia, hydrangea, Oregon grape, viburnums

bug farm). Plus you may release your expensive squadron only to see it fly immediately off to your neighbor's yard. Some claim you can deter an escape by first chilling them in the fridge. They do not mean the freezer, which was tried in my house, due to a miscommunication with a four-year-old, and produced the world's first cryonic facility for ladybugs. I can report to science the fact that none survived the re-animation thawing process. Another suggested strategy involves spraying the ladybugs with a sticky substance such as soda pop to prevent them from flying away...but isn't this sounding a bit harsh for something that's supposed to be your ally?

The simplest way to deal with aphids is to set the hose nozzle to jet and blast them with prejudice. You have to do this early enough in the attack cycle and often enough to stay ahead of the pack. Once they get entrenched, they cover up in the curled undersides of the sap-less leaves and are most troublesome to reach with water, soap, sprays or anything else.

"Simply break the soil a bit and then toss the seeds":

Fava beans
Vetch
Clover
Alfalfa
Lupines
Borage
Black nightshade
Ground cherry
Cayenne pepper
Dandelion
Sunflower
Cosmos
Wild lettuce
Marigold
Shasta daisy
Sow thistle
Curly dock
Sheep sorrel
Shepherd's-purse
Smartweed
Milkweed
Cocklebur
Lamb's quarters
Mustard
Stinging nettle
Goldenrod
Burdock
Nasturtium
Amaranth
Flax
Rye
Plantain

Keep any eye out for construction sites in your area. If they have to remove the topsoil but aren't planning to replace it after development, you may be able to get it free. Because it costs money to haul soil and the cost rises with distance, they may even pay you for the privilege of delivering it to your nearby lot. Alternatively you might rent (or better yet, borrow) a pick-up truck to shift the whole load to the base of your new garden.

A little research here could save you a lot of trouble later. You don't want to take soil from a site that may have pollution issues (such as a former gas station). If in doubt, you can always get soil tested for contaminants at an environmental lab. It typically takes a few days and a few hundred dollars.

You might also try contacting your city for compost. Some offer non-profit groups decomposed leaves and yard trimmings for free, including delivery. The arboriculture department may also have wood chips to add to the mix.

If you have some money, another option is mushroom manure. Producers go through the stuff rapidly in large volumes. I wonder how nutritious it is after the mushrooms have had their way, but perhaps fungi don't take all that much out — they're not exactly the wonders of the nutrient world. You might ask the producers about their chemical strategies if you're strictly organic.

Another budget-saving measure is to grow your own green manure. Seeds are relatively cheap for crops such as crimson clover, alfalfa, buckwheat, rye and oats. Just sow them onto the ground you wish to improve and do nothing beyond the occasional watering. The plants do the work for you by grabbing nitrogen from the air and fixing it into the soil. Finally, turn the soil and it's ready for planting.

Animal manures which enrich poor soil may be secured for nothing from owners who tend to have too much of it anyway. Not your pet dog or cat poop, though, which may have parasites or diseases you don't want mixing with your vegetables. But people who have rabbits, poultry or petting farm animals might be worth a visit. Also llamas — I know an apple grower who swears by the micronutrients they produce. Horse manure is fine too, but ask for the aged piles. The fresh stuff will be too hot to plant directly into and may contain the seeds of weeds that will be hard to get out later.

Some people add coffee grounds which they get free from the local coffee shop. These would be off the chart for acidity on the pH scale, but a little won't matter and larger amounts could be good news for your acid-loving plants such as blueberries and azaleas.

One more source of a soil helper to consider is the local lumber mill, particularly if you're trying to bring more variety and structure into a heavy clay soil. It takes a lot of organic matter to make a difference in clay, but lumber mills tend to have no shortage of sawdust and may be happy to let you take it by the truckload. This may not be what you want for a site to be planted immediately. Sawdust requires a lot of nitrogen to decompose and that could take away from the plants you'd like to grow. You also need to check into what kind of wood it is. Fir or hemlock will do well. Cedar, on the other hand, will inhibit the growth of some plants and may even be toxic to tender seedlings.

Black gold

Try this test to find out which of your friends are honestly trying to walk lightly on the earth and which are just blowing enviro-smoke: watch what they do with the rest of the apple. If the core goes into the compost bucket or straight into the garden, they pass. If it goes into the regular garbage to be trucked to some distant landfill, call bullshit.

But not too loudly. Composting is not always as easy as some have made it out to be. First, not everyone has the space for a decent pile. Yes, there are apartment-friendly bins for vermiculture, or worm composting, but they're even trickier to get right. I know I'm going against the religion here in even saying so, but watch out for those worms. I followed the directions (at least I thought I did) for a few diligent months. Then I suppose I must have let up. Somehow my worms all died. I felt bad about this, so I got more worms and vowed on the memory of their shriveled cousins to do them right. Only they died too. Nor did I get the sweet, loamy, black treasure I had expected to spread onto my houseplants. My bin produced an oozing, smelly pile of yuck.

Of course, you would do better. I mention it here only as fair warning. Basic composting is no more difficult to pull off than a school science fair project, but not everyone is going to get an A.

When it comes to urban agriculture, things are looking up.

DESIGN TIP

Advice from landscape designers, garden experts and fancy magazines is all good if you remember to take it for what it's meant to be: advice. What you end up doing is your choice and should reflect your own style. If you're curious or courageous, don't be afraid to try new things. Come up with your own new combination of colors. Try new plants nobody told you would go well together. Every garden is an experiment anyway.

One thing to keep in mind, though, if you are keen on expressing yourself, is to be bold. The meaning of a design idea is likely to get lost in a garden if it's too small or insignificant. Your best intentions may soon be overgrown unless you make them clear. If you have something to say in a guerrilla display, don't be afraid to shout.

Stick with it and you will, eventually, produce a pile of rich, fragrant, organic material your plants will love. But there may also be times when you get a reeking mess. I don't want to come across as pessimistic, because I do keep a compost pile myself and I get plenty of workable material from it, but let's just say it's not under my bedroom window.

Here's the skinny on home compost control: don't forget to add enough brown and dry (carbon) to counter the typical overload of green and wet (nitrogen) from your daily kitchen scraps. Dried lawn cuttings (which you can collect from the local park if they don't spray pesticides and the cut grass sits in the sun for a few days) or your neighbors' collected and bagged fallen leaves can be added all winter long.

There are enough sources of free information on composting (anywhere from your local library to greenie group brochures) that it isn't necessary to go into detail here. The best way to get good at it is to learn by doing, while being constantly inspired by the fact that the most sensible soil additive will always come from your own garden.

Garden goods

Clear plastic sheets stretched over a frame of curved PVC pipes stuck into the ground can turn a bare patch into a mini-greenhouse. Look for free sheet plastic in places that use a lot of it to cover something like furniture; or you could try taping together dry cleaning bags. The structure should be sturdy enough to stand up to wind and rain, but you don't need to go to great lengths since you're only aiming to get through a single growing season.

A more formidable cold frame can be made from an old window propped up on bricks, rocks or wood. Here's another technique your neighbors may call "trash," until you correct them with the proper term "cloche" from the French for "bell jar" — although in this case it describes a plastic soda pop bottle with the bottom cut off. If you put this over certain tender plants in early spring or late fall, you can extend your growing period by weeks, giving you the first peas on the block or the last tasty lettuce in winter. Keep the screw cap as a regulator vent to be taken off on hot days.

Another use for plastic bottles is to fill them with water and surround a plant such as an early season tomato. The bottles soak up heat during the day and radiate it back at night, giving your tomatoes a warming head start.

Real free trade

Gardeners are the most generous people on earth. They're also the biggest scrounges. They love to give things away, and they love to get things free. To watch a gaggle of gardeners in action is to believe the whole market economy thing never happened. Keep an eye out for plant or seed exchanges in your area. The fact that you have no plants or seeds to exchange should not keep you away. Everyone understands, because they had to start somewhere too. Just go, talk to people and vow to bring up your end of things once you're able.

Or if you can't find an organized exchange, start one. Put up a notice, pick a spot and see who shows up. Seeds and plants are popular items in spring of course, but there's nothing that says you have to restrict yourself to that. How about extra food crops in August? Or clothes? Or books? Or maybe it's not even a meet-and-exchange but a straight-forward Free Table (not the table but the stuff on it).

Seeds of death

There's more to choosing seeds than deciding what flower or vegetable you want. Now you also have to make sure you're on the right side of the line in the battle for the future of farming.

The traditional planting community is under siege. A practice of planting crops, collecting seeds and replanting the result that has been passed down for generations is now threatened by profiteers who hope to turn the very idea of agriculture upside down.

A problem with plants, as the world's biggest seed-selling corporation sees it, is that they produce their own seeds. If only that annoying biological process could be stopped, farmers would have to *buy* the seeds every year. Ka-ching! And so long as they're playing with the genetic content of life itself, why not rework the plants so that these new mutants alone have the ability to tolerate the same corporation's best-selling pesticide? Why that would make the

What can't *you grow in a pot? The world's largest tree, giant sequoia* (Sequoiadendron giganteum), *in a container near Vancouver's False Creek, or so it appears.*

growers dependent on the corporation not only for their seeds every year but also for the chemicals needed to help them grow! Ka-ching! Ka-ching!

Thus the push by Monsanto to develop "terminator" seeds. Whether a scam on a scale this huge could even have been tried in any other era but our own corporate rampage is open to question. But let's answer it elsewhere. For now we might simply agree not to buy into any technology invented to help greed flourish while crippling the last of our family farmers. So check into what you're buying. Don't go for genetically modified plants or food. Preserve and promote heirloom varieties. Grow consciously. Plant with heart. And share.

Free rain

Water, some say, will be the oil of the 21st century, a source of political strife, international intrigue and outright war. Or maybe it won't, any more than food is today. If you've got it, you've got it, and if not, sorry, and better luck next life.

Fortunately, for now, whatever falls from the sky is still free. You can collect as much as you like if you set up the containers to store it. These can be as simple as a large, open, plastic tank you

Saving seeds is not just a smart way to cut back on gardening costs. It also expands your knowledge and deepens your relationship with plants. You'll feel more a part of the cycle of things when you learn to tend plants through the entire circuit from seed to seed.

Fortunately it's fairly easy. Plants do all the seed-producing on their own, if you let them. Your only task is to pay attention and gather at the right time. Think of how things are supposed to work in nature and act accordingly. Wait until the flower or fruit holding the seeds is ripe and about to fall. That means the seed is fully developed and contains all the genetic material it needs to produce another plant for the next growing season.

Pick the seed head or fruit. Remove the seeds. If they're wet, dry them on a plate in a sunny window. Label and store the seeds in a reliable container such as a film can or baby food

dip into to water your plants, or as elaborate as rooftop drainage systems which collect enough to supply the entire house and garden for the year.

Collecting rain is not difficult. Water goes where you expect it to (if you expect it to go downhill). And because what falls from the sky is typically softer than that from your tap (or at least less chemical-ridden), you may find your plants respond enthusiastically.

Start your rain harvesting operation with something simple. Drill a hole into the side of a 55-gallon drum near the bottom to fit a spigot (or if your city encourages this kind of thing, it may sell subsidized plastic rain barrels with the taps included). Raise the barrel up on a stand (an overturned milk crate will do) where it can catch rainwater directly. Or else divert one of the downspouts from your roof. That's basically it. Fill your watering can from the barrel as needed. Or, for a guerrilla garden which lacks a municipal water source, attach a soaker hose to the tap and run it right to the patch you'd like to water. In between rains, just open the tap and let the barrel drain into the patch. For more elaborate systems, a simple library or net search on rainwater harvesting will reap plenty of designs.

The first duty of a revolutionary is to get away with it.

— Abbie Hoffman

jar. An envelope will work too — you don't need an air-tight vessel for this since what you're mostly worried about is preventing the seeds from getting wet and moldy. When you're ready to plant the following year, a net check or library run should produce enough information on the type of plant you're propagating to know if you should put the seeds through a cold spell in the fridge or nick their protective coats to get the process going. Or try a germination test by soaking several of the seeds in a wet paper towel wrapped in plastic and stored in a warm place. Wait several days (or more, depending on the plant) and check for sprouting. Then again you could just plant the seeds and see what happens. Nature does it that way, with pretty good results. Chances will be good you've successfully helped to turn the circle.

Digging for treasure

The best investment you can make in terms of future amenities for your community is a tiny thing you can probably find for free: a tree seed. Plant a tree today, and over 50 years it will provide an estimated $57,171 in benefits.[1] From reduced heating and cooling costs to air pollution filtration to stormwater management enhancement, an urban tree is a financial boon to any community lucky enough to have one…or many.

YOU SAID IT…   Loren Rieseberg

One of the world's leading evolutionary biologists, Loren Rieseberg does what Charles Darwin did with finches, only he uses sunflowers. He works at the University of British Columbia, continuing research boosted a few years ago by a $500,000 "genius" grant from the MacArthur Foundation.
     Although we were both in Vancouver, we were too busy to meet. I

Here's a tip I wish someone would remind me of next time I've got an empty container, a plant to put in it, and no potting soil in sight: do *not* fill the container with garden soil.
     Because it won't work. Garden soil belongs in the garden on the ground. In a container it's only going to get as hard and as heavy as concrete. It will dry into a solid block between watering times, and lose the capacity to transport oxygen or hold water. Your plants are already constrained by the physical limits of the container, so don't make them suffer all the more by restricting their roots with a horrible growing medium as well.
     You're better off waiting until you can get an actual potting mix, available at any garden store. The problem is the mixes aren't cheap. But wait, put that shovel down, you are not going to use that as an excuse to go back to the regular soil.
     You can instead make your own potting mix. There are many different blends possible. You don't need a soil science degree to make them. Just know that you're looking for good drainage (1/3 of your total might be sand), holding material (1/3 could be the natural rock-based vermiculite or perlite), and organic material (1/3 could be compost or something similar such

might have pressed, but then he did have his hands full trying to figure out the nature of the living universe. We did the interview via email.

On why he chose sunflowers for his life's work: The primary focus of my research is on how new species arise, one of the most fundamental questions in Biology. Botanists have often speculated that this might sometimes occur through interspecies matings or hybridization. It turns out that sunflowers are among the most promiscuous of plants (hybridization among wild species is common). Thus, they represent an excellent system for research on the role of hybridization in evolution and speciation.

On what that means: Plant promiscuity can have some surprising consequences including the origin of evolutionary novelties, the formation of new species and the evolution of noxious weeds.

On things that make the sunflower interesting: a) Sunflower is the only major crop domesticated in North America. Thus, it represents the cornerstone of the theory that agriculture was

Nothing is so interesting as weeding. I went crazy over the outdoor work, and had at last to confine myself to the house, or literature must have gone by the board.

— ROBERT LOUIS STEVENSON

as peat moss — unless one of your enviro friends is around to nag that it takes 10,000 years to produce a thimbleful of peat).

Make sure you have drainage holes in the bottom of the pot to prevent your plant from drowning. Traditional clay pots are inexpensive and offer a classic Mediterranean look, but they also breathe which means the planting medium inside can dry out quickly on a hot day. Glazed pots will retain moisture longer.

New pot designs have emerged to lighten the chore of watering. Some have wicking tapes you can connect to a barrel of water to cover you during an extended absence. Others are called self-watering, although that's a bit much since they don't exactly turn on the tap themselves. They do however include a reservoir in the bottom of the container which can extend the time between waterings considerably.

But don't feel you must buy an expensive pot from the expensive pot store. Anything that holds your growing material and plants will do, including stuff too leaky for anything else. A wooden crate lined with plastic (don't forget the drainage holes), an old toaster, a toilet, a shoe, a bathtub — you get the idea.

invented independently in eastern North America. b) The Jerusalem artichoke also is a sunflower. c) Sunflower was accepted as an oil crop in Europe mainly because it gave the Russian people a source of oil during Lent that did not break the laws of the Holy Orthodox church.

On a variety to recommend to guerrilla gardeners: Willow-leafed sunflower (*Helianthus salicifolius*) is a perennial that can survive in poor soils and competitive conditions. It gets quite tall, but can be cut back in mid-summer and will come back much shorter.

On his favorite types: When I lived in Indiana I grew about thirty different kinds of sunflowers in my yard and garden (some wild; some cultivated). Some of my favorites for looking at:
Moulin Rouge (red sunflower)
Ring of Fire (yellow tips, red interior)
Sunbright (cytoplasmic male sterile — lacks pollen)
Teddy Bear (yellow, carnation-like flower)
Italian White (white flowers — *Helianthus debilis*)
Narrow-leafed sunflower (yellow-flowered perennial, flowers
    profusely in fall — *Helianthus angustifolius*)

BEV WAGAR

Commander Orchid and crew

IF I CAN DO IT...   **Bev Wagar — Green Gang**

"In keeping with a super-secret guerrilla organization, we had our monikers. I was Commander Orchid."

Bev Wagar did at least two things right in taking on small town mentalities in London, Ontario with guerrilla gardening. She got others involved, offering an important lesson in community building as well as plant growing. And she had fun, something that helps any kind of campaign.

We communicated a few times via email in setting up an interview, during which she sent me a story she had contributed to an on-line community news site. It captured the activity so well I didn't want to change a thing.

The Old East Guerrilla Garden Posse started out as a Friday night social outing with neighbors, some of whom were community activists (or just active members of our community association). Some were gardeners and some were just along for the fun.

We were a diverse and motley bunch. Between four and a dozen people would meet at our place at dusk. In keeping with a super-secret guerrilla organization, we had our monikers. I was Commander Orchid. Donna, second in command, was Corporal Hollyhock. The rest of the crew took names like Sergeant Bloodwort or Private Petunia.

Sometimes there'd be a mission planned, sometimes we'd just do random acts of gardening. A few times the posse did "potting" missions on local streets — we'd string potted plants with wire around utility poles and attach a tag inviting people to water the plant and give it a home if they liked. Once we did a string-up right in front of a police cruiser. Obviously they had better things to do than get curious about a gang of nutty people tying pots to utility poles.

Sometimes we'd put plants in the boulevard. Once we planted seeds on the railway corridor. Another time we pulled seedlings of a gang of thugs called *Ailanthus* — a very noxious weed tree also known as Stinking Sumac or Tree of Heaven.

A very memorable mission involved a complete garden rescue. One of the posse members had been kicked out of her rented apartment. We transferred, by hand, every living thing in her garden to the new yard/garden a block away.

We did two unpopular missions at the local library, which was an abyss of clay and weeds. The library had a lot of stupid bureaucratic rules about volunteer gardening, which explained why the local branch had been so steadfastly neglected. Ignoring the rules, we pulled tons of weeds, cut a zillion dead shrubs, dug in some compost and planted stuff. Of course the authorities were not impressed, even though the gardens had never looked better. We were so put off by the attitude of the uptight library staff that we didn't go back.

One Friday only two posse members showed up: me and my husband Sean Hurley. Our mission was to weed the pathetic garden beds at the local public school and plant some lilies. By trowel and flashlight we toiled in the dust-dry "soil" that supported a surprising assortment of weeds and candy wrappers. The local police patrol noticed us and drove over for a little chat. They, of course, had not heard of the infamous Old East Guerrilla Garden Posse. After they realized we were harmless citizens bent on improving the neighborhood they drove off with much rolling of eyeballs and shaking of heads.

Sean and I are moving out of London, and I expect that the infamous gang of horticultural radicals known as the Old East Guerrilla Garden Posse will pass into legend. The group that for two summers wreaked beauty and biodiversity in the area may garden no more. Perhaps a new leader will step up, rake and spade in hand, to spur the posse onward to greater and greener acts of daring and digging.

POWER PLANT **Sunflower (*Helianthus annuus*)**

No wonder the Incas revered this plant and cast it in images of pure gold. Stand beside a 12-foot-tall green giant with its massive yellow head resembling the sun, and even moving in unison with the cosmic orb, and you can understand the appeal.

The sunflower is a visual treat that comes in many shapes and colors, but it is also an important food crop. Native Americans traditionally ate the seeds whole, ground them into flour or crushed them into oil. They also used seeds and other parts of the plant to dye their faces, clothes and baskets.

Sunflowers are easy to grow. Plant the seeds in spring, give them plenty of water and watch them soar. If you sow the giant variety two weeks before you plant pole beans you'll have a structure for the beans to climb up.

Did you know: The phenomenon by which the sunflower's head can follow the movement of the sun throughout the day is known as heliotropism.

Sunflower — Helianthus annus
Credit: Gottlieb Tobias Wilhelm "Unterhaltungen aus der Naturgeschichte" (Encyclopedia of Natural History), published in Vienna from 1810, illustration by Paul Martin Wilhelm.

CHAPTER FOUR

Growing Basics

(The Root End Goes Down)

Growing things is easy. Remember this fact. It won't help when your tomatoes wither from tomato blight or codling moths wreck your apples, but remember it anyway. It'll help keep things in perspective.

Don't believe in miracles? They happen all the time, whenever plants grow. Imagine a tiny thing like a coast redwood seed holding enough data and vim to create a tree your whole family could live in. Of all the celestial bodies in all the universe, how lucky we are to find ourselves on one crammed with living wonders that extract carbon dioxide from the air and produce the very oxygen we need to survive. What could be better than that? Only the fact that many of those living factories are tasty and nutritious as well. Photosynthesis is the greatest thing that ever happened to us. If it were a one-time annual event the nations of the world would gather to bow before plants and weep tears of gratitude. Think of this next time you're outside and could use a lift: plants *eat* sunlight.

It all happens on your watch, gardener, so you may take some of the credit. But really, your main task is simply to create the proper conditions to let the miracles appear and then stand back.

And yet there are some so stressed at the prospect of horticultural failure they hardly know where to begin. Because they know what happens when they try to help plants: the plants die. Witness their dismal record on houseplants.

If you're one of these people, I'm here to tell you it's not your fault. Or maybe it is, but don't beat yourself up about it. Houseplants were made to die. Certainly the ones in my care were. I've

The opposite of natural is impossible.

— BUCKMINSTER FULLER

*Over the past ten years there
has been a mass deception.
So many people no longer see
gardening as a process; they
think it is something you can
buy and install, like a bath-
room, and when it is in
place, you go and do something else. This approach
is a symptom of a deeper
assumption that nobody has
any time, and so they must
not be asked to do anything
that involves commitment.
This suggests not just a profound point about attitudes
to gardening; it says something about where we are
with each other. But I think
we are starting to realize that
the short-term view is hope-
less and that you have got to
be prepared to commit to
other people, to places, to
your own abilities. Otherwise, not only are you never
going to make a decent
garden; you are not going
to make much of your
own life either.*

— KEITH WILEY[5]

been experimenting with plants since I was a child. I've studied plants at the graduate level in a respectable university. I have certificates attesting to my professional qualifications in helping plants grow. Yet I kill houseplants all the time. Never on purpose, mind you. It just always seems to work out that way. I don't take it personally. And I don't give up. I like having plants in my house even though they're destined to one fate. Whenever the latest victim shrivels into the familiar brown wisp, I wonder what might have gone wrong. Was it I, plant? Was there something you were trying to tell me? Might you hold the key to the mystery that helps me break the cycle? But I really don't spend much time thinking about it. I figure it was going to happen, since none of these particular species had genetically evolved to deal with my living room. Rather than fret, I simply buy or get a cutting of another houseplant, and start the cycle of appreciation and disappointment all over again.

Compared to that, growing things outdoors is easy.

Think like a plant

Here's the secret to successful gardening, guerrilla or otherwise: put yourself in the position of your plants. Imagine the world from their perspective. What do you need? And how are you going to get it? A little research will tell you a lot about the requirements of various species, for example that beans germinate only in warm soil and peonies will not abide being planted too deeply. But before you get to details, make sure you have a basic grasp of what all plants require for survival. Remember these fundamentals when deciding what to put where, and it'll help you keep everything healthy and happy.

Planting your own seeds and nurturing the seedlings that emerge into full, healthy, productive plants is probably the most rewarding way to grow things. But it's also more work. There's no shame in starting with transplants. You can pick them up cheaply at the garden store — or even the corner grocer in some neighborhoods. Among the advantages: transplants tend to be big enough to rise above small critters such as slugs which may otherwise wipe out your seedlings.

Light

Leaves are not just ornaments bringing visual delight to our days or flavor to our tables. They're solar collectors. And also water transpiration devices. Consider how strategies in leaf size, shape and orientation reflect a plant's preferred spot in the natural environment, then try to place it accordingly. You'll know you're starting to work with nature when you put a woodland plant like lowbush blueberry (*Vaccinium angustifolium*) in a protected spot where plenty of leaf litter keeps the soil acidic and well-drained. You'll know you're stomping all over nature again when you hack out all possible competitors nearby, but that's why we say "work with" not "slave to."

Water

Like people, plants need a steady supply of water. Unlike us, they often don't get it. So they've developed various strategies to survive dry spells. Most rely on an extensive root system to collect as much water as possible in a given area. Younger plants which have not had time to develop this root system will need more attention. The same goes for container plants which may experience the localized version of a deadly drought in a single summer day. Plants will endure many forms of abuse, but not being dried out. Also, when you do water, try to do it sensibly. Many gardeners are surprisingly lame

The guerrilla must move amongst the people as a fish swims in the sea.

— Mao Tse-Tung

Easy peas, as recommended by Linda Tilgner in *Tips for the Lazy Gardener*.

I haven't tried this, but I'm putting it on my list of things to do. I can usually count on losing the list before I actually have to do anything, but this is almost easy enough to remember:

Scatter over a 10-foot-square patch of ground one pound of shorter bush peas such as the Little Marvel variety. Till or rake in the peas and then walk on the ground. That's all. Two months later come back and harvest 50 pounds of pods. You won't need a fence or supports because the peas support each other. Try it just once, says Tilgner, "and you'll never go back to the single row system, trying to get each pea just three inches apart from its neighbor."[2]

at this simple task, perhaps because they're not thinking like a plant. Don't just spray the leaves or sprinkle the soil surface a little each day and believe you're done. You'll only encourage shallow rooting. Water less frequently but thoroughly so your plants develop a deep, strong network of roots.

Air

People tend to neglect the oxygen requirements of plants below ground. They don't know you can kill a 100-foot-tall tree simply by cutting off its subterranean air supply. Well maybe not simply, but it happens more often than is recognized. Take the example of a tall, robust tree successfully growing in a place for decades when a construction project one day sets up at the site. No worry, says the foreman, roping off the tree, perhaps even using a barrier fence, to prevent accidents or collisions. All goes according to plan, the project is completed, the tree seems fine. But one or two or ten years later it dies. Why? Heavy equipment compacted the surrounding soil, closing the open pore spaces that had been providing the roots with the oxygen they needed. No air means no healthy root development and a tree that goes into decline. This is a good lesson to keep in mind when evaluating potential sites and deciding what to put in them. Urban soils are notorious for being compacted and poor.

Facts from the US Department of Agriculture's Natural Resources Conservation Service:

- Five tons of topsoil sounds like a lot, but spread over an acre it'll be no thicker than a dime.
- It can take more than 500 years of natural processes to form one inch of topsoil.
- Scientists have identified over 70,000 kinds of soil in the United States.
- It's the different-sized mineral particles, such as sand, silt and clay, which give soil its texture.
- Roots loosen the soil, allowing oxygen to penetrate. This also benefits animals living in the soil.
- Five to ten tons of animal life can live in an acre of soil.[1]

Nutrients

This refers not to the main meal plants get from the sun but the additional elements they need to complete the growing process. Nitrogen, phosphorus and potassium are the big three; these elements are listed on almost all fertilizer containers in that (alphabetical) order by their chemical symbols N-P-K. Then there are the micronutrients — magnesium and boron and a raft of others.

Providing light, water and air may seem simple next to supplying the precise amount and proper percentage of the various nutrients. I know I can never keep the things straight. I mentioned the alphabetical ordering of the three main elements because that's the only way I can remember that the P in N-P-K is for phosphorus and not potassium. Although I'm not sure why I bother. I wouldn't know phosphorus if it walked through my doorway. And potassium sounds like something to run from after a train wreck. I understand these are important things for plant development — one having something to do with the roots and one encouraging more flowers and fruit — but I'm not sure which does what, nor do I know whether the distinction is based on proven scientific studies or on everyone repeating what they've heard. I suppose if I truly cared I might bother to find out. In designing new gardens for clients I have sometimes recommended lab tests which can break down the soil's nutrient requirements into quantifiable amounts to achieve maximum growth efficiency. On my own gardens, I don't bother. I just work with nature. I get all the data I need in the food I haul out of my vegetable plot (at least in a good year, if I stay ahead of the predators, and weed once in a while). And all those forests you see thriving on the edge of town seem to do fine without anyone fussing over the chemical content of their soil. What does this mean for you? Your guerrilla garden plants will probably do just fine if you follow the first lesson in solving soil problems: add more organic material.

The dirt on dirt

Soil is made of rocks, water, air and living (or decaying) things, in that order. A typical sample would be 45 percent minerals, 25 percent water, 25 percent air and 5 percent organic stuff.

It's hard to create a healthy garden without healthy soil. Not that it can't be done. City lots that seem to be based on rubble

It might be helpful to know where your soil is on the pH scale before you consider any strategies to amend it. I say "might" because I've never done it. The garden store kits are cheap and supposed to work all right, but I've just not bothered, partly because I know my basic soil strategy already (I'm going to add more organic material). If I had a problem (like withering plants), I might be tempted to do the test.

You may remember your pH lessons from high school. The scale goes from 0 to 14, acid to alkaline, with 7 being neutral. Most plants do fine in slightly acidic soil, although if it's too acidic and they're not something like a blueberry, they may not grow well.

You can fix this by adding lime which is cheap and easy and available by the bag at the garden store. If your soil is too alkaline, you can apply pine needles, peat moss, cottonseed meal or (to get more to the point) sulfur.

over clay can support surprisingly lush growths. That's because some plants specialize in difficult sites, which they eventually turn into something fertile enough to accept a wider variety of vegetation. Even so, the plants you're likely to prefer will probably do better with a more supportive growing medium than loose rock. So it's worth understanding just what you're working with.

Soil is alive. Keep that in mind and you'll always be a step ahead of the chemical jockeys who reach for a bottle of poison at the first sign of trouble. Soil is home to an astounding number and variety of organisms. There's a teeming universe in every handful, including so many living things that some have yet even to be named. In the absence of going back to school to get that soil science degree, just promise to treat your soil as if it is alive — again, add more organic material every year — and you'll be working on a solid foundation that should help your garden thrive for years.

Fertilizers and all that crap

Maybe you've agreed with everything up to now. You've sworn to add organic materials to your garden at every opportunity. You're convinced that compost is the key to starting and maintaining a healthy growing environment. Yet you're still tempted by the lure of the fertilizer lobby to give your plants a "boost." You're thinking of a "shot in the arm" with some good old N-P-K. Although your plants look healthy now, maybe a little "fix" of nutrients would vault them into a higher category.

Let's ignore the curious fact that the same terminology for fertilizing can be applied to 'roid-riddled athletes and common junkies. Because there's nothing wrong with wanting the best for your charges. If that means providing them with more growth-inducing goods than the soil happens to hold already, who's to complain? Especially for high-production plots such as vegetable gardens where nutrients get depleted each year, regularly adding useful stuff back in is an excellent idea.

Your dilemma will be over whether to choose organic fertilizers, which may be hard to find in variety, or synthetic ones which will probably come in more types and sizes at a lesser price. But choose the organic. Your garden will be healthier in the long run if tended with a life-positive approach that supports and strengthens everything from the soil to the plants throughout the entire growing cycle. It's also a better strategy for the planet because it uses recyclable natural sources for the material rather than factory-made, artificial ones.

Plants, in one sense, don't care. They don't really know the difference between organic and synthetic fertilizers. They can only use nutrients in their molecular form. Synthetic fertilizers work fast because they've already been processed down into this molecular form, while organic fertilizers must still be broken down by microbes in the soil. That's why your annoying neighbor can dose his tomatoes with a popular synthetic fertilizer and get dramatic results. And don't they look so tall, so thick, the vegetable equivalent of the varsity squad's front line, while your wimpy organic variety is still knee-high and spindly, smoking pot behind the bleachers? The difference, according to the organic evangelists, will come later, particularly with the harvest. By more closely sup-

Whiskey is for drinking, but water is worth fighting over.
— Mark Twain

You don't have to learn the proper botanical method of naming plants, and you may feel faintly ridiculous the first few times you try wrapping your lips around the Latin, as if your toga is slipping, but it's actually a good idea. Botanical names let you talk to plant people anywhere in the world, even if they don't speak a word of English. It also helps avoid confusion. A "black-eyed Susan" can mean one of several different flowers even in the US, but if you say "*Rudbeckia hirta*" everyone knows what you mean.

Knowing the botanical name can also tell you something about a plant before you see it. The format is simple: first the name of the genus, or group, followed by the species, or specific plant. Many of the words are descriptive:

albus — white	*barbatus* — barbed
compactus — compact	*fragrans* — fragrant
indicus — from India	*laurifolius* — laurel-like
macro — large	*phylla* — leaves

So you can expect some sizable foliage on a *Hydrangea macrophylla* which indeed has large leaves (and is commonly known as the bigleaf hydrangea).

Bev Wagar, aka Commander Orchid, offers the following planting advice for newcomers:

"Recommendations are always for a specific environment, of course. In our area [southern Ontario] the winters are not consistently cold, but often we have little or no snow cover. Spring is unpredictable, and summers are normally hot, humid and pollution-filled. If I were going to do flower seed planting in a dry, sunny, urban area, I'd try native stuff like echinacea, wine cups (*Callirhoe involucrata*), certain kinds of mallow, coreopsis. In a spot with richer soil and consistent moisture maybe lupins, foxgloves or balsam — things that re-seed.

As for hints on planting, here's something for bulbs. If you put them down 8 inches deep, the squirrels won't go that far. They'll bloom later, but they'll survive. Put some compost and soft rock phosphate in the planting hole — rock phosphate works like bone meal to provide P for the blooms, but it lasts for years. With the extra 'nutrition' the bulbs will come up in the crappiest of soil and remind passersby that green, growing things are inherently good.

porting the natural growing tendency of the plant, organic fertilizers give produce time to develop the full complex range of flavors. Crops grown with synthetic fertilizer, the argument goes, grow so rapidly their enlarged cell walls hold less material and are therefore not only bland but nutritionally weaker besides. The champions of organics point for proof to the difference between home-grown heirloom tomatoes that are a culinary revelation and the typical store-bought variety that would be better employed as weapons.

I can't say since I've never tried the same plant side-by-side in a controlled experiment with the two types of fertilizer. I wish someone would, and let me taste the results. Do your own experiment if you're curious. For me for now, it's enough to know the organics work. Of course, there are other arguments to make against chemical fertilizers, including the environmental cost of producing them and problems with their runoff polluting streams and lakes. But that case has been better made elsewhere. I'll stick here to what I know from growing and eating with my own hands and mouth. My vegetables are top-grade. Trust me — or no surplus squash for you next summer.

Types of organic fertilizer include seaweed, fishmeal, green-sand, minerals and more. They may not be cheap, although you can collect the seaweed yourself, for free, if you live near the coast. Gardeners I know who do this don't even bother washing off the salt, and seem to do just fine.

You can also try pee. I know a gardener who one day looked at the ingredients of a synthetic fertilizer, saw "urea," and had a eureka moment. She began collecting her own urine (which she says isn't as onerous as it sounds if you keep an old ice cream or yogurt bucket by the toilet). She dilutes it with water and pours it into her garden every week. It could be that, or it could be something else entirely, but her plants are some of the biggest on the block.

Cover crops (see text box in this chapter) are probably the most effective way to fertilize a large spread of land, with most of the effort coming in the time it takes you to locate a supply of seeds. The rest is easy. Sow according to the directions your alfalfa, buckwheat, crimson clover, fall rye, oats or other crop. Let the plants grow. Turn them over in early spring, giving your soil a serving of fresh organic goodness. Then plant what you want. This is a wonderful way to replenish a previously farmed plot or to take over a new site that might be barren. The cover crop can make the whole place look good as soon as the sprouts emerge, and the roots also help to break up the soil below.

No mono

Whatever you decide to plant, don't make it all one thing. Do your garden and the environment a favor. Embrace biodiversity now.

A monoculture may have certain advantages. If you're growing a single type of plant for money, and you can get the crop to ripen at the same size at the same time, you can maximize your profit by harvesting faster and selling in bulk.

The world, like dreams, will never come true. Operate on intuition.

— Jack Kerouac

Cover crops may be the easiest, least expensive and most effective way to fertilize. The disadvantage is you don't get to use the land to grow other things for a season, but many of these crops are attractive enough on their own that this at least won't be a loss on aesthetic terms. Here are some examples:

Alfalfa: Sow in late summer. It adds nutrients and the roots break up soil.

Buckwheat: Sow in late summer or early spring. It brings up phosphorus from the subsoil. Turn it under before it gets too big to turn easily.

Crimson clover: Sow in spring, summer or fall. It grows quickly, adds nitrogen to soil, looks great and is a favorite with bees. An excellent first choice.

Lupin: Sow in fall or early spring. It provides edible beans and makes phosphorus available to other plants.

Oats: Sow in late summer or early spring. It fixes nitrogen in the soil. It doesn't get as tall or as fibrous as buckwheat.

Rye: Sow in spring or fall. It grows quickly, is good for a short-season area and is easy to till in.

Soybeans: Sow in spring or fall. The big beans are easy to broadcast. It helps condition the soil by secreting an organic acid that gets broken down by soil fungi.

Summer vetch: Sow in late summer. It's an effective nitrogen fixer and can withstand an early frost.

And from a design point of view, a monoculture is not always a bad thing. Those waving fields of sunflowers don't need any other colors mixed in to look impressive.

The design vs. function dilemma is played out in gardens everywhere, typified by the selection of street trees. Some designers prefer one type of tree to line an entire street. This makes a bold visual display. A row of flowering cherries in spring or scarlet-leaved maples in fall can be a soul-stirring thing.

But one problem with a monoculture is that it's unnatural. Growing a single crop may require higher levels of maintenance as certain nutrients get used up all at once. It also means the site itself will be less healthy, if you judge health in terms of the ability to resist disease. The Irish potato famine that killed more than a million people in the 1840s was the result of a monocrop attacked by a single organism, the fungus *Phytophthora infestans*.

The solution is to mix things up. You can alternate cherries and maples and still get a great visual effect, but you're less likely to suffer from a single unexpected disease or weather condition wiping out every tree on the block.

The no mono idea goes beyond street trees and big fields of crops. The more you can encourage biodiversity, the more attractive your space will be to more creatures. This brings you increasingly closer to the living, natural world. Bugs, bees, butterflies and others can make a place seem more alive for a good reason: it *is* more alive.

If there's a better goal to strive for in all our guerrilla gardening efforts, I don't know what it is.

Pests or friends

Damn…little…creepy…crawly…bug-eyed…winged things… So which are they? For us or against us?

Resist the urge to kill things you find crawling on your plants simply because they're unfamiliar. They aren't gross, and they aren't disgusting. At least not by design. They're in their own world, and now it just happens to collide with yours. Must it mean war? Before doing anything, try to determine whether they really are a problem.

If your leaves are being eaten, or the sap is being sucked out of them, and you find the culprits in the act, squashing or blasting them with a spray of water or (organic) insecticidal soap is fair game. But if you don't have a debilitating problem, why chance starting one? The bug you squash as an interloper may have been scaring off an entire squadron of aphids looking for new territory to invade.

Even if you are suffering damage, consider just how much. Sometimes accepting a small loss and doing nothing is better than breaking out the heavy artillery where it was never needed. A few chewed leaves may mean nothing to the overall health of a plant.

Consider the strategy I once heard of in Japan to deal with a human pest. If you're ever bothered by a yakuza gangster, I was told, the solution is to get a higher ranking yakuza gangster to handle it. Or to bring it back to garden terms, encourage bigger things to come in and eat the little things bothering you. Birds, bats, ladybugs and lacewings are all fond of sap-sucking bugs.

Why natives rule

Plants native to a region fit in and look as if they're at home. They help us understand what home means for a given bioregion. They

It was one of the bewitching sights in the world to observe a hill of beans thrusting aside the soil, or a row of early peas just peeping forth sufficiently to trace a line of delicate green.

— Nathanial Hawthorne
in *Mosses from an Old Manse* (1845)

Compost works. A 3-inch layer of leaf mold incorporated into the soil in a typical urban lot will increase its water-holding capacity enough to support plants for four extra days without water. That's according to a study by the Connecticut State Experiment Station in New Haven which also found a 120 percent to 250 percent yield increase in crops (depending on the vegetable) compared to those grown in soils without compost.[3]

How big should your compost pile be? Four 12-foot-wide and 8-foot-high rows will do just fine, according to the study, which is somewhat bigger than I had in mind. They must have been talking to real farmers. But try this: make your pile as big as you can while still keeping it manageable enough to turn with whatever tools you have (a front-loader would be nice, but you'll likely be limited to shovels and forks). Bigger piles get hotter and turn into compost faster, but there's a limit to what an average-sized person can handle without shirking the job because of the sheer size of it.

thrive in the local climate. They can endure the local precipitation cycles (such as our summer drought on the west coast) without expensive irrigation. They support the local wildlife through symbiotic relationships (witness the Anna's hummingbird which returns to the Pacific Northwest each spring when the red-flowering currants bloom). They also give eco-minded gardeners one more thing to hector the less-enlightened neighbors about.

Easy edible landscaping

To grow your own food is to enter into a profound relationship combining earth, body and spirit. If you don't raise at least one crop of something each year, that's a growing cycle you'll never get back. What were you thinking? Or worse, watching on TV? Don't mope about it now; just promise yourself you'll do better next season.

There's something particularly delightful in finding a plant that provides everything you want in terms of aesthetics or creating habitat or enhancing biodiversity, and which gives you a tasty treat besides.

I'm hooked on edible landscapes. The very idea sometimes seems too good to be true. Combine the pleasures of gardening and eating? Who can't see the appeal in that? The subject is a book unto itself. Let's just say for now it's highly recommended. Yes, there may be some problems with certain types of fruit or nuts in public places, and some of the plants may require extra care, but so what? There are problems with roses, too, but you don't see people giving them up just because they don't leap out of the tray and plant themselves.

Some people disparage the prospect of public fruit because it might get stolen. Oh the horror, the tragedy, if they were to go to all the effort of planting a pear tree and the pears were to be taken. But by whom, if not a member of the public? And what exactly has been lost compared to before? We lose lots of fruit every summer in the community orchard I help manage. It's not enjoyable, since we've grown it with the aim of sharing it with all the garden members, but I've learned not to get overworked or consumed by complex thoughts of retribution. Instead I try to remember it's the journey not the goal, and that growing fruit is a privilege in itself only a small percentage of the world population will ever get to experi-

---

DESIGN TIP

We all know what a farm looks like, but that doesn't mean we have to plant our vegetable crops in rows. Farmers do it to harvest things by the acre. If you don't have a combine-sized plot, consider planting by blocks. The plants you prefer can fill the space, leaving no room for weeds. This works for things such as radishes, turnips, carrots, broccoli and a lot more. Just don't make the blocks so big that you can't comfortably reach the plants in the middle without walking in. The best measure is your own arm. If you can touch every point of the planting space without straining, you've got the right size.

ence. If that doesn't do it, and I'm still steaming over a whole tree full of figs stripped bare, I try to put it down to an unplanned redistribution of the wealth. And when that doesn't work, I can always hope for diarrhea.

Think instead about the produce you might get. The triumph of gardening peaks when you can not only admire your masterpiece but eat it too. Thoreau once said the only way to eat an apple is under the branches of the tree on which it was grown. Thoreau could be a bit of a scold, but he has a point on this one. It's not just about flavor. All the senses are engaged when you're enjoying a freshly-picked, home-grown fruit. Sight, smell, touch, taste, even the crisp snap of a Gravenstein are all part of the appeal.

With too vast a topic and too many details to go into, I'll recommend only one edible plant for now you might want to consider in getting started. It can be a successful test for a public fruit tree because most of the public will have no idea what to do with the fruit, and are thus less likely to take it before it ripens.

The quince (*Cydonia oblonga*) is a noble-looking tree that will stand out in a public area. It is medium-sized and broadly spreading with gnarled grey branches that hold their interest even in winter when bare. The flowers are big, white and sweetly-scented in spring. Because they have both male and female parts, you don't have to plant two trees to ensure pollination. The fruit is attractive, looking like fuzzy yellow pears, but hard and bitter when raw so casual munching is quickly discouraged. Quince makes a memorable dessert, however, if you bake it for about 30 minutes in a 350-degree oven, then drizzle the tender flesh with honey. It can also be baked into pastries or pies or processed into one of the best jams on the planet. Lastly, the tree, native to China, is almost bulletproof in its ability to resist pests and disease.

A prize quince from a community orchard.

Seed bombs

Also known as "seed green-aides," these emerged out of New York City when owners of unused lots fenced off their properties to keep gardeners out. As if a silly thing like a fence could discourage a guerrilla gardener. Accordingly, the Green Guerrillas turned rejection into an advantage by developing the seed bomb, small hand-launched projectiles filled with seeds and soil, made to break open wherever they happen to land.

Seed Grenade Recipes
(For vacant lot bombing, or how to hide illegal dumping space)

PREASSEMBLE THE FOLLOWING INGREDIENTS:

A. <u>Old Christmas ball ornaments</u> with metal hangers removed
   Small funnel
   Pelletized, time-release fertilizer
   Small bits of moist peatmoss
   Seeds, suitable for time of bombing and desired effect --list below
   Piece of kleenex or other tissue paper
B. <u>Small balloons</u>
   Funnel
   Pelletized time release fertilizer
   Water and watering can
   Seeds, see list below

<u>ADD</u>:

seed and fertilizer to grenade membrane through funnel.
In variety <u>A</u>, add wet bits of peatmoss and stuff
                opening at top with small piece of
                tissue paper.
With variety B, be sure to add the seed and fertilizer
                before adding water.
Both varieties A and B should be handled with care.

Wet peatmoss
Pellet fertilizer
Seeds

sectional view

<u>INSTRUCTIONS FOR USE</u>:

Choose a lot that has a fence and is legally inaccessible. Calculate in advance
how many grenades will be needed to cover the area. Check carefully before
throwing seed grenade. Observe all normal safety precautions. Perfected throwing
techniques are: for Christmas ornaments--use underhand throw and for the heavier
water balloons--an overhand toss.

<u>SEED LIST</u>

for early fall	for early spring	for late spring	for early summer
Soybeans	batchelor buttons	cosmos	sunflower
Clover	dianthus	portulaca	ornamental grass mix
Winter Rye	wildflower mix	zinnia	marigold
cleome	plain old grass	nicotiana	zinnia

Seed bombs are still the guerrilla gardeners' most lightweight and versatile tool to reach tough places. They can be made at home and used anywhere, even tossed from a moving bike or car at night to reduce your chance of being stopped.

The random nature of this planting approach may make it less effective than direct sowing, but there's something so appealing about lobbing handfuls of beauty into ugly places that their popularity has spread to campaigns in London, Toronto and beyond.

On the preceding page, courtesy of the Green Guerrillas in New York, is the original recipe.

YOU SAID IT...   David Tarrant

David Tarrant should be an insufferable garden snob. He knows more about plants than you and ten of your friends together. Trained in the UK at places including Kew Gardens, he leads horticultural tours around the world, hosts national TV shows on gardening, writes about plants for newspapers, magazines and books and works at the University of British Columbia Botanical Garden. Yet he's one of the most encouraging, supportive and inspirational garden experts I've met.

On the benefits of gardening: Anything you grow yourself tastes better, I don't care what anybody says. Because you've had an intimate relationship with it since the time you put the seeds in. You talk to it — at least I talk to my plants. There's some communication there, you know. There are so many other benefits. If you're having a bad day or you're not getting along with your mate and you go out and work in the garden for a while, it all seems to become all right. You come up with an answer.

On the biggest mistake newcomers make: Most people want to do it all. Say they move into a new house. From television or a computer they get this idea, Oh this is what my garden is going to look like, the delphiniums are going to go there, and so on. Then it needs to be taken care of. It's much better to do a little bit. I say to people — and they look horrified — in the old days when farmers turned over land for the first time, they planted potatoes. I think in a new subdivision, you actually could plant your front and back gardens in potatoes instead of a lawn and a border. Live there for a year, see where the sun shines, see where the shade is, see where the moisture is, and in the meantime you've got to till

Plant maestro David Tarrant

> *Take it from us, it is utterly forbidden to be half-hearted about Gardening. You have got to LOVE your garden, whether you like it or not.*
>
> — W.C. SELLAR and R.J. YEATMAN in *Garden Rubbish* (1936)

that soil, you've got to keep it weeded, and you get a crop out of it. I know this is going to go over like a lead balloon but it's just basic common sense.

On using plants in policy struggles: I remember working with a horticultural therapy group, I won't say for which section of the hospital at UBC, but we wanted to do something and they said, "Oh, it'll never work." So we scrounged around and got three half-barrels — you know the old whiskey barrels — and we drilled holes in the bottom and put decent soil in and filled them with bulbs in the fall. We put them very close to where the supervisors could see it by their window. In the spring there were these three fantastic tubs and suddenly it was, "Oh, yes, we must do gardening!" You need to do little things like that. The same works at home — a tiny bit at a time.

On a good way to grow tomatoes: Compost is great. I used to do a bit of judging. There was this woman in East Vancouver and she had these amazing tomatoes that were the best ever. I asked her what her secret was, and she said that every year she thought about where she was going to plant them next year and then in the fall she dug the holes for them and as the street tree leaves fell on the boulevard she would gather a few and put them in with a little soil. And the next day a few more leaves and soil so that by the time she ended in November there was this on-site bed of compost that she planted her tomatoes in. Each year they were fantastic.

On containers: As long as you put decent soil in and good drainage holes in the bottom it doesn't matter what you use. The size of the container is important, though. Bigger is better because they take longer to dry out. With a lot of little pots you've got to be home all day with a watering can. But one of the things I love about gardening is it knows no social values. I saw these amazing cabbages growing in old rusty oil drums in New Zealand once, and it told me something. It doesn't make any difference what you paid for the container. It's what you put in it that counts.

On why people should stop worrying and just have fun in the garden: The thing is, there are no rules in gardening, other than having decent soil and adding some compost or manure every year. The rest is up to you. I'm always saying to gardeners when I talk to a group, you listen to everybody tell you what to do, you read the magazines that tell you what to do, possibly watch a TV show that tells you what to do, and then you go home and do whatever you damn well like in your own garden. It's freedom of expression. And I think it's important to do. The more people who plant plants and have an understanding of our symbiotic relationship, where we all come from, the better it's going to be.

IF I CAN DO IT...   Al Pasternak — Easy Growing

"A lot of people want to do this. Well, they can."

He's a Vancouver guerrilla gardener with a PhD, only it's for "piled higher and deeper" and describes the perfect compost pile he says is available through some Danish natural fermentation product he represents. At least I think that's what Al Pasternak does. He lists his occupation on one of his blogs as "observer."

One summer morning he agreed to show me his guerrilla garden. It was in an industrial area between a road and some railroad tracks and next to an onslaught of construction to build the athletes' village for the 2010 Winter Olympics. The garden was small, just three paces deep by seven paces wide, but buzzing with bugs and hoverflies and several kinds of bees.

Roadside planter Al Pasternak

I started out by talking to the people in Green Streets, the official beautification project for the city of Vancouver. They authorize people to plant the traffic circles and the bulges along the street corners. One of them directed me here to this space beside the car barn of the Historical Railway Society.

It's interesting because everyone has their little fiefdom or what they consider their turf. I went and spoke to the tram manager and he said to go ahead. There was nothing in writing, and I'm always mindful that even with this agreement it could be revoked any moment. We have an interesting arrangement where I'm asking permission to use this land. Sometimes I try to exert my authority, and sometimes I get shot down. Once I said I was going to remove the bachelor buttons that were there. He said, in an email, Don't you dare or I'll rip up every other plant in the plot. Then there was a plant where the rosemary is now that died because that summer it was turning dry, and it was a long back and forth about whether to replace it. Eventually I got the go-ahead, but it was a two or three-month negotiation.

I want plants that are easy to maintain. Annuals require maintenance, and you have to plant them every year. I figured, what if you could plant something that would grow back every year and you could eat it? So perennials was one thing. Edible was second. I went for fennel, chives, things that keep growing. And the third thing was drought tolerant. It's hard to believe in Vancouver where we have very wet winters but it's also very dry in summer.

Plants I would recommend for anybody include rosemary. After a certain point it becomes a bush and does very well. Chives. Any flower that's edible: nasturtium, calendula. I use the on-line database Plants for a Future. Google PFAF and you'll find it. They list a whole range of uses, what's good to eat, good for fuel, good for dyeing, whatever.

I think anybody who wants to connect to their food supply should try it. Even if it's just one small plant. A pot of chives in your window. You learn things. Like, radishes don't grow in bunches with elastics around them. That was my first experience seeing food and thinking, Oh, they do come from another source. And this is going to become increasingly more important as the cost of energy increases and it gets harder and more expensive for foods to get here.

If I had any advice to someone starting out in guerrilla gardening I would say, You're not alone. A lot of people want to do this. Well, they can. That's it in a nutshell. It's easy, and it doesn't cost much. You can go to the dollar store, buy some seeds and throw them on the ground. Even if it's unplanned it can be very successful.

Potato — Solanum tuberosum
Credit: From F. P. Chaumeton's "Flore Medicale" (Medical Flora), published in Paris in 1814, illustration by Pierre Jean-Francois Turpin.

POWER PLANT   Potato (*Solanum tuberosum*)

Somebody get the potato an agent. It's a fantastic plant with a PR problem.

Europeans were unimpressed with the first potatoes they saw when Spanish conquerors brought them back from Peru in the 16th Century. A few amateur gardeners grew them, mainly for the flowers, but as a food they were considered low class fare and fed to hospital inmates.

In France, an early admirer was the pharmacist and chemist Antoine Augustine Parmentier. He realized the great taste and nutritional supremacy would make the potato an excellent staple (potatoes have little fat but plenty of Vitamin C, protein, potassium and more). To overcome public apathy, Parmentier planted a large patch of potatoes on the outskirts of Paris and hired guards to protect it during the daytime. In the evenings he withdrew the guards, giving the peasants a chance to sneak in to learn what the fuss was about. Sure enough, the plants found their way into home gardens and potatoes soon spread throughout the country.

Potatoes grow best in a sunny location with rich, well-drained, slightly acidic soil. Plant a piece or entire seed potato in spring about four inches deep. You can try store-bought potatoes, but they may have been sprayed with a chemical to prevent sprouting. You're better off getting your seedlings from a garden store or an organic market.

The tubers grow not on roots but on the underground stems arising from them. Once the plants are 5–6 inches high, mound up the soil around the stem (you can pile soil right on top of the leaves) to provide growing space and to keep the sun from turning the potatoes green (a sign of the poison solanine, which can be scraped away to salvage the rest of the potato).

You can also grow potatoes in a container such as a trash can. Put six inches of soil in the bottom, add the seed potatoes, then keep adding straw or shredded newspaper as the leaves grow. At harvest time, when the leaves die back, simply tip the can over and reap.

Did you know: The potato is the first food grown in space. It happened during a 1995 experiment on the shuttle Columbia.

Our bodies are our gardens, to the which our wills are gardeners…either to have it sterile with idleness or manured with industry.

— WILLIAM SHAKESPEARE
in "Othello"

CHAPTER FIVE

Naturescaping 101

(There's Always Somebody Home in a Habitat)

G uerrilla gardeners are not all after the same thing. This is not a one-front war. Our differing goals and varying tactics have inspired a decidedly diverse bunch. One day when someone hosts the first International Convention of Guerrilla Gardeners and thousands from all over the world converge in a ballroom in some big city, expect to hear gasps as one delegate after another walks in, surveys the crowd, and thinks…I'm one of *you*? And later you should hear laughter as grandmothers and street punks discuss the best way to dye hair so it gets really blue.

Motives for planting in any particular spot can vary as much as the planters, or not be thought through at all. You may decide to improve a place that needs it because…it needs it. Shouldn't that be enough?

Results may be gauged in various ways as well. If it looks better than before, that's probably good. Maybe it brings color to a gray wastescape or uses a wall of evergreen laurel to block the sightline to a dump. Just the display of volunteer activity — a sign that somebody cares — can be enough to stop others from littering. It may go beyond that to uplift a neglected or shunned place into an attraction. People might enter a newly gardened space for a closer look, decide to linger and even mingle. It could have seating with footrests for seniors and a place for new mothers to park strollers. It could be a garden to stimulate not the eye but the nose: imagine sidewalk blooms designed to remind a commuter crowd that life can still be sweet even when the job isn't, or a grassy, earthy aroma meant to evoke the idyll of the meadow on a summer day.

Expose a child to a particular environment in his susceptible time and he will perceive in the shapes of that environment.

— WALLACE STEGNER

Perhaps the intent is to stimulate none of the five senses but the mind, inspiring a philosophical journey beginning with the question: whose space? A plot formerly considered off-limits may come publicly alive with some purple echinacea around a giant sunflower next to a giant plywood bunny painted by children. It worked that way for a traffic calming attempt in my neighborhood in which a caption above the bunny reminded impatient drivers, "Time is funny." But the message wasn't just for drivers. I liked to think at least one person one day stopped to ponder how it got there…since the government isn't using child labor…yet…this must have been done by regular people…from the neighborhood …so this space can't be off-limits after all…which must mean…it really belongs to…us!

It's encouraging to see guerrilla gardens bloom for a hundred reasons and more. But one motive, I'm almost ready to argue, rises above all others. The ultimate goal of guerrilla gardening is to save the planet. The best way to do that is by supporting biological

Bats are not the bloodthirsty savages of popular misconception. They're not creepy. They're not interested in your neck and they're not going to get tangled in your hair to cause a hysterical shrieking fit. Instead, they're one of the most prolific mosquito-eating friends you can attract to the garden. Bats eat up to 600 mosquitoes an hour, or 3,000 in a good night.[2] And after all that, all they want in return is a quiet place to sleep in during the day. A tree hollow or similar dark enclosure will provide the secure space they need. Or you could set up a bat box.

The most basic model is a narrow box with an open bottom for the bats to crawl up into. You can buy bat boxes, or make your own out of ½-inch plywood. Make it a box about 2 feet tall, 14 inches wide, with a 4-inch landing area extending below the entrance.

Place it a sunny location. Most bat houses fail because they aren't in a sunny spot, according to Russell Link in *Landscaping for Wildlife in the Pacific Northwest*. He says bats like their houses warm. He also says placing the box on a post at least 12 feet high is better than in a tree with branches that produce shade and may obstruct their flying entrances and exits.

diversity, the grand variety of life. Biodiversity is encouraged in bigger, better and healthier ecosystems nurturing a wide range of plants and creatures. So the most earth-friendly thing we can do today is provide natural urban homes, food and shagging grounds for the many other organisms with which we share the earth. I should probably qualify the word share with its own inverted commas of irony, because at present we "share" the earth the way Mike Tyson used to "share" a boxing ring. But this is precisely why we need more guerrilla gardens and more guerrilla gardeners. Because that habitat we say we're building for wildlife? It isn't just for critters. It's for us. Our last chance to live on a planet hospitable to billions of people is to create cities where nature is not just a sideshow but the foundation of all life around us.

Land claims

Naturescaping is one way to describe the strategy of creating or improving a "natural" ecosystem in a developed area. An ecosystem is all the living things and the environment supporting them in a defined location. An ecosystem can be tiny, like a handful of soil with its billions of microbes, or vast like the prairies. The ecosystems we create as guerrilla gardeners are typically on the level of a small site, such as a city lot.

Naturescaping sounds elaborate, but it can be a surprisingly simple move. Put a single wild lilac (*ceanothus*) in a pot in a parking lot, and it may come to support an entire life cycle of butterflies from larvae to adulthood and even bring in some hummingbirds along the way. Or you can get more involved. Rent a jackhammer and you could convert the parking lot into a forest, choosing your plants carefully for the canopy layer, middle layer of small trees and tall shrubs, and groundcover of flowers, grasses and more, all to maximize the amount and variety of living things the space might support.

In either case the most obvious beneficiaries are, for once, not humans but the rest of the living world. This suggests a return to a time when we lived more harmoniously with the biosphere, if not by design then by the fact that we were originally tree and grassland dwellers and later farm people who had to understand the operating systems for the land in order to survive on it. But it's really a step toward the future, because cities one day will be places where

If we envision ourselves as participants in the same grand, complex web of interactions as the forest, the planting of acorns is like planting a part of ourselves. The morality that comes from such a vision of ecosystem-as-life is a common thread that, if taught and encouraged, could unite all of mankind.

— Bernd Heinrich

> *Perennials are the ones that grow like weeds, biennials are the ones that die this year instead of next and hardy annuals are the ones that never come up at all.*
>
> — KATHERINE WHITEHORN

the landscape best reflects our collective values, and these values will no longer be about the domination, exploitation and abuse of the earth but the appreciation and improvement of it.

All of which benefits us, of course. So we win both in the short term (since we get to enjoy these pretty places) and in the long term because we increase the chances that our offspring will be able to enjoy them as well. Yes, I know. It's all about us. Again. What can you do when you're the top of the food chain? Try to be humble, don't flaunt your opposable thumbs, and promise to do your part as a true patriot of the planet. Providing homes for the living world in the very urbanized environment that threatens to destroy them is the best way I know to begin.

Designing for diversity

Not everyone gets naturescaping. This new religion is still in its early stages. Next to a city park with its manicured carpet of grass and flashy rows of petunias, your patch of drought-tolerant dusky natives, fallen trees and rotting brush may be seen as untended or abandoned. Some may even call it "messy."

You might be tempted to scoff, sneer or preach at the ecological boors. Resist the urge. The environmental movement needs a lot of things, but more piety is probably not one of them. Sometimes you're better off not leading people by the hand but point-

For all the bile we reserve for bugs, a few have managed to make it into our good graces. At the top of the list is the butterfly. Everyone loves these fluttering portraits of delicate beauty. Why other creatures — even their close cousins the moths — can't get a break is a mystery.

To encourage more butterflies to come to your garden, you could build a butterfly box. It might be fun, and look whimsical, but it's not likely to attract butterflies. At least that's the opinion of the North American Butterfly Association. On their website here's how they answer the question on whether butterfly boxes work:

"Unfortunately, no. While so-called butterfly boxes can be attractive, and do little harm, studies have shown that butterflies do not use them in any way." [3]

ing out where they can find out the answers themselves. Urban ecology is growing in popularity, and naturalized park spaces are becoming more common, but even in the most progressive areas it hasn't exactly swept town. Those who have grown up with conventional ideas about land and beauty and recreation may resist efforts to impose what can be a dramatically different aesthetic.

Perceptions do change, though — and fairly quickly once people understand what's going on. If you get the chance, explain that it's about enhancing biodiversity. And if that clunky phrase only confuses them, try switching to, "It's a way to celebrate the natural beauty of our land." Then continue with the rap on why biodiversity matters. This isn't about you or me or what we think looks nice, you might say. It's about the future of the planet. We survive on this fragile earth only because of its properly functioning ecosystems which provide us with air, water and food. Protecting an ecosystem is one of the most important things we can do. Each one is linked to the next in a complex web of life we don't even fully understand, but we can work with what we know. We can help an ecosystem by making sure it supports the greatest variety and number of living species possible. Or in other words, by enhancing biodiversity.

When we plant in a space to make a thriving ecosystem — especially in a city where it may be seen by thousands every day — we're also making a statement. We're taking a stand on the side of

Well. Kind of closed that door pretty abruptly, didn't they? And those are the butterfly people. You'd think they would be a little more delicate in their denial of all those pretty boxes set up all over North America.

Could they be wrong? It's possible. You could set up your own butterfly box (they do look attractive) and find out for yourself. Or you could follow the advice of Robert Snetsinger from the Department of Entomology at Pennsylvannia State University:

"I have yet to see evidence to support the notion that butterflies actually need or use butterfly houses. My suggestion is, if you want to do something useful for butterflies, build them a mud puddle." [4]

DESIGN TIP

In some city neighborhoods, a fence is like a taunt for thieves who enjoy a challenge. But in most cases even a simple, low structure can be enough to keep out unwanted traffic, or at least peeing dogs. One way to enclose an area that looks great and costs nothing is to build a living fence. Or make that *plant* a living fence, because there's no construction necessary.

Just take whips of fresh-cut willow roughly six feet long and stick the butt ends about 8–12 inches apart into the ground at a 45-degree angle. When you get to the end of the row, go back and plant another beside it, this time with the tips pointing up at the opposite angle. You'll end up with a cross-patterned fence that turns leafy green and gorgeous every spring. You can use a variety of plants for this kind of thing but willows are a logical first choice because they grow everywhere and they have a built-in hormone that makes rooting a snap (some people soak or boil willow cuttings and then use the water as a rooting aide when propagating cuttings or starting seeds).

Although we try to make these divisions between what people do and nature, I think the two are intertwined and integral. This is a matter for celebration.

— Andy Goldsworthy

nature. Even in a busy, built-up area like downtown, in the middle of a concrete sea, we're highlighting the fact that cities are alive. This planting (cue the trumpets) marks our pledge to help the living environment flourish. As the land is our witness, we shall rule our destiny, and it will be lived in the green cities of our own design.

Right, but what about the messy part? If your naturescaping project is likely to be controversial or not immediately understood, you must make your intent clear. Someone who has spent two snarling hours removing the weeds from his own lawn may resent your approach to plants which can seem less laissez-faire than lazy. But if you have a border of, say, a low dry-rock wall separating your naturalized project area from its surroundings, it should convey the point: naturescaping project starts here.

A naturalized space can look stunning in an urban setting. The juxtaposition of the real world (nature) with the other world (how most of us live) may provide an opportunity for beauty of head-turning proportions. It needn't take much effort to suggest that this is not a neglected spot going to seed. A log bench next to a bark mulch path winding through a grove of trees hold-

Native plants are having it rough enough lately without guerrilla gardeners raiding their last sanctuaries for material. Most native plant societies (try googling for the one in your area) have guidelines on collecting, and they generally forbid taking anything from the wild unless it's in an area about to be developed, in which case your operation is actually a rescue. Barring that, the best way to get native plants is through seeds, cuttings or a nursery. If you do collect seeds or cuttings, take only a few and keep the plant community thriving.

The following are not guidelines but a "code of ethics" established by the Native Plant Society of British Columbia. Not that *you* need any more moral guidance or precautionary admonishments. In fact, these are refreshingly positive. Each statement builds on the one preceding it and supports the one to come, somewhat like a "stream gathering fish." Members:
- Understand that plants are essential to all life.

ing birdboxes and bathouses are all indications of intent that won't ruin the effect or look imposing. I'm not a fan of signs in natural areas, and not only because people in the eco-restoration business insist on calling them "interpretative signage." I just think the lessons should come from the landscape itself. But this may be one case where a small, friendly explanation of the project can go a long way toward improving the view for everyone.

Final argument for supporting an eco-sensitive planting project with species selected appropriately for the bioregion? Native plants can support 50 times more native wildlife species than exotic plants.[1]

Will chirp for food

You may never know half the many creatures you're creating a home for when you start a naturescaping project. If it helps, think in general terms of what the majority are likely to need, and then provide it. It turns out that birds and bugs and small mammals and reptiles and lot of other things need the same things we do: food and shelter, mostly. Water is nice too, if you have it.

Amphibians may be happy to dine on your snails and slugs at night if they like your offering of a cool, dark place to lounge under during the day. Try a broken, overturned clay pot with an entrance gap in the rim big enough to crawl under and frogs, toads or salamanders might make it a patrol station.

- Acknowledge the intrinsic value of native plants and habitats.
- Recognize the botanical history and diversity of the province.
- Acknowledge human impacts on native plants and habitats.
- Are respectful of and receptive to First Nations' traditional knowledge and unique relationship with the plant world.
- Conserve native plants and habitats and maintain biodiversity of natural ecosystems.
- Preserve and protect rare native plant species and habitats.
- Promote restoration of altered land and reintroduction of appropriate native plant species.
- Encourage establishment of native plants in developed areas.
- Share knowledge and promote understanding of native plants and habitats.[8]

A public start for a public apple tree in Vancouver.

Clues on how to do this come from nature. Watch how things work in the kind of ecosystem you're hoping to create. If it's a mixed forest (evergreen and deciduous trees) watch how songbirds such as sparrows and finches flock to a food source like fallen seeds on the ground, especially if it's near a dense bush or thicket that provides a quick escape. Notice how swallows swoop over meadow grasses in the early mornings and evenings when it's easiest to spot flying insects against the sky. Birds are often used in ecological studies as measures of biodiversity, which is valid, but that's mainly because they're the easiest things to spot and count. With a narrower focus and enough time, you could learn a world of things about nature from simply sitting quietly in one place and paying attention. Follow a snail to see what a Saturday morning schedule in the Gastropoda class is all about. Watch an ant brigade deal with the crisis of the leaf you drop on the entrance to their nest. Bring an Annie Dillard book if you think you might get bored.

Whatever kind of ecosystem you hope to create, a dependable supply of water is a big help. The same popularity of the watering hole in the African jungle can apply to your little naturescape site once word gets around in the better critter circles. Not only will you attract more things, the things that come will attract yet more things hoping to eat them. When I redesigned a small area outside my office with native woodland plants, it seemed no more popular at first than anywhere else on the landscaped grounds. Then I added a small artificial stream, and the effect was dramatic. Toddlers were the first to get it. They were drawn like magnets to the gurgling water, or to drop the streambed pebbles into the sump bucket, perhaps for the pleasing sound. Their older siblings caught on and went for a more dramatic plop from the larger rocks. Somehow they both managed to leave the stream alone long enough for a flock of migrating Wilson's Warblers to discover it as well, and then for about a week the entire feathered family would return every day to bathe in a flittery yellow cloud.

Room to grow

You don't need a lot of land to start a naturescaping project. Habitat can be created in something as small as a container. It's not ideal, but this is a city, we all have to make adjustments, and you think the wildlife is going to complain?

The beauty of using containers to make natural spaces out of nothing is that they can go anywhere, including areas that are paved, or on roofs or balconies. They can also be easier to maintain. A stand or very tall container will bring the plants within reach of less flexible gardeners such as the arthritic. The confined conditions of a pot are limiting, but also a plus in helping you keep weeds under control.

Containers can be used to create a variety of habitats in a surprisingly narrow space. Imagine a prairie meadow in one pot, a thicket in another, a marsh in another, and then a pond in one more, all coexisting happily in the same driveway. Odd as this may sound, and as offensive as it may seem to some of your environmentaliban friends who accuse you of violating the laws if not the spirit of the bioregion, so what? Remind the finger-waggers: we're living in a *city*. Nature is not just what we find; it's what we create as well. Manufactured wilderness can work. If your potted version succeeds in attracting birds, butterflies and dragonflies, and gives kids a chance to play, and looks good besides, you've done your part. You'll know because the vote of the wildlife community will be made with wings, antennae and feet. Your neighbors might even like it too. A simple plank bench overlooking a bustling natural spot can become a favorite daily stopping place for some people.

Another advantage of container habitats is that they can be quite attractive, with the pots alone providing eye-appeal before you even get started with the plants. And if you don't like the look of some arrangement or if a group of plants isn't working out, just move or replace the whole thing. If only all our garden mis-hits could be dealt with so handily. One down side is, of course, that containers can be moved as easily by someone else, say someone who enjoys the view so much he must have it for his own yard. But not if you bolt the container down.

Don't be a buggist

Pests bugging you? Before you reach for the P-bomb (pesticide), consider hand-to-hand combat. Squish them with your fingers. This can not only eradicate intruders but also provide you with malicious pleasure. If it sounds icky, keep your gloves on. For larger critters, lift the bug, drop it to the ground, introduce the

It is in vain to dream of a wilderness distant from ourselves. There is nonesuch. It is the bog in our brains and bowels, the primitive vigor of Nature in us, that inspires that dream.

— Henry David Thoreau

sole of your boot, and twist. The more squeamish may keep a small can of soapy water to drop things into, although carrying dead bug soup around isn't the most pleasant thing either.

Or you could copy the generals in every war by getting others to do your fighting. If you want a private militia you have to feed the troops, so plant things that will attract beneficial insects. In the Asteraceae family there are daisies, asters, feverfew, marigolds and sunflowers with bright yellow centers enticing various bug-eating allies. In the Apiaceae family, parsley, dill, carrots and fennel appeal to ladybugs and lacewings, both of which are known to be fond of aphids.

Then again, you could do nothing. Just watch. So some bugs drop by for a visit. Big deal. I'm not sure where our urban fear and disgust of insects came from. I don't think it's inherent, but I've

TOP TEN INVASIVE PLANTS

Some magazines list the Top Ten Ways to Drive Your Partner Wild or the Top Ten Thigh-Busting Techniques. When you subscribe to publications like *Arbor Age*, however, you settle for cover stories like this one:

The US Department of the Interior estimates the United States is losing up to 5,000 acres a day to invasive plants, according to the article, which adds that the National Park Service counts some 4,000 invasive plant species. Yegads. How to select the most unwanted ones to top the list? The article doesn't explain, beyond its having consulted leading experts, most of whom were evidently from the east (a list for the Pacific Northwest would be vastly different).

Autumn olive (*Elaeagnus umbellata*)
Bush honeysuckle (*Lonicera spp.*)
Canada thistle (*Cirsium arvense*)
Cogongrass (*Imperata cylindrica*)
Garlic mustard (*Alliaria petiolata*)
Japanese knotweed (*Polygonum cuspidatum*)
Japanese stilt grass (*Microstegium vimineum*)
Kudzu (*Pueraria montana*)
Purple loosestrife (*Lythrum salicaria*)
Tree of heaven (*Ailanthus altissima*)[7]

seen my own kids go from being fascinated as toddlers to grossed out as adolescents, and they didn't learn bug-loathing from me. At least not directly. Maybe there's something biological in it. I can coerce them into at least tolerating most bugs but neither will abide spiders. Some of those arachnids in Africa might have been poisonous and worth running from.

Today it doesn't make sense to treat all bugs badly. There's no reason to see creeping things in your garden and immediately think: infestation. Instead you might congratulate yourself on providing an ecosystem which the real living world finds desirable. You're a good landlord.

No slugsidized housing

Sometimes, however, you must draw the line. A garden nemesis for many in the Pacific Northwest is the slug. The slimy bastards have taken out entire crops I've started from seed, ruining a whole season's worth of lettuce, squash and even pole beans.

It's partly my fault. In my vegetable plot when I wanted a raised bed I decided to go structurally with the free option by collecting river rocks and stacking them up into low walls. The walls looked good enough, the price was right, and I liked how I could change the whole design in an afternoon by re-arranging the pieces.

And this our life exempt from public haunt, Finds tongues in trees, books in the running brooks, Sermons in stones and good in everything.

— WILLIAM SHAKESPEARE in "As You Like It"

Eight non-quantifiable reasons to plant more urban trees:
1. We evolved with trees and still find them fascinating.
2. A cityscape without trees can seem barren, lifeless, inhospitable.
3. Trees help fill our elemental need to connect with other living things.
4. Trees rooted in the earth and aspiring to the heavens offer a spiritual link between realms.
5. Aged, venerable trees lend nobility and grace to our daily lives.
6. Their foliage can soften the harsh edges of development.
7. Cities rated the most livable typically have an abundance of trees.
8. Many religious faiths have a prominent tree connection.

The problem? I'd created a habitat of dark, moist crevices between and beneath the rocks where slugs love to hang out. No wonder they liked my plot more than the neighbors'. It was like stocking an empty dorm lounge with beer and sofas and then wondering why students showed up.

I might have gotten rid of all the rocks. Or I could have borrowed from the diligent example of a garden neighbor in setting out half-cut oranges each night and destroying the slugs found sleeping in them the following morning. So what did I do? Mostly nothing. I made a few tactical shifts, such as planting some crops later in the season when the slugs would have other (my neighbor's) plants to gorge on. But generally I ignored the problem and, sure enough, it's mostly gone away. I'm not sure why. It could be that something else — perhaps birds, or some kind of super beetle, or maybe toads — have figured out I was putting on a smorgasbord and came for a slug-feast. In any case, I left bad enough alone, and things worked out.

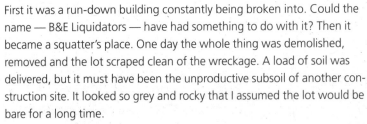

YOU SAID IT...   **Terry Taylor**

First it was a run-down building constantly being broken into. Could the name — B&E Liquidators — have had something to do with it? Then it became a squatter's place. One day the whole thing was demolished, removed and the lot scraped clean of the wreckage. A load of soil was delivered, but it must have been the unproductive subsoil of another construction site. It looked so grey and rocky that I assumed the lot would be bare for a long time.

Two years later you can hide in the foliage. What is it? And how did it get there? I asked Terry Taylor, a naturalist and ecologist in Vancouver who consults on government projects and leads public nature walks and seems to know every plant on the planet.

On how he sees the "empty" lot: From the point of view of ecological processes, it's an early successional habitat in open sunlight. When you disturb a piece of ground or have a fire or something, the first plants to come in are not the ones that form the final forest. In an area like this, first you have herbaceous plants, then you get some shrubs, then you get trees, then different kinds of trees, and finally you get a coniferous forest. So there are stages from a disturbed unstable ecosystem to a final relatively

Plant naturalist Terry Taylor

stable ecosystem. This is an example of early succession. It's not merely by chance that the weed species you see are successful here. These are the species that live in open sunlight and thrive in harsh conditions. They can compete in the first stage. Eventually if you had a coniferous forest all these things would disappear because they all need sunlight. So the first forest in the next 30 years, if it's not disturbed, would be a cottonwood forest. I don't see any alders but usually it's a cottonwood and alder forest. Eventually in this area they would get replaced by Douglas fir which would later get replaced by hemlocks and cedars.

On where all the plants came from: They're mostly European weed species. They're actually quite fascinating. When you get to an open area like this people look at it and say, They're just weeds. But this is the history of civilization. Most of the weeds aren't from here; they were brought in. They've evolved over 10,000 years. They would have started out where agriculture started out, in the Fertile Crescent and in the Ukraine, areas like this, and they moved westward, to eastern Europe, to western Europe, to eastern North America and across to western North America. They're the plants that were able to survive intense pressure. They produce seeds that lie dormant in the soil for a long time and then when conditions are good they come up, and the next year plowing takes place and they have to start over again. So these are the things that have been selected over 10,000 years. Timewise it's like a micro-evolution because the plants that couldn't withstand this intense pressure weren't successful. So these were actually weeds not just by chance but selected by human practices, by agriculture. They are adapted to urban life, or at least to agricultural life. This is a natural ecosystem. These things are competing, one against the other. They're not maintained, they're not cultivated. The forces of evolution, natural selection, and succession and everything else are working in this system.

On urban nature: People who identify with wilderness consider this to be urban blight. But nature is very subtle, isn't it? Nothing is black and white. Look at this one [points to a low, spindly plant]. It's related to alfalfa. It's called black medic. It's a legume, fixing nitrogen in the soil. Actually this isn't fixing the nitrogen, it's the bacteria in the roots of this thing fixing the nitrogen. The nitrogen that makes up all our proteins and virtually everything else is taken out of the atmosphere by bacteria. If those bacteria disappeared, the whole thing would collapse. So this is increasing

I consider every plant hardy until I have killed it myself.

— Sir Peter Smithers

DESIGN TIP

Garden infrastructure materials can be surprisingly expensive, bringing an untimely end to an otherwise fine idea. But not if you locate used things that can be brought back to life. Broken-up concrete is an excellent choice for footpaths. If you see a demolition project in your neighborhood where they're jackhammering a sidewalk, ask for some of the pieces. These can be a nuisance to truck away, so the crew may even help wheelbarrow them to your site.

Get pieces as large as you can handle. It's more comfortable to walk on oversized steps than to tip-toe on small foot-sized ones. Arrange each piece on a layer of gravel and sand for long-term stability, or just dig them in so they're flat with the surrounding grade. Some gardeners plant thyme or other fragrant herbs in the spaces between the steps.

the fertility of the soil. But it's not what people want to grow here because most people want something that's nice and ordered and simplistic enough that you can understand it.

Here are some of the plants Terry Taylor identified in a typical vacant lot in East Vancouver. We didn't keep a species list, or set up a grid to count numbers, or even think of getting everything down. At one point, in fact, I steered him away from looking closer at the ground, afraid he was about to launch into a discourse on mosses which would have been a whole other story.

Velvet grass — *Holcus lanatus*
White sweet clover — *Melilotus alba*
Purpleleaf willowherb — *Epilobium coloratum*
Black cottonwood — *Populus trichocarpa*
European hornbeam — *Carpinus betulus*
Common horsetail — *Equisetum arvense*
Black medic — *Medicago lupulina*
Red clover — *Trifolium pratense*
Hairy cat's ears — *Hypochoeris radicata*
Sand spurry — *Spergularia rubra*
Common plantain — *Plantago major*
St. John's-wort — *Hypericum formosum*
Colonial bentgrass — *Agrostis capillaris*
Orchard grass — *Dactylis glomerata*
Reed canary grass — *Phalaris arundinacea*
White clover — *Trifolium repens*
Kentucky blue grass — *Poa pratensis*
Pearly everlasting — *Anaphalis margaritacea*
Prickly lettuce — *Lactuca serriola*

Cities aren't the easiest places to make or enhance habitat, at least the way we've built them so far. As expected, the more development, the less room for natural areas and the organisms they attract. In the Greater Vancouver area more than 350 bird species can be counted, but fewer than 50 are commonly found inside the city limits, and the most abundant are euro-thug interlopers such as the European Starling (*Sturnus vulgaris*).[7] Starlings were introduced to North America by a fan of Shakespeare who thought all the birds mentioned in the Bard's plays would look good in New York's Central Park.

Before and after pics demonstrate how plants can claim an empty lot in just two years.

"Finally he looked up and said, 'You're on our land!'"

Susan Kurbis has been helping young people develop earth-friendly lifestyles and careers for more than 10 years. Not only as a manager of the
award-winning Environmental Youth Alliance in Vancouver but also in the
organization's admirable work in Ecuador, Brazil and many places beyond.

EYA's urban greening successes are found all over Vancouver, although
the people responsible are rarely recognized. Here she talks about projects
that work and projects that don't, and how guerrilla gardening fits into
efforts such as the campaign to plant an illegal potato.

It was an heirloom potato, a heritage variety, that was being eliminated because it spread so easily. It was considered a noxious
weed, according to the government. There was a movement in
the sustainable agriculture sector to protect heirloom/heritage
varieties of food, and a call went out to plant the caribou potato
to help keep it alive. It's very pest resistant and a high producer.
We got a hold of some and planted it in empty lots on Granville
Street in downtown Vancouver. This was in 1992 or 1993. We
kind of drifted off into other things so we didn't really follow up.
I'm not sure how they did.

Another time we didn't have permission was when we
started the Youth Garden in the Downtown Eastside. We had the
space so we just went and started gardening. I was working with
a group of high school students and we were looking for a project
to do in Vancouver. I said, there's a really cool community garden
already that we might add space to. It was basically a dump we
wanted to turn into a garden. It was on land that was part of the
city of Vancouver Engineering Department's right of way. So we
went in with a whole team and started a garden. We planted
hazelnuts and an Asian fruit orchard and built a pond. The official
response was nothing. There was no reaction. They didn't even
notice for the longest time. Then we applied for some money
from the city. I remember we went to the City Manager. We were
on a panel with him at some public forum as the youth represen-
tatives. One of the youth stood up and said, Youth are not
involved in any decisions in this city, you never consult us in any
way, it's terrible, and so on. So the City Manager said, You have
an open invitation to talk with us on how you want things to go,
you can talk to me about anything. Then he set up a meeting

between us and the heads of every city department. He brought us all together into the same room. The heads of everything, including the Park Board. He said, You guys have got to work with these people. And that was it: we got money, we got recognition, we got nominated for a provincial award, and we did very well.

So the engineering right of way extends for, I forget, 50 feet or 100 feet from the curb into the space. There's no question we were on it. At that point we already had a lot of stuff built on it. Hundreds of youth for two years had been really busy making it into the place it is today. We took it from a derelict trash heap to a city garden. At one point, one of the engineering guys showed up when we were there working. I'll never forget seeing him, in his suit, pacing off the dimensions, stumbling a bit over the uneven ground. His head went left and right, and he had this strange, bewildered look on his face like he was having trouble figuring something out. Finally he looked up and said, "You're on our land!" We just said, Oops. We got $25,000 from them too.

Why did we get away with it? I think it was the power of youth. Ultimately they saw what we were doing as a good thing. Every time they went they would see us there. It's impressive to see 30 youth working their butts off. Anyone walking through would think, This is cool. The lesson I draw from all that is: It's better to ask for forgiveness than to ask for permission. People want to do the right thing. You just have to be strategic so they can.

Another project we had was to do a school garden. School gardens are great learning places, but they have to be done right. There are a lot that get started but they don't end up doing well. We were at one school, I don't want to say where, so let's just call it somewhere in Vancouver. They have a rule at the School Board that gardens have to be fenced in. There are all these regulations, and the process was just daunting. So working with the coordinator — one of those fabulous people everyone loves — we just slammed it in over a weekend. Of course the School Board freaked when they found out. We just said the same thing, Oops. They went, Oh my god. You can't do this. You have to take this out. We hemmed and hawed and eventually they came around and said, Well, we'll leave it, but you have to do the following things to fit the guidelines… It was just their way of keeping some control. The changes didn't make a difference, and the project was a success. Today there are 25 school gardens in the city. Most are done together with the School Board. To a certain degree

A garden is a construct that evokes an ideal of nature. Whether real or imaginary, a garden is the meeting of man and nature orchestrated by a set of moral, aesthetic, and philosophical principles. Gardens are closely tied to the civilizations that produce them.

— HEATH SCHENKER

Where's a poor winged thing to go? Since intensive farming began in the 1940s, Britain has lost more than 95 percent of its wildflower meadows.[5]

none of them are particularly successful, but this one and one other one are doing quite well.

POWER PLANT   Apple (*Malus domestica*)

If you had limited space and money enough for just one tree, you might well choose the apple. Apples are what many of the first European settlers brought when sailing to the New World. It was the right choice, making life sweeter for millions for generations to come. The apple became the great democratic crop of North America, grown by both poor and rich in back yards and grand estates. It became prominent in each season in meals from breakfast to dessert and in the drinks between. Every home had its favorite varieties, chosen from more than 2,000 named types, each as distinctive as a well-made wine. The importance of the fruit to daily life is reflected in our speech even today as we may refer to someone who's lovable as the "apple of my eye" and someone who's not a "bad apple" or "apple polisher" or "crab."

Then came agribusiness with its advances in refrigeration and mass marketing, leading to grower preferences for a few manageable types. Many heritage apples were lost, to be recalled now only in literature. The average American today samples no more than six kinds of apples in his or her lifetime, writes Roger Yepsen in the delightful 1994 book *Apples*.

Apple trees sold in nurseries have typically been grafted onto dwarf root stock. Dwarfing here doesn't mean smaller or fewer fruit but a reduced tree size, making the tree itself easier to inspect, prune, treat and pick without ladders or machines. Even orchardists plant trees on dwarf root stock now, because it makes sense from a human (picker's) scale. But if you have ample space, it might be worth planting at least a few trees of the old-fashioned standard size. There's something magical about a tree full of apples that's also big enough to climb in or picnic under. While some of the dwarfing types are flimsy enough to need staking throughout their lives, standard-sized trees are known for resilience. In British Columbia it's not uncommon to visit old homesteads and find long-forgotten apple trees still producing fruit after a century or more.

What kind of apple should you plant? That's no easy question. The more you get into apples, the more you open the door to a vast and fascinating world of horticultural and culinary adventure. Start at your local nursery, or even better, local organic apple grower's place. Taste, talk, compare. Once you get hooked, you'll be grafting your own 400-year-old Dutch varieties and watching the results develop with all the pride of a successful parent.

Apple — Malus domestica
Credit: F. P. Chaumeton's "Flore Medicale" (Medical Flora), published in Paris in 1814, illustration by Pierre Jean-Francois Turpin.

Did you know: Each bite of an apple represents about one hour of sunshine, if you start with the number of leaves needed per fruit (40), calculate the number of days it takes for an apple to reach maturity (about 180), figure that ½ to 1 percent of the solar energy falling on a leaf gets converted to apple tissue, and conclude that each apple represents about one day of sunshine. Does the math hold up? Who cares? It's a lovely thought.

CHAPTER SIX

Get Off the Grass
(Make It a Meadow)

Eco-friends, cover your ears, I'm about to say something shocking: not all lawns are evil.

How can I even think that? With all the evidence against them?

Because turf grass can be a wonderful plant. It has been a friend to humans for many years. Who hasn't had at least one, and more likely dozens, of memorable experiences that would be unimaginable on anything other than sod? Picture playing soccer in a forest …rolling with a lover on asphalt…attending an outdoor wedding on tumbleweed.

Love of lawns cuts across the ages. Kids run to an inviting expanse of grass. Watch as they get right down to the blade level in tumbling and leaping games. Seniors are just as enchanted. Although less fun as tumbling partners, they appreciate the serene environs of an open space set apart from the urban bustle. A patch of urban turf can offer a cool respite on a hot day, especially if you go barefoot. A lawn and a recalcitrant mower may provide some men the only exercise they're going to get all week, and a legitimate reason to drink afternoon beer. Grass attracts a variety of birds and insects, too, particularly if a few other species such as dandelion and clover get into the mix.

So don't call grass boring. The grass family, Poaceae, is the most important plant group in the world, for humans. We live on grass (also known as grains) or else we eat the animals that we raise on grass.

Grasses have evolved over 65 million years and are now found in a vast range of ecosystems all over the world. They are one of the largest groups of flowering plants in the plant kingdom. Yes,

Sentiment without action is the ruin of the soul.

— EDWARD ABBEY

You don't need soil to make a lawn if you bring your own turf.

flowering. They will if you let them, although most in the turf variety aren't planted for that purpose and produce only tiny flowers when left to grow that long.

I mention all this so that you might check your sanctimony at the garden gate when dealing with people who obsess over their lawns. If only all our garden experiments encouraged such active participation. There's nothing wrong with caring for a patch of soft green plants that encourage people to play, sit, relax, nap and more. And I didn't even mention the incomparable aroma of mown grass wafting in a warm summer breeze.

Why, then, all the fuss?

Good crop, bad crop

Oh yes, the down side. It's hard to know where to start, but let's begin with a question. Do we need so many lawns? In countless generic sites all over the city? And in front of every suburban home? When everyone knows they're likely to stay untouched all week, until maintenance time, when they become mini-war zones of mowing, weeding, edging, aerating, power-raking and top-dressing — all so they can go unnoticed and unused and unloved for another six days?

The evolution of the suburban lawn can be traced back to the pastureland set aside around the homes of the upper classes in rural England. And is there not something oddly eccentric, in that wacky British way, in the aspirations of the modern lawn-fixated suburbanite? The original version may have served as a status symbol, offering the rich an opportunity to display their wealth by leaving good land idle, but the present style of identical tiny patches in front of every suburban home seems more of a cruel joke.

Marketers love an obsession, though, and in the lawn fetish they've got a gold mine. Advertising helps convince suburbanites they must spend mightily to produce a crop greener than the rest. If that means using synthetic fertilizers and toxic pesticides, the consumer responds by pouring them on. Imagine being able to convince anyone to pay money to poison their own land, yet it's done to an astonishing degree. Americans lace their yards with more than 100 million pounds of pesticides every year. They apply it even thicker than on the modern chemical-laden agribusiness farm, according to the National Coalition for Pesticide-Free Lawns.[1]

Like a lot of good things turned bad, the lawn is in some ways really a problem of scale. Turf grass is like a friend on a 'roid rage. How big and grotesque has it become? You need a satellite to get the real picture. A NASA study found lawns occupying 32 million acres of land in the US.[2] That makes turf grass the largest crop in the country. It occupies three times the area devoted to corn. Keeping all these lawns green also requires water, and a lot of it: 200 gallons per person per day nationwide. And what happens when you spread all those poisons onto the ground and then flush everything with water? Chemicals from this toxic tsunami end up in our food, water and air whether we're the ones dosing the environment or not.

So. Still keen on that paltry rectangle of bondaged plants? Well, maybe. The benefits shouldn't just be ignored. Some people are always going to love their lawns, no matter how many statistics you throw at them. Lawns are still better to look at than asphalt, and they do help cool the air. It seems counterproductive, then, to hate them outright. It would be more prudent to support them when they're done well: at an appropriate scale, within the local context and with some sensitivity toward the surrounding environment. In fact, you can have an organic lawn that gives you everything you want in a grassy space and helps the environment besides. Just add some attractive bunch grass or wildflower species

Controlling the lawn is controlling the family. Taming the space between the street and the house with the latest equipment symbolizes the taming of that which is within the house. The lawn acts as the public image of private life. To threaten that image is to threaten the normative view of domesticity and unleash a wide range of anxieties.

— MARK WIGLEY

Herbal lawns can be an alternative to the same old, same old sod. Try peppermint-scented pennyroyal (*Mentha pulegium*) or the tiny-leaved Corsican mint (*Mentha requienii*), chamomile (*Chamaemelum nobile*) which will be more tolerant of dry conditions or creeping thyme (*Thymus species*). Broadcast the seeds in freshly tilled soil and keep them moist until they germinate, or go with more reliable starter plants. It will take some effort in the first year or two to help your plants get established over all the weeds which want their space. Once they're settled, the effect can be most attractive and the aroma unforgettable to someone traipsing across barefoot on a dew-spangled morning. However, more people (such as groups in boots) may be too much for the plants to handle. For heavy traffic areas, consider putting in a footpath or stepping stones.

in a few places, and let the turf itself grow longer between mowings. The whole thing will look great, and far more impressive than your neighbor's spray-painted green brush-cut. Now that's a status symbol.

Public lawns can be an intriguing challenge for guerrilla gardeners. Their powerful iconic presence makes them a tempting target. How many people even know it's the continent's No. 1 crop? This is a vast opportunity ready for innovation and intervention.

But you wouldn't want to ruin a successful site that is being used. Kids would not appreciate having their favorite disc-throwing spot taken over by earnest adults with big ideas. In places where the lawns really are pointless, however, where all those chemicals,

GLOSSARY OF FLOWERING PLANT TERMS

Annuals — Plants that complete their life cycle in a single year.

Perennials — Plants that live for more than two years (or are supposed to). Many perennials started from seed will not bloom the first year.

Biennials — Plants that complete their life cycle in two years, typically blooming only in the second year.

Self-seeding — Plants such as California poppy that may live only one year but put out enough seeds to provide a returning crop.

Wildflower — A flowering plant that can grow without human help.

Native — A plant indigenous to a particular area.

Naturalized — A non-native plant that has adapted to local conditions and can grow without human help.

Introduced — A plant brought to an area outside its native range, intentionally or otherwise.

Exotic — A foreign plant growing outside its native range, usually referring to plants in cultivation.

Invasive — A non-native plant that takes advantage of local conditions to spread so vigorously it crowds out more desired species.

Weed — A plant growing where it isn't wanted.

water, fuel and maintenance hours add up to nothing that a big green carpet couldn't provide, you might be justified in thinking about how the space could be better used.

Kick your grass

Everyone loves a meadow, by which they envision a spread of wild-flowers waving in the summer wind. But a real meadow, to go by the definition, is a field producing hay for livestock. Maybe you have a large field, a posse of Amish friends, a hay wagon and a barn to make all this happen?

No. Perhaps then you were thinking of a pasture? Another excellent idea. You bring the sheep.

Yes, I'm quibbling, and it doesn't really matter what we call it. I introduce the idea here to make a point. It may be more work than you think to turn a lawn into a meadow. But we can make it a little easier by first claiming the term in its broadest sense, using meadow to mean an open space with self-seeding grasses and wild-flowers.

Now let's suppose you are indeed starting with a lawn, in which case you have to get all that grass out of there.

You could cut and remove the sod in sections. Lifting out the grass is the most thorough way to do it, and the soil underneath is usually ready to plant in right away. But it's a grunt job you may find discouraging as each piece confounds you by hanging on with those troublesome things called roots. An easier strategy involves covering the grass with a plastic sheet. Clear plastic will let you see the experiment progress as the unwanted turf cooks from green to yellow to brown over the next six to eight weeks, but black plastic will get hotter and do the job faster. Once that's done, remove the sheet and plant at will. Don't worry about removing the remaining grass. Once dead it should decompose on its own.

One problem with this strategy is that it takes time. The area will look scrubby for most of a season. This might not be a factor in a neglected site, but in a prominent place you could get complaints. Another approach offering faster gratification is to spread newspapers 10-sheets thick over the lawn. Most papers these days use vegetable-ink dyes (which is what you want), but if you're concerned about toxins you could call the head office and ask.

When I die I'm going to leave a piece of ground better than I found it.

— Dwight D. Eisenhower

> *If a man owns land,*
> *the land owns him.*
>
> — RALPH WALDO EMERSON

Add 3–4 inches of topsoil on top of the newspaper. The paper will decompose over the next five to six weeks while the grass beneath gradually dies, and then you're free to plant what you like. Cardboard will work as well.

Fields of dreams

Once you have space and soil, what to plant to make your meadow the flower-laden, grass-waving haven of your dreams? Here's where you want to do a little research to learn what works best in your area. Different regions favor different grasses and flowers. Even in a given region tastes vary, and it's impossible to say one type of meadow is best. Think of your space as a painting, a unique creation that can never be replicated anywhere else. Where will the tallest grasses go? Should it be every color everywhere or will you try for masses of plants grouped together?

Garden stores these days carry an increasingly complex selection of wildflower seed mixes. The packages tend to have one thing in common, a delightful picture of a veritable Eden. You can safely ignore that, but do check the ingredients. Some of the mixes will

---

DESIGN TIP

God, the devil, whomever, it really is all in the details. The big ideas are what get you started and guide your main efforts, but how well they work comes down to the finer points of just what goes where.

"The placement of plants and trees may appear simple," wrote the Zen monk Zoen back in 1448, but of course it wasn't then and isn't now. "Disharmonious rocks should not be used. All the rocks should go well together."

And how are you supposed to know? Relax. You know disharmony as well as anyone. If it doesn't feel right, it isn't right. Keep trying.

What can you do with a lawn that isn't yours and wouldn't be right to take up, but still clearly needs something — in the way that lovely German word *Backpfeifengesicht* describes "a face that cries out for a fist in it"?

I thought I read how to get a message into a lawn on the website of Primal Seeds,[5] a lively "network to actively engage in protecting biodiversity and creating local food security." But when I checked back later for the reference, I couldn't find it. Maybe I was wrong, or maybe they've withdrawn the suggestion, which was, admittedly, bordering on rude if not illegal. And it's a fairly involved operation with results visible only after a considerable delay. But the payoff could make it worthwhile. Here's how it works:

Cut into an old bedsheet the shape of your message, logo, symbol or whatever. Bigger is better, obviously, but remember, simplicity counts. Place the sheet-stencil flat on the lawn and apply fertilizer in the open places you've cut out. A 4-4-4 organic fertilizer ought to do it. The point of the fertilizer is to create a marked difference between your stenciled area and

have been assembled thousands of miles away, and include plants that have nothing to do with your growing conditions, and may in fact become invasive if introduced.

Plants native to your region will naturally be your first choice. Some consider them the only choice, but I've softened my own hard stance on this. I still favor natives, and will always choose a local over an exotic when all other things are equal — particularly for land that isn't going to be carefully tended. Natives with their 10,000-year head start in adapting to the local elements are more likely to succeed. But for managed sites, it's not a crime to plant something that might not have been growing there on its own without human help. Even many of the plants sold as native will have come from beyond the particular ecosystem you may be looking at. And in any case, if we're working in an urban environment we're dealing with cultural blends, a world of species thriving in some kind of harmony. Moreover, plants love to travel. Consider all those clever strategies from helicopter wings to sticky burrs. If some plants are smart enough to have duped humans like me into carrying their genes for them, I can live with it.

Go to the pine if you want to learn about the pine, or to the bamboo if you want to learn about the bamboo. And in doing so, you must leave your subjective preoccupation with yourself. Otherwise you impose yourself on the object and do not learn.

— MATSUO BASHO

the surrounding grass. Taller and thicker growth is one possibility, although if the lawn gets regularly mowed it may not be noticed. What should be apparent, however, is a different color. Depending on the condition of the grass already, this could be distinctive, especially when seen from above such as out of the windows of a tall building overlooking the site. As in, say, a corporate headquarters, a government agency or a courthouse building.

The source added that an even more pronounced effect could be reached by using not fertilizer but herbicide. The message would then be marked in dead grass. Eye-catching, to be sure, but scorching plants by lacing the soil to prove a point may not sit right with some in the public who tend to side with people growing things. Then again, pet owners let their dogs pee over plants every day and it amounts to almost the same thing. Use your own judgment on this one. Respect is usually the best yardstick. What strategy would show the most respect to the place, the people and the planet?

Whether it's all-native or a blend of local and introduced things, planning your grass and wildflower meadow can be half the fun. Get the catalogues and guidebooks and web site addresses out on some cold February evening, pour a drink of something comforting, then transport yourself to a balmy July day as you plot your earthly paradise.

From the ground up

Before planting your meadow, you may want to check the soil. In most cases you'll do fine working with what you have. Some claim you can only hurt your cause by trying to improve the fertility because wildflowers do best in poor soils. Well, some do and some don't. Generalizations work for general situations, not necessarily yours. You're better off choosing the individual species you want and then meeting their requirements.

If you do have to amend the soil, bring in a lot of organics. If you have to buy it, and if you're talking about a meadow bigger than, say, 10 paces in one direction, you'll want to buy in bulk. Order it by the yard rather than trying to haul bags from the garden store. The bags add up quickly in cost and weight, and you still never seem to have enough.

Should you till your new site before planting? Look at what was growing there before. If the soil supported a blend of plants, don't bother to plow. You're only likely to stir up some of the thousands of weed seeds lurking in every square yard. Once these get going they can change the character of a meadow dramatically, crowding out all the lovely flowers you were anticipating.

If you do have to till and weeds are likely to be a problem, finish by adding a layer of sand on top to plant your wildflower seeds in. The sand will repress the unwanted growth beneath to give your chosen plants a big head start.

Meadows have to be maintained — at least for the first few years until they get established with the proper mix of plants you want. A scythe (what the Grim Reaper carries) or a power weed-whacker can help you keep things under control. If you've put in only annuals, let them bloom before you cut everything down to ankle-height. If you have only perennials, keep the meadow cropped fairly low during the first growing season to prevent weeds of annuals from setting seed and becoming established.

Frank J. Scott, one of America's first landscape architects, in *The Art of Beautifying Suburban Home Grounds,* declared, "A smooth closely shaven surface of green is by far the most essential element of beauty on the grounds of a suburban house." An even more influential 19th century landscape designer, Andrew Jackson Downing, equated a badly kept lawn with a "rude and barbarous people."

No two meadows are alike. Even in the same area, varying histories of land use can turn one field into a poppy emporium and its neighbor into a blackberry thicket. If you know what you want, to get it will require ongoing work, but it will all be worth the effort one day if you stick it out.

You don't need massive space to make a meadow. A smaller size can even help it make a big impact. Context is everything. If you're slogging across a bare parking lot on a hot day, wouldn't you look twice at a single stall given over to corn cockles (*Agrostemma githago*), love-in-a-mist (*Nigella damascena*) and Flanders Field poppies (*Papaver rhoeas*)?

When weeds appear (which they will) try not to let them go to seed. Remove them first, by uprooting if possible, although beheading is better than nothing. In the bare spaces where you remove weeds you will be offered opportunities to retouch your masterpiece. Perhaps a butterfly weed (*Asclepias tuberosa*), Shasta daisy (*Chrysanthemum maximum*) or California poppy (*Eschscholzia californica*)?

Don't worry about following the combinations I'm suggesting. I'm just pulling names out of the plant book. You could do the same, only it'll be more fun if you do it while envisioning the result in a glorious symphony of bursting color.

One more thing to keep in mind: you can't expect everything in the way of brilliant flowers. No meadow blooms all year long. There are times in every meadow where it will look droopy, brown, bare and tired. This is natural, and not something to be overcome. Consider it a chance to appreciate the natural cycles of growth, bloom and decay in a fascinating ecosystem you've helped bring to life. A meadow after the big event of the main blooms can be a thing of even more beauty when you learn to appreciate its own quiet charms.

A scythe makes a pleasant alternative to the noisy gas-powered weed whacker.

Imagination is more important than knowledge.

— ALBERT EINSTEIN

YOU SAID IT...   Bill Stephen

Bill Stephen is a Vancouver Urban Forester Technician. He helps monitor and treat the city's street trees. It's a big job — there are more than 130,000 trees to be cared for on his to-do list. But like a true plant person, his interest doesn't stop just because the working day is over. He also finds time to

Because of its heavy cultural implications and instant familiarity, turf grass is a great plant for making a statement. And what other plant do you know that can be cut out and picked up and rolled under your arm like a carpet to be planted somewhere else? Take it wherever you like, set it on a bare patch of soil, give it some water and — *voilà* — instant lawn.

Or this: an instant seating area in the middle of a blacktop, such as the one I saw at a recent eco-related event in Vancouver. The design was appealing in part for its simplicity — nothing but rectangles of sod placed over a box so people could "sit on the grass" (signs instructed them to do so) which also doubled as a stoop.

A more elegantly designed example of the power of turf is the Sod Sofa by forward-thinking architect Greg Tate, as seen in *ReadyMade* magazine.

The Lawn Lounge makes a case in L.A. for more earth-friendly furniture.

GREG TATE

Sod Sofa design: Greg Tate. Graphics: Shannon Wheeler

The campaign to save endangered species involves more than pandas and whales. Many of the plants with which we share the earth are threatened with the prospect of disappearing forever. Imagine after the millions of years of evolution it took them to get this far, we get the reins for one short blip and they're lost forever. The shocking but true story, from the Center for Plant Conservation:

- More than 200 native plant species in the US have already gone extinct.
- There are 730 plant species in the US federally listed as endangered or threatened.
- Twenty percent of our native plant species are in decline and on a conservation watch list.
- A single plant species going extinct can cause the disappearance of up to 30 other species of plants and wildlife.[3]

beautify his own neighborhood outside the city with a little guerrilla gardening. Here's a tactic that's free, easy and available to all.

On what plants work well: I use foxglove. It's an exotic but it does well here and looks great. The flowers come in whites and purples on plants that grow 5 to 7 feet tall.

On where to get seeds: Take a plastic milk jug and cut off the wide end on the bottom but leave the cap on. Place this open end under the foxglove — you can bend the flower right over the jug — to harvest the seeds for about a month in July–August. Foxglove flowers from the bottom up so you've got a long window to work with. You should get 300 or more seeds falling into the jug with each knock.

On how to plant them: If you wear steel-toed boots and scuff the ground a bit and just drop the seeds in, basically you're doing what nature intended, so I don't worry about cold-storage or marking the seeds or anything. The only thing is you may have to wait two years for the flowers to develop, but after that, if you've dropped seeds all around the neighborhood you might get five or ten patches of flowers that look really good. They prefer moist, loose soil, but not hardpan. Drop 20 or 30 seeds in each patch and that's it.

IF I CAN DO IT...   **Mark Yardas — Gone Native**

"It's a way to connect this often alienating urban reality to the larger ecosystem. It's part of a quest for greater depth."

Mark Yardas is a publisher and independent filmmaker in Los Angeles who does sound work for film studios, a job he likens to "renting out my nervous system."

He's also a gardener who likes native plants. Although "likes" doesn't really describe it. He wants others to see the light. He touts native plants to friends, he writes about them in the Neighbor2Neighbor homeowner's resource guide he publishes, and he's even followed the passion into guerrilla gardening.

I don't think of myself as a "guerrilla gardener" per se. I just like getting the natives back into the urban landscape.

I started with my back alley, which is weed infested. I had plenty of extra poppy and clarkia seeds harvested from one season's bloom. So I thought, why not spread the love? The kids and I just dug up weeds and planted seeds. The local gardeners destroyed most of the plants, though, which turned out to be one of the typically discouraging constants in the "guerrilla gardening" biz. Gardeners are always wiping out my little natives before they bloom and people can see what they are. It's to be expected, I guess. It even happens when I give seeds to friends and they plant them themselves.

I harvest California poppy seeds from my yard, a big jar of them. Then I plant them all around the back alleys and vacant lots near the film studio where I work. On occasion, some poppies have even been discovered blooming on the lot itself. I don't know how they got there, though.

I also fling them along the bike path that travels along Ballona Creek. The goal is that one day I would like to be able to ride from my home in Venice Beach to work and always have some sort of native plant within eyesight.

I'm always giving my native plant spiel to folks. I try not to be too dogmatic about it, but it's a challenge. People always love seeing the poppies, and that promotes them better than anything else. I explain why I love them. Because they're so beautiful…and endangered. Los Angeles' native plant community (coastal sage scrub) is the most diverse and arguably the most endangered plant community in North America. Yet the vast majority of Angelenos wouldn't know a native plant if they saw one.

For me, it's been very healing to discover the plants that were here in centuries past. It's a way to connect this often alienating urban reality to the larger ecosystem. It's part of a quest for greater depth.

What helps most is going into the local wildlands and discovering inspiration there. Drawing from nature. I love wild California, as do so many residents here. I just keep asking, How can we get more of that in our urban landscape? Why should we have to get into a car and drive to it, instead of just living in it?

As far as planting the seeds in public spaces is concerned, it just feels good. I don't think about the legal aspects much. Mostly, I plant the seeds where people will be happy to see the wildflowers bloom. I don't want to give natives a bad name.

Anybody can do it. Down here natives are best planted right before the winter rains in November or so. I try to do most of my work then. I don't just toss the seed. I dig up the soil a little and tamp it down after I've spread the seed. Mostly, I use California

Remember when we blamed the Exxon Valdez for spilling all that oil in Alaska? Spare some wrath for right here at home where we do even *more* damage every year. The US Environmental Protection Agency reports 17 million gallons of fuel gets spilled each year, much of it as gasoline that doesn't make the simple transfer from the gas can to the lawn mower.[4] People. Come *on*. It's called a funnel. We're not asking you to steer a freighter between icebergs. Pay attention or something. Sheesh.

DESIGN TIP

It sounds obvious, but it's one of the first things beginners tend to overlook when gardening a new site: plants grow. And if the plants are trees? They may grow massively. Try to imagine how your garden might look in a year, and then ten years. Don't doom some of your other favorite specimens to a withered life of struggle in the shade of a more vigorous neighbor just because you didn't think ahead. If you want to create an immediately filled-in look, plant annuals in the spaces that will be taken up later by your more lasting perennial plants.

poppies because they're so hardy and recognizable. They're also great at reseeding themselves.

Caring for them isn't a big issue. Native wildflowers shouldn't need a lot of maintenance or resources. They're from here, so they can hack it on their own.

Discovering native plants has definitely changed the way I view Los Angeles. You begin to realize how completely artificial everything is, even the living plants in a sense. They're not from here, and it's questionable how they affect the larger ecosystem. It's a fundamental disconnect. One feels as though one is walking around in a theme park, even amidst trees and plants. So going out and planting native seeds serves as a small antidote to this problem.

Advice for others? Get into the wild, discover what you love there, find its name somehow (you can ask a ranger or take its picture and drop by a nursery that specializes in native plants), then sow those wild seeds wherever it will make you and others happiest.

Lavender — Lavandula angustifolia
Credit: F. P. Chaumeton's "Flore Medicale" (Medical Flora), published in Paris in 1814, illustrated by Pierre Jean-Francois Turpin.

POWER PLANT   Lavender (*Lavendula species*)

The Romans and Greeks both had a thing for baths that somehow passed the rest of Europe by. Maybe because the Euro-barbarians didn't know about the clean, fresh scent of the gorgeous plant and bathwater additive known as lavender. The name itself derives from the Latin term *lavare*, "to wash."

This attractive evergreen shrub has inspired a variety of uses beyond soap. It can be a food flavoring, an oil to scent hair, a tonic water for sensitive skin, an antiseptic against acne, a sachet to protect linen, a tea to cure headaches and a painkiller for insect bites and stings.

Lavender is easy to grow in sunny, well-drained soil. Once established, a single bush can spread to surprisingly wide dimensions, producing enough flowers for every use you care to try. You can also grow more than one plant as a low, sweet-smelling border hedge.

Check your nursery for variations on plant size, flower shape and fragrance. If you shop while they're in bloom you can make sure you get precisely the type you prefer — the tiniest shift in scent can make the difference between a beloved bush and one you'll go out of your way to avoid.

Prune lavender in spring by cutting back to last year's growth but don't cut into old wood. Old plants can get woody and scraggly, in which case you may wish to replant using new stock rather than keep trying to prop up the current bush.

For the longest-lasting fragrance, pick the flowers in the morning just after the dew evaporates. If you know how to make an infusion, a dose of lavender is said to restore a lost voice and "calm the tremblings and passions of the heart."

Did you know: The dried stems can be used as incense or scented fire-lighters.

If you want to see an endangered species, get up and look in the mirror.

— JOHN YOUNG
former Apollo astronaut

CHAPTER SEVEN

Grow Your Own Community Garden

(It Takes a Village to Raise a Turnip)

Some people claim the natural world is always in a state of flux, and they're right, but there are ecosystems which reach a stage of such maturity they actually settle down and become stable. In an old-growth forest, for example, all the plants that are going to grow up have grown up. They've won the battles. The upstarts and interlopers have been pushed aside. The ecosystem enters something known as the climax stage, and it can last for hundreds or even thousands of years. Its stability is based on a complex balance of relationships relying on diversity. Countless organisms will still come and go, but in a sense they're working together now in a vast harmony of beneficial relationships that make the whole stronger than any of its parts. Guerrilla gardeners, to stretch our metaphor, are usually resigned to the ephemeral beauty of random acts that may be destroyed in an afternoon, but there is a climax stage here as well. It's called the community garden.

I joined my local community garden seven years ago. I didn't know at the time it was one of the most successful in North America and a model visited by people from around the world. It didn't look perfect, because it isn't. I know now it takes a lot of work to keep things going and there are constant stresses, but like a climax forest it seems to have achieved the strength and diversity to withstand anything as simple as a single pathogen or bad idea. It's been there 20 years, and last year secured a lease from the city to stay 20 more. Translated into municipal bureaucracy years, that's a lifetime.

No fault is greater than possessiveness.

— Lao Tzu

People create and join community gardens for different reasons, including some you might not guess. I recently asked one of my community garden neighbors, a tall, graceful artist named Liberia Marcuzzi, what brought her. I'd assumed by the prodigious crops of food and the gorgeous flowers she raised that she was one of those people so good with plants they just had to garden. But that wasn't it.

"After my son was murdered in February 2003 I remember thinking if I put my hands in the soil I would be OK. And then — I don't even know how — I found this place. I didn't even know it existed. To this day I consider it my sanctuary. I put my hands in the dirt and get this primal connection, not only to him but to the beat of the earth.

"That's how the garden saved me. In the midst of the madness, it's become my life. One of the things I've learned is that no matter where you go, there are always good people. There are always positive things happening. If you throw yourself out into the world it comes back to you. That's how I've gotten this far."

Liberia Marcuzzi in her sanctuary.

Garden grail

What else is it? A community garden can be a school, church, nursery, playground and laboratory. It can also be a fitness center, picnic spot, habitat refuge, recycling depot and meeting place.

People use it to grow organic food to feed their own families, but that's only a part of the much bigger picture. It's a way to connect, in an age of alienation, with the land and with other people. In our inner city location, the poorest postal code district in Canada, we've had the landless sift soil they could call their own through their fingers for the first time in their lives. We've had seniors spend their own time and money to come from miles away to teach street kids how to graft apple trees. People who could not afford or endure formal education have learned about solar technology, green building and graywater recycling strategies. Other educational opportunities have come from projects involving beekeeping, plant propagation, community-scaled composting, organic orchard management, wetland habitat creation and more.

I could go on, but you get the point. Community gardens are more than gardens. They're community-building resources that use the ripple effect of good ideas to spread beyond the immediate area and time. They can create social legacies that last generations. They can turn lives around and reshape derelict city spaces into urban wonders.

So how do you start one?

Choose the right place

There are sites in every city that could become community gardens. Vacant lots, street ends, railroad right of ways, abandoned park spaces, unused schoolyard areas, empty rooftops and more. Where *can't* you find land that would more productive and environmentally improved by letting folks on it to raise their own food and flowers?

Community gardens come in all sizes. Smaller ones may fit into narrow leftover spaces such as the strip beside a schoolyard wall or a single unused city lot. These may be managed by a half-

The highest reward for a person's toil is not what they get for it, but what they become by it.

— John Ruskin

Volunteers are not free labor to be exploited but the co-creators of your collective dream. Here are some tips on how to handle volunteers, borrowed from the Green Guerrillas and others:

- Find out what your volunteers are interested in so you can match them with appropriate events as they arise.
- Get your volunteers involved from the start in planning and setting policy. But don't think you're doing this just for the volunteers' sake. These are the people who will become the future leaders of the organization.
- Match new volunteers in groups or pairs with more experienced ones.
- Keep your volunteers in the loop. Whether the news is good or bad, they deserve to hear it and help deal with it.
- Let your volunteers know their role is important. You can't say thank you enough, but you ought to try. Use words, notes, certificates, awards, newsletter announcements, whatever.
- Don't expect too much. Volunteers have outside lives they must manage as well. Accept that it takes time to build up a good volunteer program.

dozen or so neighbors who lack their own space to grow things. In such cases the sites may well suggest themselves. Convenience and accessibility are the priorities guiding the search.

For a larger garden that can accommodate more people and more than just personal plots, take the time to find a place that will be good for you and for the area in years to come.

Context is king. Don't just look at the site. You must take in everything around it as well.

RIP THIS — COMMUNITY GARDEN COUNTER-THEFT STRATEGIES

1. More gardeners mean fewer opportunities for thieves. Think of ways to minimize times when you have no "eyes on the crops," particularly during harvest season. Schedule events, coordinate visits, get volunteers to keep watch. If your garden is in view of homes where neighbors might be able to keep an eye on things, make sure they know what's going on.

2. Hide your prizes. Most thieves are opportunists. They aren't likely to go digging through straw to uncover your champion pumpkin. Yellow tomatoes are as tasty but less tempting than red ones. Grow desirable and easily-picked food (such as raspberries) behind less popular crops like parsnips or beets.

3. Figure out security/prevention strategies before problems come up. Work out a common strategy on questioning unfamiliar visitors. Would-be thieves hate a place where people talk to them, even if the questioners are friendly. "Can I help you find the plot you're looking for?" Or "Would you like to sign our waiting list for a plot?" may be all you need to say to turn intruders away.

4. If a thief is spotted, make sure the gardeners know what to do. Most pilferers will slink away when confronted, muttering excuses so lame they're embarrassed to air them at normal volume. Consider keeping a cheap throwaway camera nearby to use in gathering evidence. A picture is worth a thousand threats. One year we had a bad harvest season with vegetables disappearing almost daily throughout the

DESIGN TIP

Don't have water where you need it? Collection barrels linked by hoses can do the job of hauling water to various parts of the garden for you. So long as your target barrel is lower than your reservoir, a hose from one to the other filled with water will keep your target barrel topped up no matter how far away.

Make sure it can provide trouble-free access for everyone whether they come by foot, bike, car, public transit or something else. Check the parking options and also see whether there's room for trucks to drop off bulky deliveries such as loads of wood chips or manure.

You need sun. A minimum of six hours is recommended, but all day would be better. Check the surrounding vegetation and look into long-range municipal plans to make sure you won't be

A fallow field is a sin.

— JOHN STEINBECK

grounds. We were convinced local crime rates had soared and were debating the effects of the various social trends behind it, when the real cause was spotted, a few streets away, selling our "fresh organic" vegetables. Once someone got a picture of him and posted it around the neighborhood, he wasn't seen in the garden again.

5. Keep the plots in good condition. Fallen fruit, overripe vegetables and general disarray send the message that no one cares. A well-managed site is harder to steal from because it makes the crime more obvious.

6. Put up a sign. Do Not Steal is one option, but will the thieves get it? You might see better results with a message explaining who gardens in the area and why…and how anyone can join if interested. Or get creative. You could dust your ripening corn with a harmless white powder such as flour and then install a sign warning of some weird scientific test in progress. How about "Penile Reduction Powder — Sample at Own Risk"?

7. Grow more than you need in a variety of crops so you won't get cleaned out of an entire season's bounty by one sack-toting robber. With an extended harvest you'll always be more successful than the grab-and-run criminal types. But if you do have things taken, try not to dwell on the missing goods. Don't give in to dark visions of the culprit collapsing under the weight of the loot in the middle of traffic, no matter how delightful. Invent some better scenario where the stolen food somehow ends up in the stomachs of people who need it. Consider that in a future life, they may be growing things for you.

Most of us walk unseeing through the world, unaware alike of its beauties, its wonders, and the strange and sometimes terrible intensity of the lives that are being lived about us.

— Rachel Carson

heading into a shady future from maturing trees or new high-rise developments.

Of course you want a site with fertile, dark, fluffy and well-draining soil. And people in Hell want ice water. Urban areas are known for having poor, degraded, unproductive soils. Yours will probably be no better. You'll just have to improve it, over time, by adding plenty of organic materials. Start your compost system right away to get the cycle going.

When evaluating size requirements, don't just total the dimensions of the plots. Make sure you have enough space for everything you hope to do, now and later. Think of what you'll need for other features, perhaps an orchard, a herb garden, a picnic spot or a pond. Anticipate future needs. If you're popular and dozens more applicants show up, will there be room to expand?

Before you roam the city checking on places, prepare a checklist to be filled out at each site. That way you'll have something to evaluate later once you've seen a dozen places and they all scram-

A city lot covered with a mass of weeds can be a daunting site, but all that growth means fertility. If nature can grow a jungle there, so can you, only it will be a jungle of plants you prefer.

The weeds already present may help you determine what kind of site you're on. "Weeds want to tell a story," says biodynamic growing pioneer E.E. Pfeiffer. Weeds often survive where cultivated plants, softened by years of pampering, cannot. Identify the weeds on a site and you can learn something about the soil condition:

Previously cultivated: lamb's quarters, plantain, chickweed, purslane, buttercup, dandelion, nettle, prostrate knotweed, amaranth, ragweed, mayweed, prickly lettuce, field speedwell, mallow, carpetweed.

Sandy and poor: goldenrod, ononis, broom bush, yellow toad-flax, flowered aster, sandbur.

Slightly acid: daisies, horsetails, field sorrel.

Increasingly acid and compact: sorrel, dock, horsetail, finger-leaf weed, lady's thumb.

Very acid: hackweed, knapweed, cinquefoil, swampy horsetail.

Hardpan: field mustard, horse nettle, morning glory, quack grass, chamomile, pennycress.[1]

ble together in your memory. Your clipboard list might include answers to questions such as:

- What's the neighborhood like?
- Does it change at night?
- Would gardeners feel comfortable going there alone?
- Will theft and vandalism be issues?
- Will fences be necessary?
- Are there nearby schools, community centers or senior facilities that might hold potential partners?
- What's the history of land use on the site?
- Is it easy to reach by public transportation, by bike, by car?
- Are traffic patterns likely to change?
- Is there room for parking and for trucks to make deliveries?
- Does the site get adequate sunlight?
- Will any nearby trees grow to shade the growing spaces?
- Which way do the prevailing winds blow?
- How's the soil?
- Will testing for contaminants be required?
- Does the site drain adequately?
- How much work will be involved in making the soil fertile?
- Does the site have access to water?
- Is there a master plan for the area that might affect the garden?

Choose the right people

There are a lot of things you can do yourself, but starting a community garden is not one of them. The key word in "community gardening" is the first one. Think of the garden as what grows only after you've tended the community.

Pick your comrades carefully. Spend more time on this than you do with the seed catalog. Your colleagues don't have to be like you, and in fact offsetting skills are beneficial, but you do have to get along. And not only when things are new and exciting and full of potential, but also later when you get bogged down and have to face obstacles such as financial setbacks or official jerks. You'll want to know you're in it together with people you both like and trust so you can deal with the crap effectively.

How many people you choose for your core team is probably not going to be up to you anyway, especially once word gets out and would-be gardeners come looking for land. At the start, though,

Before and after Vancouver views of barren Strathcona Park land in 1973 and 30 years later once community gardeners had their way.

you'll probably have a small group. These will be the ones who end up doing the majority of the work. It's important to get this group's dynamics off to a productive start.

Call to order

One of the first things your group must do is decide exactly what it wants. It may sound obvious — you want to start a community garden — but it helps to spell it out. Yes, that means get it in writing. If you hold regular meetings and keep minutes, not only will you have something to refer back to 18 months later when you forget a key strategy, but you'll be writing a legacy for future gardeners when it comes time for them to expand or change or start a new project elsewhere.

If your site is big enough to merit more than four or five small plots, you may want to register as a non-profit society. And because you're now a recognized group, you must have a purpose, so determine your mission. You do this by agreeing on a mission statement. Consider it your lofty aspirations crystallized in written form, a sentence rather than a paragraph or page. This can seem a little pretentious at the opening stage, but it's worth doing

Ain't no sunshine when you're gone, or so it can seem when trying to raise a crop surrounded by skyscrapers or trees. There may however be more light than you think. If the plot gets at least some morning or late afternoon direct sunshine, it may still have enough to produce something edible. The following list of vegetables recommended for a partially shady site is adapted from oldhouseweb.net:

Arugala	Rhubarb	Rutabagas
Beets	Broccoli	Brussels sprouts
Sorrel	Spinach	Cauliflower
Summer Squash	Celery	Turnips
Cress	Endive	Garlic
Kale	Borage	Kohlrabi
Leaf Lettuce	Leeks	Parsley
Parsnips	Lovage	Peas
Mint	Potatoes	Pumpkins
Thyme	Radish	

because you will return to your mission statement in those dark hours when you're wondering why you ever wanted to get involved with this blasted project. Or when two sides in an argument both claim they have the group's best interests at heart in debating a new policy.

The beginning stage is also the best time to establish the garden rules. This may sound too bureaucratic or authoritarian to be fun, for gardeners, but do it anyway. It may save you from despair later when a dispute comes up that can't be solved with common sense. A single anti-social garden member can screw things up for everyone if you have no rules. Try to handle an aberration without them and you'll long for a more bureaucratic and authoritarian stick to set things right. Make sure the rules are understood by newcomers before they join. If the membership agreement form they must sign includes the rules all neat and numbered, even better; no one will be able to say later they weren't informed.

How to ward off developers (and their offspring)

An empty city lot may be empty for a reason. No one else wants it. It might be in a scary part of town, or downwind from a chicken rendering plant. But let's say some guerrilla gardeners with more verve than real estate savvy or brains move in, do all the heavy lifting, and lo, it becomes a garden. Somehow the community grows with it, perhaps even because of it. The neighborhood becomes desirable. The chicken factory moves out. Now even people with money want to live there.

Suddenly trashy lots where meth-heads previously would have been embarrassed to be seen are being listed in the real estate pages for millions. Developers, politicians, investors, civil servants and regular folks all get caught up by the lure of hot property and big money. The core values of community and justice and health and ecology aren't exactly tossed out, but can you believe they're asking two million dollars for that place? Now it's a boom, and any city commitment to the neighborhood left from the time the garden was launched withers like a chestnut tree with blight. Developers begin snapping at the land like jackals after a fawn, and it becomes increasingly more difficult to justify why you should be able to keep growing your broccoli there when so many others want the site and are willing to pay top dollar for it.

But it'll *never* work... There's someone in every crowd convinced that whatever you try is going to fail. A community garden here? Noooo. It's too busy, or polluted, or cold, or wet, or something, anything, really, so long as it confirms a glum outlook on life and drags everybody down into it.

Let these people moan and groan — to each other. Listen instead to the positive types who see a tough situation and start looking for opportunities. Like the 100 or so people in Inuvik, in the Northwest Territories, growing everything from squash to muskmelon 125 miles *north* of the Arctic Circle.

The Inuvik Community Greenhouse took an old hockey rink scheduled for demolition and turned it into a neighborhood amenity. Even some residents without plots use the facility, coming for family picnics in the warm, flower-scented air, two things not usually associated with the Arctic.

You want to prevent the debate from ever getting to the point where it's your vegetables against their dollars. From the start, design your space not just as a collection of allotment plots but a true community garden. That means as much or more space for communal activities as for personal plots. If you're also a recreational area and a habitat preserve and serve as a crucial link in an ecological chain to other wildlife-friendly sites, you'll be that much more difficult to turn into condos. Money still talks, but it doesn't win every argument, because what price can anyone put on a community's right to gather in the outdoors, enjoy nature, learn eco-based living skills and tend the fragile earth together?

In my community garden, before the first shovel went in, a design was created that divided the space into three roughly equal parts. The 200-plus plots take up just one third of it, and include gardens used by schools, community groups, the handicapped and others with special needs. Another third goes to collective uses including a community orchard with more than 300 varieties of fruit trees, a picnic area, a kids' play area, a herb garden, a solar-powered meeting house with the city's first licensed composting toilet, a native plant nursery and more. The remaining one-third is set aside for a wildlife habitat, a crucial sanctuary in the busy downtown area for a region where more than 90 percent of the original wetlands have been lost.

I mention my own community garden here not to brag — because I didn't do any of it — but to illustrate how taking the land now would mean paving over not just some home grown greens but a complex infrastructure supporting a successful community stewardship of an ecologically important site.

Or if you think your garden might one day be threatened (and if you're in a city, you're probably right) why not just buy it now? Not you personally, maybe, but enough people pooling their spare change together have made it happen elsewhere, together with land trust groups and other funders. In return for promising to keep the space going as a community resource, you might even get the government to pony up.

In places where "progress" is inevitable, you might try working with developers who, as a condition of being allowed to make a profit on a local building project, would agree to set aside a portion of the property for a community garden. This will be easier

Security can be designed into containers so they can be safely left out in public in high-theft areas. Of course they'll never be truly secure, but this should work for most places unless the thieves are both industrious and bored.

Drill an extra hole in the bottom of the pot large enough to fit a heavy gauge chain. One end of the chain sits in the bottom of the pot with a bolt through it so it doesn't slip out. The other gets wrapped around and locked (or cemented onto) a cinder block buried beneath the pot.

It sounds like a lot of work, and it can be — at least to dig and bury the cinder block. But it doesn't cost much for a short length of chain and a cheap combination lock from the hardware store (or you can even close the loop with wire). Once it's buried, the chances of someone digging everything up are slim. Give it a tug to test. If it doesn't come up easily, you're probably safe. Most thieves hate to linger and will move on to easier pickings.

to envision if you're already on the site. Here as with any urban design issue, creative thinking can catch on. When a community garden site in Montreal was about to be devoured by a huge building, the gardeners got the developer to include a 7,000-square-foot community garden on the roof, and even pay for the soil and water.

You might also try to get your city to enact a law like the one in Munich mandating certain areas to be used only for public vegetable and flower gardens. If you find park space that would fit your needs, offer to maintain the site as a public amenity with no fences, plenty of open space, and plots available to all on a first-come basis. You could even work up a maintenance contract that explains how you will do the regular landscape chores, pick up the litter, provide security and so on — all things that normally cost a city money — in return for, say, water services or professional tree care.

Link it or lose it

A community garden is more than meets the eye. It should also be considered an ecological link to natural corridors that may help turn a scoured city into a wildlife haven. Most creatures can't follow our traffic grid set-up of asphalt and cars, so natural byways and stopovers are essential. A corridor can be as simple as a row of street trees over varying shrubs, yet make all the difference in supporting a variety of living things.

The wildlife potential for your community garden site is probably quite high. Food and flowering plants attract a great number of insects, birds and more. Think of adding areas which have brambles, a mixed selection of deciduous and evergreen trees and maybe a small pond. With every move you're adding to the area's habitat value and making your city more hospitable to a world of creatures.

What have you done for me lately?

Some cities have caught on to the social benefits of having an active citizenry engaged in community gardens, especially as more urban dwellers move into anonymous apartment complexes lacking gardening opportunities. Municipal officials in Seattle and Montreal even run the community garden programs themselves. City staff

Raised beds are often recommended when starting a new garden. If you have poor soil to begin with, rather than going to great lengths and a lot of time to amend it, the simplest solution can be to bring in better stuff, pile it right on top and plant away. Advantages include improved aeration and drainage, along with soil that will warm earlier in spring, which could mean a longer planting season. Disadvantages include the need to water more often due to faster drying times and the prospect of more freezing in winter. But here's one more advantage: less bending.

take care of the planning and organizing — no small tasks. They also ensure the grounds are properly maintained, deal with malcontents who don't tend their plots, and keep things going through the seasons by overseeing everything from the year-end clean-up to the spring opening.

This may not be what you want. Particularly if you have a dedicated community group already, this system may strike some as overly bureaucratic. For those just starting out, however, all that structure can be a plus. If your city isn't doing its part, ask why not. The following questions are all taken from examples of what taxpayers in other jurisdictions are getting, so you're not out of line in wondering whether your own city can provide them as well. Ask the city staff, or perhaps the candidates in the next municipal election, whether your city is willing to help community gardeners in:

• Donating office space or administrative help.
• Buying or leasing land.
• Providing insurance under the city's umbrella insurance policy.
• Awarding grants for startup expenses.

Seven things you probably didn't know about tomatoes:

1. Tomatoes picked when showing the first sign of pink and brought indoors to ripen at room temperature will taste just as good as those left to ripen on the vine.
2. You can tell whether a crop of green tomatoes will ripen off the vine by cutting into one. If the seeds are surrounded by a slippery gel that moves away from the knife, your tomatoes can be picked. If you can cut right through the seeds, picking now will leave you with green tomatoes that won't get ripe. They can still be tasty though, fried in butter.
3. Tomatoes are vegetables, not fruits. Unless you insist otherwise.
4. Tomatoes first came out of Central and South America.
5. They were introduced to Europe by Spanish conquistadors during the early 16th century.
6. They were originally called love apples.
7. They are extremely rich in lycopene which may help prevent cancer.

- Doing maintenance around the garden site.
- Offering design help from city landscaping experts.
- Loaning skilled city workers for construction projects.
- Offering city greenhouse space.
- Planting trees and shrubs near gardens.
- Installing playground equipment.
- Writing letters of support to help with fund raising.
- Collecting leaves and delivering compost to the site.
- Providing water systems.
- Donating heavy equipment for clearing, plowing, hauling bulk materials.
- Advertising plots through city channels.
- Starting gardens at public housing sites and city parks.

What was paradise but a garden and orchard of trees and herbs, full of pleasure and nothing there but delights.

— WILLIAM LAWSON (1618)

Grow your own

The following ideas from the Strathcona Community Garden in Vancouver have been tested on the land and found to work. Your socio-political climate conditions will vary, of course, but these successful ideas can at least make a good starting point when thinking of ways to grow your own community garden.

1. A work party on the last Sunday of each month in which all members take part. Gardeners share communal chores such as weeding paths, picking up trash, pruning trees and turning compost. The work parties are held rain or shine from 10 A.M. to 2 P.M. with a break at noon for lunch. Yes, some people do come just for the lunch, but they end up working too.

2. An annual Open House/Plant Sale. Neighbors are invited to learn more about the gardens through educational workshops, site tours and a big bargain sale of plants and things donated throughout the year.

3. Fun events for gardeners such as workshops, field trips, harvest parties and seasonal celebrations. Community gardening can involve a lot of work so sometimes it's good to schedule events that almost force you to have a good time.

4. A monthly planning meeting open to all gardeners (or those interested in becoming gardeners) to schedule tasks for the work parties, debate new policies, work out disputes, whatever.

5. A Free Stuff table where gardeners can leave surplus crops and things for anyone to take away. Zucchini anyone?

Activist grower Muggs Sigurgeirson

The Strathcona Community Garden is known as an urban oasis in Vancouver's Downtown Eastside. For a sanctuary it's a pretty busy place, attracting more outside visitors than gardeners, including delegations from as far away as Shanghai who come to learn new ways to encourage urban agriculture and citizen-stewardship of the land.

It takes a major group effort to keep all the activities in a garden this large going. There is clearly power in numbers, because a lot of the tasks could never get done without the help of a crowd. But a few particularly devoted individuals end up taking on the most responsibility and doing the bulk of the really important work. Strathcona was fortunate from the start in enlisting one of Vancouver's most dedicated community activists, Muggs Sigurgeirson. The heart and soul of the garden since it was founded in 1985, she offers advice here from decades of experience on the enviro-political front lines.

Q: How do you start a community garden?
A: Lots of people have asked me this over the years. I would say you need at least three solid committed people. One person cannot do it. Well, one person can get things started. What happened here was two people went around putting up notices in the neighborhood to hold a meeting at the community center to start a community garden. And people came out. There was a clear demand.

Q: Is there always a demand for this kind of thing?
A: That depends. If you're in a neighborhood where everybody's living in a single family home and has a back yard, no, it's not going to work. It works where there's a high density of people and low availability of land. In that kind of population I think you will always find a core group of people who really want to garden.

Every city has extra fruit trees, ones that may have been planted by well-meaning gardeners in their yards years ago but have since become neglected. If only every city had something like this: the Fruit Tree Project in Vancouver sends crews of volunteers out to pick the fruit. Residents ask for them so they can avoid a ripe mess and perhaps share in the crop, while the local food banks appreciate getting fresh apples, pears, cherries and more.

Then you have to have three people who are prepared to build an organization. You can't have a community garden without the infrastructure.

Q: What do you mean by infrastructure?
A: You have to have people who are prepared to make signs, call people to meetings, come to meetings, open a bank account, keep track of the money, solicit donations in an organized way.

Q: An organization.
A: Yup, a group with structure.

Q: You can't just do it with you and your pals even though you're all really keen?
A: That's the thing. The overwhelming number of people just want to come and garden and get away from it all. The difference in this garden from most community gardens is in the fact that people really believe in the ownership of it. Look at the P-Patch gardens in Seattle. We went down there to look at them, and we were shocked. On one hand it's absolutely fantastic you've got the municipal infrastructure that will pour money and resources and staffing into setting up and maintaining gardens for people, but people have no feeling of ownership or of building something.

Q: Is that bad?
A: It's not bad, it's completely different. It's not what I call a community garden. It's an allotment garden, where an individual goes and grows their own thing and goes home. And they take no overall responsibility. And actually in Seattle each year there's a staff person who opens it up and you apply for a plot, you don't necessarily get your own plot, they just allot them out. There's no feeling that this is mine. Whereas if you maintain your own organization, then there is a community feeling of ownership and responsibility for that area.

Q: So keep walking us through the steps. We've put up the notices, we're at the meeting.
A: We actually met every two weeks, I think, to talk about the principles of the garden. Number one was that it would be organic. Number two was that it was community, it wouldn't just be allotment, there had to be space here for people who weren't actively gardening or people who didn't necessarily need a plot but had to have access to the community. Which we've honored and maintained all these years. We came up with five principles,

College of the Compost in a community garden.

but the first was organic. So what does organic mean? If somebody brings in slug bait, is that non-organic? We went through all those discussions.

Q: Before you got to the details of the size of the plots or anything else?

A: Yup. Maybe it wouldn't unfold that way for other people but I think it saved us a lot of grief. Every so often a wave of new people come in and they want to garden the orchard or they want to garden the top area. I remember these two guys came in and they had fabulous plots and one was a landscape architect and they wanted to change the entire top area and turn it all into garden plots and open it up. We said, we have a design we've all agreed on, these are our principles, so you'd have to go through a whole process to change that. And it was too much trouble for them. I think having these principles saved us a lot. So then, we started pulling the community into it for support and resources.

Q: You mean money?

A: Well, in the beginning it didn't mean much money. It meant getting places like Finning Tractor to donate a tractor for the day and the union to agree to provide a driver and a truck to bring it over here. A gardener had a partner who was working there so she asked him. People did that who were good at it. It wasn't me, for sure, I wasn't good at getting donations at that level in those days. And them coming over and doing it. We organized the community to come out for coffee and 50 people, working with their bare hands, showed up to pick out all the rocks. Not only gardeners. Landlords from the Downtown Eastside, people who were so poor they didn't want to garden but were completely excited by the concept of the community, all building it together. This was like the worst farmer's field, full of rocks. So we spent

Watering works best when it reaches the roots — not the leaves, not the flowers, not the top $\frac{1}{8}$" of soil you see get damp and think you're done. To make sure you water in ways your plants appreciate, try simple props like plastic jugs with holes in the bottom half-buried in the soil. Fill the jug and let the water seep in at its own pace. If you use a sprinkler, put an empty tuna or cat food can in the garden. Once it's filled, you've sprinkled enough.

the whole day just picking out rocks with our bare hands. We didn't even have money for gloves. And this was in February or March, not summer.

Q: So now you've got the place and you're ready to plant.
A: We started but it was still a lot of work, mostly because of water. The Downtown Eastside Women's Center were growing potatoes in stacks of tires, but they had to pack buckets of water over from the park field house. The biggest turn-about in terms of developing things was when the Ray-Cam Community Centre gave us $3,000 to put the first water line in. That's when the whole place turned around.

Q: Water was key.
A: It was. You've got to have three things. You've got to have people, you've got to have location, and you've got to have access to water. Once you have those three things, I think the garden can go in any which direction. That's the lesson. If you've got committed folks, and you've got a site, and you've got water, you'll have a community garden.

This City is what it is because our citizens are what they are.

— Plato

IF I CAN DO IT...   Les King — Roses Rule

"People pick the flowers sometimes. What are you going to do, break their legs?"

Les King owns an auto repair business in Vancouver that seems to be doing well. It's larger than most, in a building that's practically factory-sized, in an industrial area beside the port. The work apparently leaves him enough time to garden. His guerrilla plot occupies a long strip of grass and trees across the street beside the port's chain-link fence.

His rose garden provides a gorgeous splash of color in a gray neighborhood where a sex trade worker arriving for a 10 A.M. shift looks right at home. Signs tell people to leave the flowers alone, which they don't, and also explain who's behind the financing and care of the site.

It's a rose garden. I planted about 65 rose bushes. Well, 60 at least. They're all different varieties. Heritage roses.

No, it isn't my land. The space belongs to the city. I just keep it clean. I do it because I think it looks nice. People walk here sometimes with their dogs and they're surprised to see this. They say, It looks nice.

Rose master Les King

No, I didn't ask the city for permission. They knew once they saw what I was doing but they didn't say anything. In the beginning it was a garbage dump. I just started cleaning it out. Then when I was about a quarter of the way through, the city came and helped to clean one end. But they didn't plant the trees and flowers. I planted those. That one's an Italian plum. It has fruit but they're not ready yet. This one is Japanese, a purple leaf plum. I planted the ones across the street too. Once day the city came in and counted all the trees for their inventory. I say, if they want it, let them have it. I didn't talk to them.

People pick the flowers sometimes. What are you going to do, break their legs?

I just watered so now it's looking pretty good. Watering is not so bad. I've got a pick-up truck with a 45-gallon drum. Just drive along and water. It's easy to carry the water that way, better than running a hose all the way along.

I don't know if gardening like this is within the law or not, but I never think it's wrong. It should be right because it's nice for the city. They say the east side is not a good area, but it's a nice area. Even the people, as long as you don't bother them they don't bother you. They're just picking flowers — but the flowers come again.

POWER PLANT   **Sweet pea (*Lathyrus odoratus*)**

All the beauty that goes into making a flower has a higher purpose: sex. It's meant to attract enablers such as bees or butterflies that might help with pollination. Another strategy uses an irresistible scent. A few flowers try both, often the result of cultivation in which breeders have selected out types to emphasize desired traits.

The sweet pea is one of the most managed flowers on earth, having been tweaked since the early 1700s. There are now hundreds or even thousands of varieties in almost every color, many with a lovely fragrance that makes a fresh bouquet a welcome addition to any room.

Although originally from Sicily, the sweet pea varieties we tend to grow today are cool weather plants which won't endure a site that's too hot or windy. Other than that, if you have fairly rich soil which you can keep moist, they're easy to grow. Some gardeners pre-sprout their seeds by placing them in a damp paper towel for a few days before planting out in spring (or in fall for areas where the ground doesn't freeze). Nicking the seed coats is also said to help.

Perennial Sweet Pea — Lathyrus laifolius
Credit: From William Baxter's "British Phaenogamous Botany" published in London in 1834, illustration by Isaac Russell.

Once the sprouts get four or five inches tall, pinch out the growing tips to encourage strong branching. The plants will dutifully climb to six feet or so with support from a fence or trellis or string. Pick the flowers often to encourage more to develop — once the seeds pods form the blooms will stop. Note that the print shown here is not *Lathyrus odoratus*. It's a tough perennial cousin much praised for its resilient beauty but without a scent. Sweet peas can also be considered invasive so choose your spot carefully.

Did you know: Despite the common name, this sweet pea isn't for eating. The pods and seeds contain the poison beta-aminopropionitrile, although you're unlikely to ever eat enough to do real damage.

CHAPTER EIGHT

When to Work Within
(The Art of Aikido Politics)

There's a time to fight, and a time to fight without looking like you're fighting. In other words, to work within the system. What? To march, lamb-like, right into the lion's den? Am I mad? Probably. But why pass up the chance to do some of your best guerrilla gardening work just because the people who own or manage the land you're after happen to agree with you?

If it's private property, the owners of an unused lot may see the point in letting volunteers in to clean it up, care for it, stop people from abusing it, make it look beautiful and probably raise its market value in the process. A simple letter or phone call may be all it takes to arrange a meeting to work out the details. If permission is indeed all you want (which may be the easiest route), get the approval in writing and go to work. Some guerrilla gardeners have done this by signing a lease which agrees the owner is free to retake possession at any time. Although "any time" sounds a little restrictive, especially if you've got tomatoes about to ripen. Try at least for a fair severance period, say the 90 days it would take to grow corn. If that won't wash, 30 days is better than no time, and no time is better than a slammed door. While working the details out, get a sense of how cooperative your owner could become: you may be able to get the materials and plants donated in return for your promise to keep the site secure.

Sometimes your toughest decision in a guerrilla gardening project is not what to do but whether you should first ask for permission to do it. Before you reach that point, it helps to get as much information as you can. Find out who owns the property through a trip to City Hall where it should be part of the public record. The

Certain gardens are described as retreats when they are really attacks.

Ian Hamilton Finlay

name alone may not be enough, however, if it's been bought as an investment by an absentee owner who could be half a world away and waiting for the rest of the neighborhood to improve before cashing in. Or the property could be registered in the name of some company that isn't easy to track down like Tax Off Ltd., Nowhere Lane, the Cayman Islands. Sites such as these make the best candidates for simply taking over and planting. If you do, and then hear from the owners, or their lawyers, express your delight at finally making contact and proceed accordingly with the ask-permission strategy. In some cases, while the initial idea may be repellent to the owner and raise terrors of the landless everywhere rising up to question the divine nature of property rights, one look at the difference between a trash-riddled lot and a blooming neighborhood garden can be the difference. That's another argument for planting first and explaining later.

If you've been reading carefully up to now, this marks the third time you've heard the same advice. That should be enough to make it the underlying theme of the book: it's better to ask for forgiveness than for permission.

Advice from Sun Tzu and *The Art of War* that was intended for ancient Chinese warriors but might work as well for guerrilla gardeners:

A military operation involves deception. Even though you are competent, appear to be incompetent. Though effective, appear to be ineffective.

When you are going to attack nearby, make it look as if you are going to go a long way; when you are going to attack far away, make it look as if you are going just a short distance.

Use humility to make them haughty. Tire them by flight. Cause division among them. Attack when they are unprepared, make your move when they do not expect it.

By taking equipment from your own country but feeding off the enemy you can be sufficient in both arms and provisions.

Therefore those who win every battle are not really skillful — those who render others' armies helpless without fighting are the best of all.

To unfailingly take what you attack, attack where there is

The care and feeding of city officials

Getting permission to plant on city property can be a hard row to hoe. Not because the territory itself doesn't provide plenty of opportunities for improvement, but because the official approval process can require negotiating through a Sargasso of desks where on any given day any timid or mean civil servant can stop the whole thing. Why? Because we've never done it that way. Or the liability issues. Not to mention the budget constraints. And you might poke your eye out with that stick.

There's no one set of instructions that will work for all cases in taking on the local government. Each city is different, each department has its own style, and even within a department the sub-sections may be run according to their own peculiarities.

I learned a few things working inside the bureaucracy one summer on a landscape architecture internship with the Vancouver Parks Board. I expect they could be applied elsewhere. For example, it's good to keep in mind that you are, despite the pointy-headed evidence before you, dealing with normal people here, and these people are likely to say yes or no to your proposal for the same

A simple frame, a little soil and a few seeds turned this city street tree into a flower fest.

no defense. For unfailingly secure defense, defend where there is no attack.

Be extremely subtle, even to the point of formlessness. Be extremely mysterious, even to the point of soundlessness. Thereby you can be the director of the opponent's fate.

When on surrounded ground, plot. When on deadly ground, fight.

Those who come seeking peace without a treaty are plotting.

Therefore those who do not know the plans of competitors cannot prepare alliances. Those who do not know the lay of the land cannot maneuver their forces. Those who do not use local guides cannot take advantage of the ground. The military of an effective rulership must know all these things.

Thus one advances without seeking glory, retreats without avoiding blame, only protecting people, to the benefit of the government as well, thus rendering valuable service to the nation.[2]

We are all indigenous to this planet, this mosaic of wild gardens we are being called by nature and history to reinhabit in good spirit. Part of that responsibility is to choose a place. To restore the land one must live and work in a place. To work in a place is to work with others. People who work together in a place become a community, and community, in time, grows a culture. To work on behalf of the wild is to restore a culture.

— GARY SNYDER

reasons other people say yes or no to a new idea: because they like it (or don't), because they think it will work (or won't), because it will make their life/job easier (or won't). Other motivations can be fear (siding with your kind could be a bad career move), ambition (just the opposite) and spite (if residents in your neighborhood won a previous skirmish over resources they may have a difficult time winning the next battle, especially if the last one got personal).

In more cases than some suspect, however, you may find a city official who genuinely wants to help. The trouble is, getting something done, especially something such as a new initiative, usually involves a complex process. Most staff members will be too busy

EIGHT THINGS YOU PROBABLY DIDN'T KNOW ABOUT WORMS

1. An acre of soil can contain 1 million worms.
2. Compost worms are hermaphrodites, having both male and female genitalia.
3. Worm poop holds up to nine times its weight in water and is rich in nitrogen, potassium and phosphorus.
4. The ancient Greeks understood the importance of worms to soil health. Aristotle (384–322 B.C.E.) referred to worms as "the intestines of the earth."
5. In ancient Egypt farmers were not even allowed to touch an earthworm for fear of offending the god of fertility. Cleopatra (69–30 B.C.E.) declared them sacred.
6. Charles Darwin studied earthworms for more than 40 years. He wrote a book about them called *The Formation of Vegetable Mould Through the Action of the Earthworm*. Clearly a page-turner...if you agree with him that, "It may be doubted that there are many other animals which have played so important a part in the history of the world as have these lowly organized creatures."
7. Earthworms are not native to North America. They came from Europe in the soil used as ballast on ships. Some consider them an invasive species.
8. Earthworms are 82 percent protein, a fact worth recalling if you're ever starving.[1]

keeping the old initiatives going to be bothered with the prospect of trying new ones. You won't be able to convince them to take up your cause, and it isn't worth trying for long. This doesn't mean they're stupid or heartless, necessarily. More likely they just realize it could become a tough, draining and ugly process with plenty of ways to fail along the way, and what's in it for them anyway? Every bureaucracy has plenty of staff who won't stick their necks out, and if we're honest, we'll admit that we have met the enemy and they are us. Many people have joined institutions for fine reasons, including some idealized version of their working life meaning something in the creation of a better world. Later, having dealt with the grinding reality of how things really work (or don't work), most will have settled for doing a decent job, and that's how you can find them, perhaps living for the weekends, collecting the paychecks and counting the years until the pension kicks in. I used to think worse of people for settling, but who was I to judge? I realized during my own term in the office that I wasn't much different, and that it wasn't the people so much as the systems they have to operate in that may be flawed. Has anyone anywhere ever worked in a large organization that wasn't kept running largely by compromisers quietly going through the paces?

Your biggest drawback in figuring out how to get a municipality to move on your project may be a lack of information. Everyone on the inside may know where the black hole of decent proposals lies, and will accordingly avoid steering projects they favor in that direction. But you don't know that, and all they'll tell you is that your call is important to them, although not quite important enough to pick up.

Here it may help to probe the staff contact list until you can find a human with whom you can work. Every bureaucracy has them — people who remain sincere and sympathetic and compassionate even on the job. They understand how it feels to deal with a faceless wall of regulations. Your contact, even if in a different section, may help you maneuver your proposal through the system. He or she should be able to tell you the most effective routes to try, the proper formatting of things, the right timing and so on.

If you do get an ally on the inside, and you establish some kind of relationship, you must be responsible and carry through with whatever you say you'll do. Find out what's expected from your side and be sure to deliver it. You may be asked, for example, for evidence of community support. Letters from concerned citizens, nearby school officials, local merchants and anyone else involved will help. You may be asked to demonstrate constructive partnerships. Community centers, non-profit organizations, civic clubs and school groups may be pleased to help you improve the neighborhood by writing glowing letters describing the prospects of working together.

All this will enhance your project's chances by lifting it from an intriguing idea to a broadly-supported plan. The more paperwork you can provide to back up this plan, the better its chances of success. The lingua franca of the bureaucracy, even today, is still the paper report. Meetings and more meetings are the daily gruel of office communications, but it's the written report that gets read and passed from one desk to another and referred back to weeks or months later when it comes time to make a decision. So yes, more paper often means a better case for your side, but not if you're padding your stuff. A single pithy page is better than ten meandering ones. Despite the popular image of the bureaucrat toiling under stacks of useless information, the preferred style for staff reports is actually fairly snappy. At least it is for the readable ones. A well-written report is smart, factual, on-target and interesting. Your documents should be no less.

Push or pull

So now we have our proposal, with the supporting documents, and they're all on the desk of an insider with the very government agency that has the authority to make it happen. But we're not done. There will probably still be more hoops to jump through, some entirely unanticipated. Even your ally won't know all the ways things can turn sour. The logical blocks may be explained and dealt with accordingly. The illogical ones may not be. If you're not on the inside yourself, you'll probably never know that your idea is languishing because it was picked up and promoted by someone whose efforts are being sabotaged by a rival who can't forgive what happened last Christmas at the office party.

All you can do here is keep pushing the idea forward. Remember that this is one of a number of proposals the bureaucrats must

It's fine to add used newspapers to the compost pile, but if you just throw them on in stacks they'll stick together and make a gluey, gloppy mess. You need to shred the paper first. An office shredder will do it. So will a dedicated group of children old enough to handle scissors. The shredded material makes a good source of "brown" to counter the "green" of your kitchen scraps.

consider. Remember also — and remind them of the fact if you must — that considering things like this is what they're hired to do. Gentle pressure can help keep your project up on the to-do list, but do it kindly, with humor if possible, and if not, at least humanely.

But don't be so nice that your project gets ignored and slips into a bureaucratic eddy beyond the reach of your main supporter. At times you just have to push harder. Don't threaten — remember the ally is on your side — but it's fair to emphasize that you're serious and will not give up, and then suggest a date by which progress must be made or you'll consider alternatives. You'll probably have to take them, so don't even think of bluffing. This could mean moving your proposal to another, perhaps higher, desk in the bureaucracy. But that's a dicey move. Bureaucrats hate attempts to play one off another. Since no one wants to have the same thing happen to them, most will not even entertain the thought. Although with someone in another section who doesn't care about the infighting, or a superior who may appreciate the chance to demonstrate personal clout, you could have a chance.

If none of this works, you may have to shift directions from the bureaucrats to the politicians. We elect politicians to improve our lives, so here's a chance to let them earn their keep. The right politician with enough influence can make a sluggish bureaucrat jump like kangaroo, if the will is there. This works better during an election campaign, of course, when every politician is your friend.

And if the will isn't there? You weren't going to get far with that political hack anyway. Why that lying, thieving, graft-mongering… but let it go. Because you were prepared all along to take your case directly to the people. And finally we're on friendly turf: the parliament of the streets where you probably belonged all along. If you are going to make a public case of your project, refine your message until it's clear and resonate and exciting enough to generate media attention. If that happens, the whole thing can curiously come back full circle. One thing almost guaranteed to make both politicians and bureaucrats tremble is the prospect of a public account of their incompetence. Controversy to public officials is like garlic to vampires, and they may go to great lengths, including agreeing to your proposal, just to avoid it.

You don't have to be in close proximity to a grandmother to grow some of these antique flowers. They've stood up through the ages because they have features a lot of people (not just grannies) love:

Bleeding heart, bells-of-Ireland, Christmas rose (hellebore), columbines, corn-cockle, English primrose, gillyflower, hollyhock, lady's-mantle, lungwort, lupine, nicotiana, pulmonaria, rugosa rose.

Drops of water make the ocean.

— Tibetan saying

You're blocking

What are you likely to hear from City Hall if you propose something new such as a gardening project on an empty city lot?

Pat answers, most likely. Have a response ready that will keep the conversation going and the options alive. For example:

- "I'm too busy to deal with that." Ask to schedule a more convenient time. If you can't get one, ask for the name of a supervisor to whom you can address your concerns about this staff member's scheduling difficulties.
- "We don't have the budget." Explain that you'll pay for it yourself. Or look through the budget for openings that might apply to your case.
- "But we've never done it before." Remind them that they also hadn't used electric light bulbs before, at some point, until someone finally decided to give something other than the gas lamp a try.
- "I loved it but, hey, my supervisor wouldn't budge." Ask for a written explanation from the supervisor detailing why. You'll at least know your proposal is being heard. And you may be able to use the objections to find areas where you share common ground.

Oh bother

All of this sounds potentially vexing and may suggest that your first instinct was correct: just do it and don't worry about getting tangled up in the bureaucracy. If it's going to be so bothersome, why bother?

Because the payoff can be worth it. And anyway, it isn't right to give up on the local government simply because it's hard to move. Yes, it can be work — but it's necessary work, and not just for your project. The system is there to serve us. Some of the people running it don't always understand that, but the more they get to meet dedicated and persistent gardeners who believe public spaces should be good for the public, the more the whole churning apparatus is likely to change for the better. Even if it does take a long time.

Vancouver residents, for one example, used to be civically harassed for planting beyond their lawns in the narrow grass strips between the sidewalk and the street. It was city property,

By its form, as by the manner of its birth, the city has elements at once of biological procreation, organic evolution and aesthetic creation. It is both a natural object and a thing to be cultivated; something lived and something dreamed. It is the human invention par excellence.

— CLAUDE LEVI-STRAUSS

Before and after shots of a traffic calming circle tended by volunteers with city approval in Vancouver.

but people did it anyway, and in such numbers that it eventually made sense to not only allow it, but encourage it. Now there's even a section of the Engineering Department that works to help residents plant boulevards, corner bulges and traffic circles. It's called Green Streets, and it's a good model demonstrating how a city can not only tolerate but encourage the public desire to improve the shared environment. I know it works because I'm part of a group that tends the traffic circle on my street. The city was good to us, letting us do our own design and then providing the soil and plants we requested to fill it. They even gave us an official safety vest, but no one uses it. We found that neighbors will go out of their way to thank anyone working in the plot — unless you wear the vest. In that case they think you're a city employee and can't wait to rag on you about potholes and taxes.

City official Alan Duncan

Q&A   Alan Duncan — Key to the City

Alan Duncan also knows about the Green Streets program from personal experience, although from another side. He's been working for the city of Vancouver for 16 years, serving as an environmental planner and designer for various departments of City Hall and the Parks Board.

He's also a landscape architect who occasionally teaches at UBC, which is where I met him. He was one of the tougher profs but also one of the hardest working himself. I liked his practical and straight-forward approach to design problems, and hoped he might be equally as direct when asked for advice on working with city officials.

Q: Are there any common misconceptions about the bureaucracy? Something we've always gotten wrong?
A: No. They're actually made up of people. Some people are more receptive to ideas than other people are.

Q: What about: You can't fight City Hall. True or false?
A: Interesting word to use. I think if you actually want to do something, fighting is not the way to go. Most people who fight end up putting someone in a defensive position. I think the way to work with City Hall is actually work with them. To act as if you're actually partners in the process. And to approach them as partners, not as taking an aggressive stance. A lot of people come forward and say, Look what they do in Seattle. Why aren't you doing that here? It's like, well, we all do different things for different rea-

sons. I wish people came forward and said, I was in Seattle and I saw this and talked to all my neighbors and we'd like to try it out on my block and we've had fundraisers for the last six weeks so we actually have some money to put into it and we've figured how much it would probably cost and we figured we could put in this much sweat equity. Then you've got city going, Oh, they've actually thought it through, they've researched it and they're willing to contribute, they're not just demanding that we do something for them.

Q: A lot of people think that when they run up against the bureaucracy the default answer is No, we've never done it that way. Is there some way to get past that initial no?
A: When I first started with the city we spent an awful lot of time saying no and sending out letters. We noticed you planted a tree in front of your property, you have to remove it or we will remove it for you, stuff like that.

Q: Which is not what you'd want to be doing with your day.
A: Of course not.

I am led to reflect how much more delightful to an undebauched mind is the task of making improvements on the earth, than all the vain glory which can be acquired from ravaging it.

— George Washington

TREES RECOMMENDED FOR IMPROVING AIR QUALITY

City air can get dirty (which you already knew). But did you also know it kills? An estimated 60,000 people die each year in the US from health problems brought on by air pollution. Shocking, yes, but there is one thing we can do about it right away: install more filters. In other words, trees.

The following trees are recommended for their air-cleaning properties:

English elm — *Ulmus procera*
Linden — *Tilia europa*
Western hemlock — *Tsuga heterophylla*
Paper birch — *Betula papyrifera*
European ash — *Fraxinus excelsior*
European larch — *Larix deciduas*
Tulip tree — *Liriodendron tulipifera*
Dawn redwood — *Metasequoioa glyptostroboides*
American beech — *Fagus grandifolia*
American elm — *Ulmus americana*

Q: But you have to because that's the law and if people don't follow the law, my gosh, what would we have?

A: So there was an attitude shift saying, People want to do it, why don't we find a way to accommodate it, what's the big problem? The problem is people plant inappropriate species or they overplant the boulevard so you can't get out of your car. Okay, let's just make some guidelines we can live with. So that's what we did. Now when someone phones up and says, I want to plant my boulevard, we say, Great, go online, we've got guidelines for how to do it. It's all common sense stuff like leave space so someone can get out of their car if they happen to park in front of your garden, have a couple of stepping stones so people can actually cross the boulevard.

Q: Why did that work here and not other places?

A: I don't know, maybe lack of imagination. One thing they figured out here fairly early on is it was way cheaper to have the public plant and maintain a traffic circle than it was for them to pay a crew to go out and plant it. When they first started out they used to provide money for people to go out and buy plants. Then they figured they didn't even need to do that. Let's say it costs $400 to plant a traffic circle with junipers, something really mundane. If someone is going to do it for free, and look after it, what would you figure? If you have to a run a program which maybe takes a third of one person's time, it's a huge savings over time. Plus it makes the streets more beautiful. I think it makes the traffic circles and corner bulges more unique, and it does slow traffic down. People are actually looking at it not as something in the way but as something to look at. It's a matter of a win-win here. I think for Engineering it was doing the simple math and realizing they would save a fortune.

Q: What about getting something that does cost money? Is there a strategy that works when you can't use the budget savings argument?

A: Windsor Castle is an example. It's a lot on Windsor Street. It was acquired originally for road-widening. It became clear we were never going to wider the road, in fact it was to get narrower, so some of the people during this greenway consultation process said they'd like to have a gathering place there. Maybe a kids' play area, whatever. They organized themselves and we met with them. We kind of told them what the situation is: we don't have a lot of money, it's not a park so it won't get park maintenance, so if we even do anything it's kind of your baby. They said they were OK with that, and it went through a design process and came out with a pretty simple design. The ideas came from them, and they were different from what we would normally do. It was called the Windsor Castle. Of course, that sounds very English, right? How politically incorrect is that? And yet all these ethnic people were going, Hey, that's a great idea, it's so obvious. So we said we can provide some basic stuff. OK, put in a gravel walkway and a sandbox. We said, You don't want a sandbox because that's where needles go and cats poo in them and they said, Well we don't have drugs in our neighborhood and there's no reason a cat would go out of their way to use this sandbox instead of a garden anywhere else and anyway we'll look after it. And they have, every year, and it's been 10 or 12 years now.

Q: Does it pay to get to know city staff? It could take a lot of energy.
A: Yeah.

Q: Suck up?
A: Buy them. I'll take real estate.

Keep a garden journal. It can provide you later with valuable inside information you would probably have forgotten otherwise. Or at the least it can give you an entertaining way to review successes and failures long after the fact.

Among the things you might record are: plant purchases, harvest results, pest control experiments, unusual weather events, soil amendment techniques, tree pruning strategies, tips learned from neighbors, seed collecting projects, hopes and dreams for the future, and anything else that goes through your mind at the time you pick up the pen.

I took the easy route in buying an already formatted 10-year gardener's journal, and it's great, but you could make your own over an ambitious weekend. The point is to get something attractive and durable enough that you make it a regular habit, even if only to record the temperature and weather before jotting down one observation or fact or garden note of interest each day. Thomas Jefferson did it, and he was kind of busy too, so you can forget that excuse.

*Degged with dew, dappled
 with dew
Are the groins of the braes
 that the brook treads
 through,
Wiry heathpacks, flitches of
 fern,
And the beadbonny ash that
 sits over the burn.
What would the world be,
 once bereft
Of wet and of wildness? Let
 them be left,
O let them be left, wildness
 and wet;
Long live the weeds and
 wilderness yet.*

— Gerard Manley Hopkins in "Inversnaid"

Q: I was actually thinking of smaller gifts of non-value.
A: No.

Q: I mean like flattery. Platitudes.
A: Tell me how young I look. My god you look good. Oh really, you think so? Sometimes if you just phone in it's easy to brush someone off. But if you show up with drawings or pictures, it can help.

Q: With or without an appointment?
A: Either or. If you were showing someone something they might say, You know, that looks like something the landscape architecture technicians handle. They might go, you know what, that's actually a Green Streets program and they'll be able to help you. And the only reason is because you went in and showed them something. If you phone you get a receptionist who gives out numbers but may not actually know what people are doing.

Q: Speaking of the phone, something I've always wanted to know. When we call and you're not there, is our call really important to you?
A: Oh, some people still say that. I think it's so hokey.

Q: E-mail?
A: E-mail's good. It's easy to respond to. And now you can attach anything. Copy it to other people.

Q: What about dealing with the psychopath? There's one on every staff list. The person who, for whatever reason, is very difficult and makes it impossible to get things done.
A: There are psychopaths on both sides of the fence. We have to deal with psychopaths too, and there are some real wackos out there. Sometimes you just have to say, I'm going to hang up now because I don't want to go through the whole story again because nothing has changed and I'm sorry but get a life. A psychopath on the inside is certainly a challenge. I've been on projects where engineers especially change a lot — they want them to have a lot of breadth, while we in planning have a different approach, or maybe there's more commonality. But sometimes you'll be on a project that's going really well and the engineers are really with it because they're young and hip and then you get a deadbeat or malcontent who comes on board and that's it. And all you can say is, I'll let that one sit on the shelf for a while and I'll focus my efforts somewhere else. Sometimes it works going around them,

Die when I may, I want it said of me by those who know me best, that I always plucked a thistle and planted a flower where I thought a flower would grow.

— Abraham Lincoln

but sometimes it doesn't. Sometimes if you're not getting anywhere with someone on staff because they're so obstructionist it's better to just go ahead and do it and then invite the City Council to the opening. Make it look like it was their idea and they were so helpful and staff kind of go, OK, I can't exactly speak out and say I think it's stupid now that Council thinks it's great and the community loves it. There's no one size fits all either. Sometimes you just have to do it in a guerrilla way. Just be smart. Whatever you're doing make sure it's neat and tidy, make sure there's not a liability, make sure there's no danger.

Q: Any last tips? Or advice on what not to do?
A: Be respectful. When you do something think about what impact it'll have on other people. Try to think about the long term. One of the issues when people do stuff is what happens when they lose interest or move away. That was a big one for the Engineering Department with Windsor Castle. A lot of projects depend on one or a few people, and the worry is what'll happen when they're gone. Interestingly, the go-getter on that one has left. The city's part was, we have to have faith and hope for the best. And you know what? It has worked out. I think again it's your approach. And to have a really good project with strong support from neighbors who say, We want to do this.

IF I CAN DO IT...   Tom Wuest — Downtown Farmer

"We thought if we started doing something the owner would show up. Before then this lot was trash and weeds."

Downtown farmer Tom Wuest

Vancouver's Downtown Eastside is home to Canada's largest concentration of poor, jobless, addicted, mentally ill and socially challenged people. It also attracts a lot of folks who aim to help, including the ones who run Jacob's Well, a Christian group. Two years ago they went beyond the level of most do-gooders by getting more involved in the neighborhood, right down to the soil level. They took over an empty lot to grow food.

They now sell the harvest to project supporters on a commissioned basis. This practice, called Community Supported Agriculture (CSA), is gaining popularity all over North America. It's a response to the crisis of the family farm and the growing interest in securing local, organic produce, but this is the first time I'd heard of it being tried from an inner city lot through guerrilla gardening. Tom Wuest took a few minutes from dividing the

This community-supported farm was a rubbish-filled lot just one year ago.

weekly harvest — a generous supply of beans, blackberries, kale and more — to explain how it happened.

We saw this empty lot and did a land title search but couldn't find the owner. We got the name of a company but couldn't locate it. So we decided to come in and clean up the lot ourselves, really in an effort to find the owner. We thought if we started doing something the owner would show up. Before then this lot was trash and weeds. It was completely overgrown. Fenced in, locked up, signs saying No Trespassing. We picked up a lot of needles, an old carpet, beer bottles. In this neighborhood you can imagine the stuff we pulled out.

We started by shaping the growing beds. The soil was pretty poor. There had been a house 14 or 15 years earlier, but it had burnt down. We decided to truck in compost. We got in touch with the landfill for the city of Vancouver. We were a non-profit organization so they gave it to us for free. They didn't ask anything about ownership, and at that point we still didn't know whose land it was. That first truckload, 14 cubic yards, took care of only a small portion of the front. We moved our way back like that, through 10 or 15 truckloads.

We got in contact with a turkey farmer nearby and brought some turkey manure in the fall. Also Home Depot every week donated about a vanload of perennials that people weren't going to buy. On the alley side of the garden we planted roses and lavender as a way of beautifying the area. People walking back and forth can enjoy it now. We wanted this to be a beautiful space.

It's really amazing how well it has worked out. We've gotten a lot of feedback from people on the street. One woman said, You have no idea what this garden means to us. But it's just to look. It's not open to the public. That's to prevent theft and also out of respect to the owners who don't want to keep it open. We do unlock it when we're working in here, and the other garden we started across the street is open all the time.

What did the owners say when they found out? At first they said they felt violated and excited at the same time, so it was an interesting mix of emotions. Since then they're quite excited. Their main concern was liability. They had it insured as a vacant lot so knowing we were here was a problem for them. But they liked what we were doing. One person in the family has a background in landscape architecture and the other son is in Toronto doing some work with homeless advocacy so it was a great family that ended up owning this lot. Now that we insure the liability, they're happy. A lease has been drawn up, and we're just waiting to sign it. Basically it says we're here until they decide to develop it, and we're fine with that.

From the beginning we wanted to use the produce, which we are, in the community kitchen every Tuesday when we have a meal with our friends down here. We're also distributing it to ten or twelve families in the neighborhood. But we realized when we started growing that we had far too much for that alone. We really want this to be eaten. It's organic and local so we had the idea to sell five shares in the program for $200 each.

We did it through word of mouth, just by talking to people, most of whom were connected with Jacob's Well. For eight to ten to twelve weeks — however many weeks we have produce growing — every Wednesday they can come here and pick up their food. We harvest and separate each share.

Does it work out to be a good deal for them? I don't know. Probably not. But we still have to see what happens. We told everyone in the introduction letter, This is an experiment. What you'll get is local organic produce and you're helping us start an experiment on what can be produced in a vacant lot. Everybody's real excited to see what can happen in an abandoned area. We hope it works, enough to do more, maybe expand it to at least one other lot. I'm sure other communities could do it too.

POWER PLANT   Scarlet runner bean (*Phaseolus coccineus*)

This may not be the plant of "Jack and the Beanstalk" fame, but it is a close cousin with the same genetic vigor. In the Pacific Northwest where the summers never get so hot that the flowers will drop early, we can plant a few of these attractive purple and black beans into the warm soil and then step back to enjoy the show. The speed and enthusiasm with which a runner bean develops is impressive. It's a robust vine with winding stems and heart-shaped emerald green leaves that will power its way up anything close by. Put it next to a building and it quickly shows its disdain for the ground floor in a race for the roof. Put it next to a 10-foot-tall pole and it will scale the pole and then some, waving about in the clouds until gravity finally sends the reluctant tip back down.

Then come the flowers, a generous spray of pea-shaped blooms in a splash of color pretty enough to please anyone. Hummingbirds and bees love them. And as if all this were not enough, there's still a crop to come.

Scarlet runner bean — Phaseolus coccineus
Credit: From Gottlieb Tobias Wilhelm's "Unterhaltungen aus der Naturgeschichte" (Encyclopedia of Natural History), published in Vienna from 1810, illustration by either Paul Martin Wilhelm or J. Schaly.

Pick the pods when they're young and tender and you can eat them raw or cooked like any other green bean. If you don't get them in time, the pods turn thick and fuzzy, but that's OK too. Just wait a few more weeks to harvest the dry beans inside to cook in soups or stews the way you would garbanzos or lima beans.

Scarlet runner beans are an excellent way to transform an ugly chain link fence or wall into a floral display you can also eat. They also make a good cover for a child-friendly teepee. Start with a base of three bamboo poles stuck into the ground and meeting at a point in the center. Plant three or four seeds about one inch deep around each pole. Later that summer you'll have your own green-themed hideaway.

Did you know: The flowers and the tuberous roots are also edible, and still enjoyed by indigenous people in Central America.

CHAPTER NINE

Start Spreading the News

(Information Is Just Fertilizer With Better PR)

Last chapter we swerved off the path of the classic plant-and-run guerrilla gardening operation to suggest that some projects might be done openly with prior approval. In those cases, but not only those cases, you may also wish to promote your efforts to a wider audience. We're now moving into public relations.

Why talk about media in a book on guerrilla gardening? Because this campaign is all about planting the seeds of hope, and the biggest public space is between the ears.

Then again. You may resent the notion of having to explain the deeper meaning of your crusade. Because it may not even have one. You saw an empty lot and you decided to make it bloom. Enough said.

A case may also be made for *not* putting any time or energy into propaganda, by which I mean, raising public awareness. Because we're flooded with information already. Useless information, mostly, and yegads, what an ocean of it. From wake-up until bed-time we're wading in facts, lies, advertising, news, entertainment and all the hybrids in between. The barrage is relentless. A typical eight-year-old child growing up in North America today can recognize more corporate logos than the sound of his own father telling him to turn the bloody TV off. So if you elect to conduct your entire guerrilla gardening campaign without adding to the cacophony, because you feel plants can do all the talking necessary, more power to you. You have done your part. You are a true and valued guerrilla gardener, and let no one say otherwise.

On the other hand, as we saw in the last chapter, the battle to build a more enlightened ecological city will be fought on many

Gardening is civil and social, but it wants the vigor and freedom of the forest and the outlaw.

— Henry David Thoreau

One thing is sure. The earth is cultivated more than ever before…swamps are drying up and cities are springing up at an unprecedented scale. We have become a burden to our planet. Resources are becoming scarce and soon nature will no longer be able to satisfy our needs.

— Quintus Septimus Tertullian, written more than 2,200 years ago

levels, and that includes the airwaves. If in addition to reshaping the land you feel your successes might also be used to help build the movement so that others understand the importance and appreciate the beauty of it, perhaps even enough to join in and begin transforming their own cities…read on.

Mass media and how to move it

I don't know how it happened, although I suppose I should, since journalism imploded in my own time. When I started in the business, journalists were almost heroes. They had just stood up to a government that had lied about the Vietnam War and Watergate and more. Reporters were society's collective crap-detractors, rumpled middle-class warriors taking on corporate crooks, political tinpots and ruling juntas. The prospects of unearthing rot, greed and corruption in high places had never seemed better. Kids I knew wanted to be reporters because reporters upheld a stirring tradition of truth-telling for the common good.

And then…what the hell happened? What do we have now? Phht. Things are even worse than the doom-mongers had predicted. The greedy won. Welcome to their world. Common sense

The creation of an event merely to attract news is known as a publicity stunt, and there have been some doozies over the years. Most of these examples are not from politics but entertainment. And is there any difference anymore? These may not translate directly into garden work, but they could give you some ideas.

A Charlie Chaplin Look-Alike Contest that drew hundreds of Little Tramps (and plenty of reporters) for one of his film openings. More news was generated when Charlie Chaplin lost one of his own look-alike contests.

An audition for "beautiful" cats to be used in (and promote) an upcoming cat calendar.

A letter to the editor denouncing the P.T. Barnum display of the 161-year-old "nurse of George Washington" as a fraud because it was not an old woman at all but "simply a curiously constructed automaton, made up of whalebone, India rubber and numberless strings." Of course the letter was written by Barnum himself, using one of his favorite tactics.

is now an endangered species. Elections have become gong shows. Oh, we still have courageous journalists writing and broadcasting important stuff. If you can find it. Because the truth crusaders don't own the newspapers or radio stations or TV networks. Big corporations do. And when a big corporation has billions of dollars invested in a status quo that's working well for its investors, no wonder we can follow the news all week and end up knowing more about Tom Cruise's baby than who's winning what in Iraq or why the polar ice caps are melting.

Cynical? Me? Nah. I only mention it here because, like it or not, big media is still the main way we share information, and if you want to get your word out, it helps to know a bit about how it works. I say "a bit" because I'm not sure anyone knows for sure anymore how it all fits, not with information distribution in such a state of upheaval.

The main daily newspaper used to be the first medium of choice for any local group with a message, but that was back when the papers were still locally-owned, or at least locally-run. As they increasingly took on the personality of franchise strip malls managed from a distant head office, they grew less relevant to people's

John D. Rockefeller went from being one of the most hated men in America to one of the most beloved after a strategic campaign which saw him handing out shiny new dimes to poor children whenever photographers were present.

Yippies promoted a campaign to get people thinking about capitalism by throwing dollar bills from the gallery of the New York Stock Exchange. The fracas managed to stop trading for several minutes.

Comedian Buck Henry got on "The Today Show," "The Tonight Show" and several others by pretending to be the vice president of a citizens' group protesting the indecency of naked pets.

John Lennon and Yoko Ono staged a bed-in on their honeymoon, getting a solid week's worth of press to talk about world peace.[1]

lives. But it's still worth trying to get your message in there first. People continue to use the morning newspaper to get the pulse of the place, if not directly then through the relay of morning radio and TV news stations where producers and editors begin their shifts by checking the local dailies. The newspaper is still the arbiter of local events, and a thing hasn't really happened for many until it gets written up. So just getting your project into the paper means people will read about it, discuss it, maybe like it enough to join in. Even members of your own group who slag the paper as a capitalist rag will hustle to the corner store for a copy if it includes a mention of them. Everyone feels curiously legitimized at seeing their own efforts confirmed in print.

Do not, however, mistake the city's biggest paper for the media in total. It's not even the only print medium on which you should focus your attention. You may well get a more intelligent treatment from your alternative weekly or free community paper. In a lot of

Don't be reluctant to put your message in writing: big, bold, colorful writing. The advertising industry captures our eyeballs for most of our daily lives. No point being shy when it comes to contributing your own ideas. Remember, you're competing against pros here and they have fat expense accounts.

On some streets in my neighborhood the residents have erected colorful signs depicting animals in kid-friendly shapes telling motorists to slow down. The drivers may know a plywood raccoon isn't legally binding, but they understand they're entering a neighborhood where kids could run into the street at any time. Or it may have parents willing to stare down or confront reckless drivers. Homemade signs may also deter drug dealers and sex trade workers who would rather not enter a neighborhood where people obviously care about the street activity. It doesn't have to be a sign. On one block nearby they've gone with a huge banner, stretching from one side of the street to the other. It's probably not worth asking the city for permission to do something like this. Just put up the sign or string up the banner and let the officials decide if it's worth trying to get the neighbors to take it down. If you're on the side of safe kids and cleaner streets, they're unlikely to bother.

cities these are now on the upswing, and getting better as more readers catch on. Once belittled for being free (and worth it), in cities where the sole remaining daily has lost touch the community papers offer some readers their only media connection that feels like home.

Everything I've said up to now has been about print, but of course TV is the Emerald City. This is the glittery faux palace everyone turns to, so it's worth cultivating any contacts you can find to get on the air, especially if you have really nice hair.

Radio can be the most effective route of all. Not as flashy or frenetic as TV, yet still spunky, it can move at a pace that lets people absorb complex thoughts. Good radio is a great medium for ideas.

And then there's the Internet, where you now find the whole world of fact-slinging in hyper-speed. It's already so big and volatile I don't even know where to tell you to start, except to say that if you blog me I'll blog you.

No matter which medium you choose (and you won't choose just one, because one feeds off another anyway), there are a few things worth keeping in mind when dealing with journalists, editors, producers, webheads or whomever you hope to convince to cover your case.

What's the news?

Here's a clue to help you answer that question. Read the first three letters of the final word. New information is what sells newspapers and news programs…or is supposed to. Naturally there are limits. It can't be too new. Journalism relies on formulas. Precedent means a lot. Partly because journalists are busy, partly because they're lazy, but mostly because they fear being publicly wrong, they read and watch each other voraciously and then steal/borrow/pay homage. This is not the same as copying. It may sound like a dereliction, but I'm not sure it's as bad as that. The formula works in most cases for most of the reading public. Not many wake up every morning with an appetite to have their beliefs challenged before breakfast. You have to pick your places. So to get your case covered, try to get a sense of how the formula works for the medium you're considering, and then make sure your story fits in.

A vision without a task is a dream; a task without a vision is drudgery; but a task with vision can change the world.

— Black Elk

DESIGN TIP

You can go a long way relying on English poet Alexander Pope's famous garden advice to "Consult the genius of the place in all." But what does it mean? One reading: work *with* nature, not against it. Instead of planting the same lawn you saw in some New York magazine at your Palm Springs site, discover what makes the Sonoran desert so striking and capture the essence of it. Mother Nature will reward you just for trying, as surely as she will thump you for being ignorant or rude about local conditions.

Help your media contact do his or her job by having something truly newsworthy to offer. Do it smartly and you'll score points as a reliable source that may come in handy later. Remember that your journalist contact doesn't control what goes into the newspaper or network. They may believe they should, because they would do a better job of it, but alas. So even if they like you and think your story is interesting, they'll still have to get it approved by an editor or some other supervisor. Help them sell it by offering the best package possible.

You wouldn't call a publication or network to say you're forming a really important group to do some really cool stuff and could sure use some coverage. But you might let a reporter know in advance about a midnight planting of a well-known site in town that will look great in before-and-after pictures. For a visual event like that, decide whether the coverage is open to just one media outlet or all-comers, and then stick to it. If you know you've got something really appealing, you might want to make it into a news conference. But a small-scale operation might better fit a single source at a time. If so, you may be able to use the lure of an exclusive as bait. Journalists are suckers for anything that smells like a scoop, a legacy from the days where there was real competition among news-hungry dailies for the freshest stuff.

ACTUAL HEADLINES ABOUT GUERRILLA GARDENING

Green-thumbed guerrillas hatching secret plots! — *Christian Science Monitor*

The Revolution Will Be Fertilized — *Globe and Mail*

Garden rebels say sod it to neglect — *National Post*

Guerrillas in the Garden — *Washington Post*

Resistance Is Fertile — *Globe and Mail*

Guerrilla War: Urban diehards reclaim flowerbed in dead of night — *Stratford Guardian*

Plotting Revolution — *Now* magazine

Vandalizing with nature — *Eye Weekly*

Guerrillas in Your Midst — *The Big Issue*

Guerrillas in the Mist — *Organic Gardening*

Labour of Love — *Rise* magazine

Timing is important, so keep your eyes open for events that can be used to your advantage. The most fertile case is a media frenzy, when journalists are swarming and anything can and will become news to feed the voracious beast. These are rare, but a fantastic find because you can use them to attract attention the way a bucket of chum attracts sharks. When funny newspaper columnist Dave Barry and some pals decided to test how long it would take to get coverage at the 1988 Democratic convention, they put cardboard boxes over their heads and marched in a circle outside the convention hall. The answer was seven seconds.

Related events that can make the difference between your story being covered or killed are called pegs. Is there an event coming up, say the 10th anniversary of the death of someone notable who donated a nature preserve? The seasonal opening of the local pool in an area where obesity rates are off the chart? An important City Council decision on whether to create a park? Look for ways to tie your story into other news items. If the bird society just announced the imminent demise of 28 more species, you might mention the habitat you're creating at a new site and how it fits into the campaign to stop the death count before it can rise any higher. Or maybe you know that the government is about to release a report on childhood nutrition — which could be a good time for a story on your group's attempt to bring edible landscaping to schoolyards.

On a slow day, of course, almost anything can turn into news (just flip through the paper). The chances rise if your story can be considered alarming, funny, quirky, revealing, scandalous or includes a celebrity connection, even if the connection is no more than a comment from Brad Pitt's former pool cleaner.

Right on time

If a journalist does agree to meet you, make sure you follow through on anything you promise, starting with showing up on time. Especially showing up on time. The only sacred thing in journalism is the deadline. Everyone in the business knows this, and accordingly, finishes their job on time, which is why you don't open up your paper to find a big white space on page eight or get three minutes of blank screen time during the evening news. And don't try to coax a reporter out of the office with the lure of more

Our cities — old and new — do not only need to be fixed, they also need to be reimagined…places where we live can be places of hope.

— Martin J. Rosen

Signs of the changing times.

or better information than you really have to deliver. Try to pull a bait and switch like that and you'd better hope they decide not to cover you, because if they do it will only be scathing.

Every interview is different, but you can improve the chances yours will succeed by being prepared. Know your message beforehand, and try to steer the conversation in that direction. You should be able to anticipate at least some of the questions so they don't come as a complete surprise. But don't respond with rote lines or form answers — you'll only bore everyone including yourself. It's better to explain things in a cordial voice, as you would to a friend. Unless it's for radio or TV, in which case advance preparation is even more important. You still want to relax and speak comfortably, but you won't have the same time to develop themes and provide background explanations and make allusions that you might with a print reporter. Particularly for TV, you need to come up with sound bites. Consider how to crystallize your main message into a few short, snappy phrases or questions or ideas: Why shouldn't the public be able to improve public spaces?… Who are they for anyway?… This is just graffiti using plants… I don't know anyone who couldn't use a few more flowers in their life, do you?

When the interview is over, be sure the reporter has your phone number or e-mail address or some way to get in touch with you in a hurry. They may need to follow up or clarify something just before deadline. If they asked a question for which you didn't have the answer, offer to help find it. But only if you mean it. You won't win any points by pretending to be helpful if you actually aren't.

I'm busted

This isn't for everyone, but those determined to turn their case into a cause might consider the benefits of getting arrested for it.

Controversy makes news. One of the best ways to generate controversy is to create a dispute. Boxing matches are interesting because we're fascinated by the narrative of a fight, the drama involved in a soon-to-be-revealed winner and loser. You could do the same with your guerrilla gardening campaign by setting yourself off against the all-mighty authorities who would, for shame, deny the community a chance to smell roses. A courtroom can make a fine pulpit, for a while.

Of course this won't always be easy. The police are unlikely to care enough to do anything on their own, so you may have to flaunt your lawlessness with something such as a prominent planting demonstration. Alert the media first. Make sure your group is at its most representative when the cameras come out. If you've got a diverse bunch, don't let the grandmothers and children hide in the back. Who can resist that delightful shot of a scandalized senior being dragged away by burly cops while angelic toddlers wave protest signs? It always helps to think visually. An environmentalist in Victoria finally won his quest to get the city to stop dumping raw sewage into the ocean by dressing up as a giant turd.

From the time of your publicized arrest until the justice system eventually produces a decision (which may well be dropped

Thank you for your input but… wouldn't a tree have said it better?

DESIGN TIP

You can learn a lot from a walk around your own neighborhood where other gardeners will be growing things which do well in the local climate. But you needn't limit yourself to the present or the local. You can also get ideas from pictures of historical gardens or those in far-off places where they may do things quite differently. Whether you copy outright, and try to reproduce a perfect Balinese pond on the North Dakotan tundra, or you simply get inspiration from other places, keeping an open mind and an appreciative attitude will help you create more interesting gardens. The following terms from Japanese gardening, which tends to encourage a philosophical or spiritual relationship to the space, could help spark some ideas for your own guerrilla gardening project:

Muho — Buddhist term for without rules, free from restrictions of form

Karesansui — without water, a dry garden using rocks to evoke water

Oshakei — triangular group of rocks in vertical, horizontal and diagonal shapes

Yugen — hidden depth, a mysterious beauty beyond the visible

Mono-no-aware — sensitivity to the evanescence of life

Mitate-mono — old objects reused in a refined way

Fuzei — literally "breeze feeling" for something tasteful, elegant

Hai-seki — a large, flat stone from which one may view the garden

Aware — a quietly emotional response to the ephemeral nature of life

Sabi — elegant simplicity

Shakkei — borrowed scenery, as when incorporating a distant view of mountains in a local garden

charges, since no authority would enjoy prosecuting someone for gardening), you'll have a stage to tell the local world what you think about public space, encroaching corporatization, loss of natural habitat, global warming, you name it.

There is a risk, of course. You could run into a streak of bad luck that includes a harsh response and ends up with actual jail time. But we hear prisons are ripe for consciousness raising.

Alternative media options

Media means everything, not just the big prominent firms, so don't rely on stuck-in-the-box thinking limited to the usual outlets. Consider the many ways you yourself get information and then brainstorm on how to get your own message into that mix. Is it by visiting interesting Internet sites? A school bulletin board? A community radio show? Word of mouth at the local gym?

Public speaking is another way to distribute ideas. The old-fashioned appeal of a living, breathing person standing up to make a case for something is still unmatched by digital technology. People will always appreciate the chance to hear an unfiltered message straight from the source.

Creativity is its own reward here. Where might you find interested audiences? You could sign up to teach a community center course. Offer to facilitate a coffee-house salon talk on the rights of people to reclaim open areas. Host a seed-bomb making workshop at your local community garden or nursery. Find out whether any senior centers nearby would be interested in an afternoon lecture on planting techniques for empty park spaces. Ask about high school classroom visits or even assemblies — they sometimes book provocative speakers to get the students' minds off each other for an

Are you trying to make a political point with your project? Define your message, then refine your message. Boil it down to a size anyone can handle in the midst of a busy day. Most people won't have the time or inclination to dally, ponder what it might really mean or consider qualifying statements. When I started pushing the idea for this book I told people, "It's on guerrilla gardening but it's really about saving the world. And I'm not joking." Actually I was joking. But not entirely.

hour. Keep up on political events and rallies, especially during election time, to see if anyone's interested in a populist take on public space and the potential to improve it.

If you are taking your case to the public, try to have your message broken down into digestible pieces. You should be able to explain your campaign in an elevator ride, and be able to expand on it during a wait for a bus. The more easily you can convey what you know, the better your results will be. It helps if you determine beforehand what you want from people. Are you looking for votes? Volunteers? Donations? Petition signatures? Hearts and minds? If you have a clear goal you're working toward and can let people know it, your talk will make much more sense throughout.

Signs that work, signs that don't

A word can be worth a thousand pictures and help people make the connection between an act and the motivating idea. Most guerrilla gardeners never bother to explain their work with a sign, but maybe some should, if only as a way to further the cause. It can elevate your site from a pleasant diversion appreciated at a glance to a thought-provoking challenge of a passerby's basic beliefs.

If you are putting up a sign, take some time to think before you pick up the marker or sit down at the keyboard. Not only to properly block it out, so you don't end up with those pathetically crowded letters at the far edge, but also because you must use a little to say a lot. Memorable messages tend to be direct, sharp and lively. Think of "Don't Believe the Hype" and "Bring the Noise," written by those word wizards who missed their calling as ad copy writers in becoming the rap group Public Enemy.

Consider your message, its audience, and then the shortest distance between the two. What do you most want people to know? That this site has been planted by guerrilla gardeners? That would be easy enough. Especially if your group already has a name: "Planted By the Downtown Lawn Liberation Front." Or if you don't have a name: "Another Guerrilla Garden for Public Appreciation." Or "This Garden Was Created By Someone Like You."

The sign doesn't have to claim responsibility or explain motives, at least not directly. It might instead say, "Please Water

Welcome to the beach at Santa Monica, now assume the position.

It looks like art but, we really do want your change.

Road work from street artist Peter Gibson.

PETER GIBSON

The challenge of discovery lies not in seeking new landscapes but having new eyes.

— MARCEL PROUST

Me," with a brief mention of how the garden got there. Or perhaps, "These Are Your Flowers, Please Do Not Pick Them." Or come up with a slogan you can use for your pamphlets as well: "Greening the Big City One Plant at a Time."

Hand-made signs are fine for this kind of message, and may even help give your project a no-budget, folksy look. But it might also look good printed up and laminated, suggesting a more organized and successful group. If you have a group logo it would look good here. Also an e-mail address (use an anonymous free site if you don't want to be traced) to offer people the chance to learn more. The first question you get may be, How can I join you guys?

Q&A   Peter Gibson — Road Warrior

The first time we met, on the Internet, he was identified as Ronda. But I knew he was more famous as Roadsworth, the legal cause célèbre in Quebec. I also knew that neither was his real name.

Peter Gibson, a Montreal-based artist originally from Toronto, adopted Roadsworth to reflect his medium — stenciled art on public streets — and to reference British landscape artist Andy Goldsworthy. Ronda, it turned out, was an attempt to hide.

Q: Hello. Glad you could make it [to the free net chat site where we'd arranged the interview]. It's Peter then? Not Ronda?
A: Yeah, it's Peter. Ronda was just for security purposes back when I was feeling paranoid about electronic surveillance.

Q: Were you right to feel paranoid?
A: I don't know but when I was arrested a few people were telling me that my phone was probably being tapped, etc. I don't know how realistic that scenario is, but my apartment had just been searched and I had my computer and other personal effects confiscated so I guess anything is possible.

Q: Yikes. You're scaring me already. Can you walk us through a brief history? Maybe starting with who/what you are?
A: That's kind of an existential question but I guess I'm a street artist as far as this discussion is concerned. When I began doing street art in 2001 I didn't think that what I was doing was necessarily art. I starting by painting bike symbols on the street in an effort to replicate the bike path symbols the city was using to designate bike paths. I guess I thought of myself more as an activist

of some kind rather than an artist even though I did have some embryonic aspirations in a more artistic sense.

Q: So it was a political motivation? You wanted to change people's minds to some social end?
A: I've been a cyclist for most of my life and I guess I've always been struck by the absurdity of the one-person-per-car phenomenon that seems to take place in most North American cities, given the problems associated with cars and the fuel needed to run them. I began doing these mock bike paths right after 9/11 which had a certain psychological impact for me in the sense of urgently wanting to express certain feelings. At the time I remember feeling angry about a hypocrisy inherent to our lifestyle in general. For me, car culture epitomizes that lifestyle.

Q: How did the arrest happen?
A: I was basically caught red-handed, or as they say in Quebecois policing lingo, *en flagrant délit.* I had gone out one night in late November 2004 in what was supposed to be my last run of the season. I was doing Xmas ribbons at pedestrian crossings. I had just completed one when I noticed some headlights approaching. I stopped what I was doing and assumed my "innocent bystander"

You cannot carry out fundamental change without a certain amount of madness. In this case, it comes from non-conformity, the ability to turn your back on old formulas, the courage to invent the future. It took the madmen of yesteryear for us to be able to act with extreme clarity today. I want to be one of those madmen. We must dare to invent the future.

— Thomas Sankara

PETER GIBSON

posture which in the night in question was a little more suspect considering the amount of paint covering my sweater (I was usually more conscientious about such things, but I guess I had gotten a little more cavalier and therefore sloppy by that point). Sure enough the headlights in question belonged to a police cruiser which promptly beeped their lights and pulled up alongside me. It was four in the morning and according to the officer on duty, there had been a lot of robberies in the area lately. The officers questioned me for a few minutes but didn't seem to notice the stencil I had just laid down, not to mention a bag full of spray cans nearby. I gave them some lame excuse about being an insomniac artist working late at night and having just stepped out of my studio to get a breath of fresh air. To make a long story short, they let me go at first. I got on my bike, spray cans clanging in my bag, and biked for a few blocks. Just when I thought I was in the clear I saw a police cruiser pull up in front of me and one coming toward me from behind. I knew at that point that the game was up. I was brought to the police station where I spent about 24 hours in a cell during which they searched my apartment. I was released the next morning and the rest is history.

Q: It did become part of the history of Montreal, didn't it? You became famous.
A: People keep telling me that I'm famous, but I'm not sure what that means. I guess I did achieve a certain level of fame by Mon-

PETER GIBSON

treal standards but it's a relatively small town so…it seems like everybody I know in Montreal is famous to a certain extent. I think maybe we've reached that point in history that Andy Warhol was referring to when he supposedly said "In the future, everyone will be famous for 15 minutes."

Q: Did you get off? I'm not clear just what you were charged with.
A: I was charged with, I think it was called mischief.

Q: Mischief?
A: Yeah, mischief. Initially it was about 82 counts but it was brought down to 52 counts.

Q: That sounds like something Dennis the Menace would do.
A: Yeah, I was pretty proud. I was considered a menace to society. That was pretty much the tone of discussion if you followed it in the media or online. Most people felt that the prosecution was overly zealous. It kind of worked in my favor that they were so heavy-handed. More people got involved in the discussion. Luckily it swung in my favor. I ended up getting it brought down to 51 or 52 charges. Finally after various preliminary hearings I had my trial date on January 17, and I was completely absolved of the charges. I ended up paying a small fine and having to serve 40 hours of community service.

Q: So you were guilty then?
A: Well…I guess, technically, yeah, I pleaded guilty, in a way. I don't really understand that part of it.

Q: But how can you not understand it? Weren't you the guy doing it?
A: I know, I know, it's hard to believe. The thing is, it was an out-of-court settlement. As far as the precedent, yeah, I pleaded guilty. I had the option of fighting it. But my lawyer kind of advised me against it. There would be several more years of legal implications. From a legal standpoint I guess at the time I wondered, should I fight this and try to set a precedent? I didn't know. So yeah, I ended up pleading guilty, I guess.

Q: Well, maybe it's not such a stretch because you were, technically, guilty. You did do what they said you did, right? You were mischievous.
A: That's the thing. Technically, yes. Had I been absolved or had I been found innocent it would have set a precedent for all kinds of things, possibly other forms of unsanctioned expression, so the

whole question of precedent was up. Just prior to the hearing I had to decide whether to accept the offer with no criminal record, pay a minimal fine and do 40 hours of work, or fight this thing by taking it all the way, possibly, to the Supreme Court. I remember thinking at the time, Do I want to be a hero? And my lawyer was kind of strongly advising against it. I had to make a decision on the spot. I don't know what might have happened. I probably wasn't as well informed of the whole process as I could have been. So that offer seemed the right thing to do at the time.

Q: It could be that there's a great fight on these grounds, but this wasn't the case. What did you have to stand on?
A: Yeah, not much. Technically, again, I guess we would have argued for the freedom of expression. That was the foothold that we had, but our defense was that what I'd done constituted an

WHOSE PUBLIC SPACE?

Jerold Kayden teaches urban planning at the Harvard Graduate School of Design where his research topics include the use of public space. He studied the effects of a decision in 1961 by the New York City government to let corporations exceed normal zoning regulations in return for providing public amenities such as plazas and parks. It seemed a good idea, on paper.

But Kayden looked closer at 503 partnered public spaces to see how it really played out. He found 41 percent of them serving no public purpose. From locked gates to non-existent bathrooms to plazas selling retail goods, he unearthed a land grab worthy of a book: *Privately Owned Public Space: The New York City Experiment.*

Once when he was documenting a public atrium filled with retail displays, a store official told him he wasn't allowed to take pictures in the area. "And you're not allowed to have a department store here," Kayden replied.

The lesson, it appears, is all in the details. While a public-private agreement might sound like a win-win situation on paper, without public scrutiny in the follow-up, how are we going to know?

"If we allow our public spaces to be privatized," says Kayden, "we suffer a self-inflicted wound."

infraction of a municipal bylaw which meant a minimal infraction rather than a criminal offense. So in a way actually we did have a relatively solid defense. I was arguing that the charges were much heavier than what was warranted. There are municipal bylaws against things like postering. You get caught postering and you get a $100 fine or something; it's like a parking ticket. That would have made more sense. But I don't know, I'm still a bit confused about what happened. I don't know if this is how lawyers operate, but my lawyer throughout the trial was full of confidence, telling me how sure he was of our case, and then right before trial we were presented with this offer and he said, Well, we have a chance but I wouldn't advise we try it. I also had a legal aid mandate so he was acting as my lawyer pro bono. But he was suggesting that if we continued and I needed his legal services it would not be pro bono, and I didn't have any money to pay him so there were a lot of considerations like that.

Q: Apart from the legal aspects, what about the philosophical or ethical questions? Some people wonder about acts like this and who gets to decide what's acceptable. Did that come into it in your case?

A: Oh for sure. That was a big part of the discussion. I was surprised actually at how lopsided the general discussion was in my favor. Montreal is a pretty liberal, pro free expression town but I was still surprised that people didn't bring up that side of the argument. Well, a few people did — but even in conservative newspapers and editorials that argument didn't come up. You do hear that argument sometimes, though: Oh if we let this guy go we open the door to hate crimes. My response to that is, my personal ethical moral justification for doing what I want or doing this rebellion is that there already is a body deciding what's there. I mean who decides what advertising goes on? I didn't decide. I didn't vote for the advertising all around. I didn't vote for how we use our public space. I think the way our public space is used is not democratic. It's not healthy. It's not in our best interests. A lot of these decisions have been made by certain various special interest groups which are not democratic. In light of that reality I feel completely justified saying what I want. And in light of that I think anybody should feel justified and we should be open to it. And that includes graffiti writers. I would argue that even the most unskillful and the most hastily executed examples of graffiti are more interesting and more beautiful than a lot of the crap that

Every bird that sings, and every bud that blooms, does but remind me more of that garden unseen, awaiting the hand that tills it.

— EMILY DICKENSON

we're subject to as a result of our lifestyle. Yeah, the law is important, but at the same time I think we've got to a point where we have to see the law as malleable. It needs to be flexible. Laws only change when people go out on a limb and challenge them. I don't know my laws well, but it seems like if they aren't challenged the laws just reflect the status quo and as far as I'm concerned the status quo is an extremely dangerous precedent.

Q: Are you still stenciling?
A: Yes, but now I'm commissioned.

Q: You're legit now?
A: I'm legit. I'm actually getting contracts.

Q: Good for you.
A: I just did a large project with the city.

Q: On the street?
A: Outdoors, but not on the street.

Q: It doesn't mean they've bought you off, I hope.
A: Did they buy me off? I don't know. I wouldn't look at it that way. They're paying me to do a job. Like everybody else, if you're an artist or whatever, you need to eat. I guess my instincts for self-preservation are present enough that I'm not going to go out and work on the street since I'm still on probation.

Q: Ouch.
A: So until next July if I break the law or do anything in that way then it's another legal battle I'm not prepared to do right now. If I do do anything it's not going to be for another year. But I've been doing things in other cities. I went to Barcelona and France last year. But in terms of illegal activities, no, not in Montreal anyway.

Q: Finally, you've gone further than most in dealing with the possible official response to these things. Any advice for others?
A: You don't want to get caught. Your anonymity is your best tool in terms of longevity.

Q: What do you mean?
A: Once you get caught you become known by the police. On the other hand there are people like Banksy in London, he's quite well known in the art scene and he's never been caught. So, don't tell anybody. It's hard to keep a secret, but you have to. I don't think it's necessarily healthy. Maybe tell your girlfriend but don't even tell your friends. Aside from that, think of your message. If you

DESIGN TIP

Transitions are important. Think of how people enter and leave your space. A gate that needs opening or grapes that must be ducked under can turn a normally unthinking act into a conscious event that heightens the experience. An arrival may be exciting and a departure bittersweet when they happen in the transition zone between the normal chaotic world and a thoughtfully-designed site.

put out a very antagonistic, one-sided message, then people react harshly. If you write Fuck Bush or that kind of message it's not very effective. Be intelligent with your message. More than Fuck Bush or Down With Capitalism, use language that gets people thinking. If you really want change, use a method that's going to create dialogue. People don't react well to attacks. Say something intelligent, something thoughtful and do it with some kind of sophistication. That's going to go a lot farther.

POWER PLANT Jerusalem artichoke(*Helianthus tuberosus*)

It isn't from Jerusalem and it isn't an artichoke. The name Jerusalem artichoke is believed to be from a corruption of *girasole*, the Italian word for "turn toward the sun." It is indeed a member of the sunflower family. And it does taste a bit like an artichoke (if you use your imagination and haven't had artichokes for a while). This native of North America was introduced to Europe in 1616, becoming more popular there than in its own home. It could be the Jerry Lewis of the plant world.

Urban agriculturalist Hartley Rosen calls it "the food of the future." That has something to do with its growing needs, which are basically soil, and maybe some sun and why not a little water — but don't go to any trouble on its account because if you simply drop part of a tuber into a hole and refill it, by mid-summer you'll probably have a head-high plant whether you remembered it or not. (Note that some consider Jerusalem artichoke a weed because it tends to come back every year with the tenacity of an unwanted relative).

It's not a bad-looking plant. The flowers are too small and the leaves somewhat gawky, but it can work well as a seasonal fence. It makes a fine choice for a guerrilla garden you hope to harvest because it's tough, fast-growing and most people won't know what it is, so you can be fairly sure of getting a tasty crop even in a busy area.

The treasure lies underground in the tubers you get when you pull the plants up. They look like raw ginger and taste like…well, not much. Call it a subtle flavor, one that appeals to discerning palates when sliced raw for salads or dipping, or cooked as you might a tender potato (too long and you get mush). Dig them up anytime from October to May, although some say the mild taste gets sweeter after a frost. I actually quite like them, but then I don't mind bland foods.

The "future" designation also comes from the way these plants store their carbohydrates in a complex sugar called inulin. Eating inulin is said to provide one with the sense of being filled, but, unlike normal sugar, inulin is not absorbed by the body. Jerusalem artichokes have been touted as an ideal food for diabetics and anyone on a weight-loss program. If the Britney Spears Jerusalem Artichoke Diet book hits number one, remember you read it here first.

IF I CAN DO IT...   Matthew Green — Street Smarter

"We talked about values and caring for your community, that these were the streets they grew up on and they thought were worth fighting for in their little rival gang stuff."

We don't often dream beyond the short-term life of our gardening projects. Our visions tend to end at the triumphant stage with everything in glorious bloom. And what about a year later? Or two years? Or twenty-five? If our campaigns are going to be rooted in ecological principles, how long must we wait until we can declare success?

Matthew Green is a director of adult education and special programs at a community college in San Luis Obispo, California. Several years ago his community development work turned him into a guerrilla gardener when he saw it as a way to get at-risk youths off the streets of a small coastal town and into an empty lot where they might learn some earth-based lessons. Was it all worth it in the end? You decide.

I was the coordinator of a program for at-risk youth. The youth were 90 percent Hispanic. The at-risk description refers to the

> *If you don't live it, it won't come out of your horn.*
>
> — CHARLIE PARKER

Trees to plant now for future treehouses:
   Maple — *Acer species*
   Hickory — *Carya species*
   American beech — *Fagus grandiflora*
   Tanbark oak — *Lithocarpus densiflorous*
   Apple — *Malus species*
   Spruce — *Picea species*
   Pine — *Pinus species*
   Douglas fir — *Psuedotsuga menziesii*
   Oak — *Quercus species*
   Elm — *Ulmus species*

From the World Treehouse Association (treehouses.com)

biggest risk which was dropping out of school, but also the risk of getting into trouble with the law, slipping into this gang wannabe lifestyle. It wouldn't be accurate to call them gangster boys, but they played with the symbols of the gang world, doing the signs to each other and the little teardrop tattoos. The initiative of the project was to give them activities that would allow for other options.

We got permission from the owners to use the land, because it would have been very obvious who was doing it. We got permission to use water from next door, and got support from local nurseries which was lukewarm but we did get a discount for the purchase of plants. We got some donations from the community for supplies like shovels and rakes, and we also went to thrift stores. We focused on native plants because of water concerns and the very sandy soil.

The boys were all for it. It was presented as an option so there was a sense that they decided it was for them. They felt they could really make a mark on the community, and could show what good they could do. It included cleaning up years of trash. We put up a sign saying "Male Voices Community Garden Project."

It was hard work, but we got the garden planted. One obstacle was the waning interest of the boys over time. At first everyone was excited. They knew they had the image as sort of undesirables, a troublemaker group of boys. We were trying to work on their image as a group that did care about their community. That part was successful. But other things like the actual work were difficult. Getting them out there to actually work in the garden is easier said than done with 15-, 16-, 17-year-olds. Monitoring the work was always important. I once got a boy to weed and out of not knowing he pulled up the first crop of native plants we planted. Just the challenge of keeping the gardens in good shape and a high priority was hard.

The program was completed a few years ago so I guess it's a good time to look back. Some of the plants are still there. You can still see elements of it, eight or so of the original plants surrounded by weeds and trash. When I left the program the next guy never really got going on the thing. He did try once to get it cleaned up, but you just get overwhelmed with all there actually is to do. Eventually, just out of respect, I took the sign down because it was neglected.

Was it worth it? What I realized, what I take away from my experiences, is these boys find their way. A small percentage end

To make a great garden, one must have a great idea or a great opportunity.

— SIR GEORGE SITWELL, in "Essay on the Making of Gardens" (1909)

up in jail. The majority find jobs to survive with, although they're not necessarily breaking the cycle of poverty or discovering their potential or a confidence within themselves. But a few of them did; they found the push and the connection to education to get back to school and that probably never would have happened. I see these programs as a way to give a sense of connection and belonging. Underneath the antics that we see them doing at 16-17, they're going to find their way as they turn to 20 and 25. It's not really the programs that are pulling them through. But I do think that these things have value.

I just wish I had more experience because it could have made a difference. Maybe a little more community involvement, figuring a way to get more people involved. There was a continuity that the boys couldn't bring, there was a presence that I couldn't ensure, there was a concern with building within community that would have made it a bigger project but more likely successful.

So I have no regrets. It's almost like looking back on a girl-friend. You didn't get married but there were adventures that you explored and it gave us a grounding activity, for better or worse. We talked about values and caring for your community, that these were the streets they grew up on and they thought were worth fighting for in their little rival gang stuff so the underlying story of the garden was trying to deepen what they thought was worth fighting for. OK, so fight for what it looks like too. Fight for how much trash is there. I can tell you there are boys who look back with pride, who believe that their time in the project was mean-ingful. If nothing else it gave them a venue and a context to build relationships within the community.

POWER PLANT   Blueberry (*Vaccinium species*)

Blueberry muffins? Hmm? Hot from the oven? Or blueberry pancakes per-haps? Wait, wait. Blueberry pie. There. I said it. The mere mention of fresh blueberries should be enough to make the gastronomically advanced drool, and vow to go to whatever effort it takes to grow them.

It isn't complicated, although there could be some chemistry involved. Blueberries love acidic soil. They grow well in the same conditions that favor rhododendrons and azaleas. If your soil is too alkaline, you can sour it by adding plenty of pine needles, composted oak leaves, cottonseed meal or sulfur. The target range to keep blueberries happy is between 4.5 and

5.0 pH. But you needn't get too technical. Plenty of backyard blueberry growers never buy a pH testing kit and do just fine.

Blueberries are a good guerrilla gardening plant because they're low maintenance once settled into the proper conditions. They're hardy, don't really need pruning and provide year-round beauty as well as fruit for people (a tasty example of the benefits of edible landscaping) and for birds and wildlife.

Types of blueberries vary with the region, so a trip to your neighborhood nursery will be instructive. You might also try your local native plant society to see if there's a homegrown version. If you don't need a cultivated form of blueberry for the big, fat, juicy fruit, there are dozens of plants in the same underrated vaccinium family worth planting for their attractive foliage, fall colors and intricate winter twig arrangements. Vacciniums are like the shy hotties at the back of the class whose beauty no one recognizes until they're swept away by some stunned visitor.

If the acid soil part is still worrying you, blueberries and other vaccinium species do well in containers where it's easier to control the local conditions. Peat moss makes a good growing medium.

Did you know: Blueberries are grown commercially throughout North America, making a long harvest season that stretches from spring in Florida to a late variety ripening in October in British Columbia.

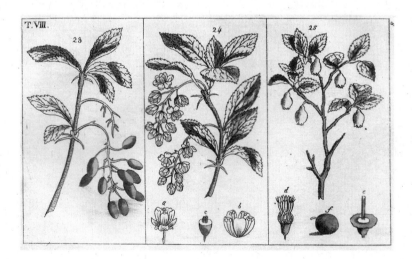

Blueberry — Vaccinium corymbosum
Credit: Gottlieb Tobias Wilhelm's "Unterhaltungen aus der Naturgeschichte" (Encyclopedia of Natural History), published in Vienna from 1810, illustrations by Gottlieb's brother Paul Martin Wilhelm and J. Schaly.

Where to Go from Here

(Make Your City the Salvation of the World)

A plant produces a million seeds, and who knows how any single one will do? A tiny acorn becomes an oak forest. Another gets squashed by a bulldozer clearing ground for the new condo complex.

Every act of guerrilla gardening is a seed. It might germinate, it might not. It might lead to another act. That one might get noticed. Someone may become inspired. More people could join in. Who knows how big this thing could get?

Never underestimate the potential spread of a cool idea. Rollerblading down the streets of Paris at night seemed like a fun thing to try for a few guys one Friday in the early 1990s. It was late, traffic was light, why not? They had a good time so they decided to repeat it the following week. Some other people saw them and wondered if it was a regular thing. Soon it was. And today thousands of skaters assemble every Friday night to take back the streets in a mass rolling tribute to democracy in action, a French revolution of fun. The week I was there, 18,000 skaters joined in, including a squad of skater cops who helped keep things rolling along. How could it get so big? The question might be put another way: How could it not? It was a great idea.

We know gardening is massive. It's a hobby (or obsession) enjoyed (or endured) by millions. We also know the environment is emerging as the most critical issue on the public mind. We're beginning to sense the looming catastrophe in every weird weather story. Although our general fascination with disaster draws us like magnets to the boy-trapped-in-the-well story on TV, we will rush out our doors at the first call for help to get him out. It's our human

The garden that is finished is dead.

— H.E. Bates

The best time to plant a tree is 10 years ago. The second best time is now.

nature. We rise to a challenge, and we find the struggle ennobling. Give us a crisis and we will work together, until we win — or drop. One day soon we'll understand that we're all trapped in the well, and then we'll find the collective will to fight for the planet's future. For now, guerrilla gardening will do, in small doses but growing all the time.

Living *la vida local*

If what you've heard up to now about using guerrilla gardening to save the world has you curious enough to try…welcome aboard. The environment is happy to have you. Your brothers and sisters in the global movement greet you with open arms, and probably a few tools you can borrow until you get set up yourself. Or they would, if there were an organized campaign with an international headquarters and all. But no. Although that's not necessarily a shortcoming. Because this global movement is, like others, really a local struggle at heart.

It's happening in the streets and parks and alleys and forgotten fields of our own towns, wherever people see how their own public spaces are being used or abused and get riled up enough to do something about it. If this happens to you, and you grab your trowel and head out the door, know that your determination is a product of your community. And this is how you give something back. In the long run, sure, your contribution will be pooled with others and measured as part of the greater campaign to improve the world. But you needn't think that far ahead for justification or inspiration. Your own corner of the planet is a perfect place to start. It's worth it.

Go team go

Guerrilla gardening at its best is a team sport. It doesn't have to be, of course. I have met a number of people doing it successfully on their own. It seems to be one of those activities that attracts the lone operative, the strong and silent type. If these people aren't inclined to get involved in setting up an organization, with all the time-consuming and perhaps contentious effort that implies, we should think no less of them. They're doing their part.

But there's something even more praiseworthy in a person who leverages his or her abilities into a community effort. If your goal is to improve a place, you may be entirely competent to do it on your own, and may even work better this way, but if your goal is not simply a better place but a transformed city in a more uplifting world, talk it up. Find out who else is interested, then figure out what you might do together. The exchange of ideas alone should be exciting. Even if you thought you had it all worked out, you didn't. Many hands make light work, the saying goes, and many brains create more effective solutions. In the grand picture, the best thing you can do as a guerrilla gardener is not simply to improve places. It's to set up a structure for improving places that's so formidable it will go on doing good work even when you're no longer directly involved.

You are the culture

But what if nobody cares what you think? What if you have no influence? Ha! Why does big capital spend billions of dollars to get inside your brain? Your mind is a valuable resource. Your views create the world. So don't let a corporation decide important things for you, or determine your tastes. They would like to tell you what beauty means. You know already. Hollywood wants to choose your heroes. Find your own — people who celebrate your values and exemplify your aspirations. Chances are they will be peers in your own community who are strong, confident, kind and engaged, as opposed to distanced celebrities who have great bone structure.

The reality of working on the land is tough and hard and it brings you right into the face of life and death every day you go out into it.

— Andy Goldsworthy

Which way do we go? Commercial Drive in Vancouver is reclaimed by pedestrians celebrating car-less culture.

The profit-seekers try to steer us into a hysteria of supposed need, but they're always just guessing. We don't have to buy into any of it. We can decide for ourselves what's good, what's bad and what it all means for the kinds of places in which we would like to live. We are our own urban designers. We create our own culture. Guerrilla gardening is proof that we can do it.

Live in the city of your dreams

Once you have your organization — which can be you and a friend, or better yet you and a bunch of friends — you're ready to take on the world. Starting with your city. Which starts with your neighborhood.

So what do you do now? Imagine the future. Picture the kind of area you would most want to live in. If that's too hard to do in your present circumstances, think of the kind of place you'd choose to leave to a loved one, say your children or grandchildren.

I thought it might be tempting to tout Johnny Appleseed as the patron saint of guerrilla gardening, but then I did the research. It turns out he was a bit too loopy even for a pursuit like this. It's probably no accident he was a loner all his life.

The man properly known as John Chapman was born on September 26, 1774 near Leominster, Massachusetts. He became a nurseryman in his 20s, helping to plant apple orchards in New York and Pennsylvania. When new territory opened up to settlers in the early 1800s in what is now Ohio, Michigan, Illinois and Indiana, Chapman took off for the unknown.

He spent the next five decades clearing land to plant his apple seeds, working diligently and alone. He spent most of his time outdoors, apparently as comfortable with animals as he was with the people to whom he would sell his trees for a few pennies.

He would espouse to all who would listen the Swedenborgian brand of Christianity by which he was guided. But just what people made of the wandering plantsman and his message is hard to know today. One lasting image is of a barefoot

You might even describe in a sentence or two the city you believe they deserve. That can be the basis of your mission, your guiding light. Once you have a goal in mind, it'll be easier to keep whatever you do in perspective. Then even setbacks won't be debilitating — just inevitable diversions on the path.

Get up and grow

The time has come. Don't wait. Don't think this all sounds like a good idea and then do something else. Get up right now and — but it's raining? Oh, all right. Go get a pen. Write down what you're going to do. Make a promise to yourself to carry through. Then do it.

Is your first move a planting project? Good for you. Something simple and elegant enough for you to complete on your own in a single burst of effort can be an excellent introduction to the campaign, and an ongoing visual stimulant to inspire more.

Public tree, public sidewalk, why not a public playground?

and oddly dressed man (apparently he was sometimes paid in used clothes which didn't fit his frame) who liked to wear his cooking pot as a hat.

All of which might even make sense — you have to carry the cooking pot somehow — but I can't help wondering why he didn't make more of a movement out of his movement. If he had not simply toiled away in solitude but had taught others to dig orchards and care for trees, his impact might have been realized ten-fold. He might have come in contact with seasoned apple growers and grafters (the technique had been known for centuries) who knew better than to plant seeds of dubious provenance collected by bulk from cider mills, as Chapman did. He might instead have touted superior varieties handed down through generations (apples grown from seed vary wildly from their parents, rarely in a good way, while grafts are perfect replicas of their desired types). If just a little of his enthusiasm for fruit-growing had been spent on farmer-teaching, Johnny Appleseed might have inspired an entire nation of apple-growing experts.

Your relation towards things has changed. If it rains you say that it rains on the garden; if the sun shines, it does not shine just anyhow, but it shines on the garden; in the evening you rejoice that the garden will rest.

— KAREL CAPEK

Is your first move a meeting? Good for you. A sign on the target site that includes your phone number or e-mail address may attract the compatriots with whom you begin building your movement.

No matter where you start or what strategy you use, there is nothing as important, and perhaps as exciting, as your initial step. Before you dig that first hole or drop that first seed, take the luxury to pause for a moment to reflect on the journey you're about to begin. You may not know how smoothly it will run or how long it will last, but you can expect an adventure. Thanks to you and people like you in cities all over the world, it will lead to a greener, brighter, happier future for everyone.

Welcome to guerrilla gardening.

Q&A   Jim Diers — Crowd control

When the Mayor of Seattle "chickened out" of a campaign promise to support stronger neighborhoods, Jim Diers marched into his office with a group of activists to release a live chicken. A few months later he met the mayor again, only this time after being hired as the first director of the city's new Office of Neighborhoods.

For the next 14 years, three mayors and hundreds of community projects, Diers helped put Seattle on the map of enlightened urban centers. Its grassroots participation process is now copied around the world. Diers, however, lost his job when an incoming mayor, whom he hadn't backed in the election, fired him. The Office of Neighborhoods was scaled back, although it is still intact. Diers went on to write *Neighbor Power: Building Community the Seattle Way.* He started another community organizing job and continues to spread the message that neighbors can be the most powerful force for good in an urban environment.

Q: I'm looking for advice from the front lines for guerrilla gardeners.
A: Here in Seattle we have a program called the Neighborhood Matching Fund. It supports neighborhood self-help projects. The vast majority of projects in Seattle involve greening and the environment and so forth. So we now have 75 community gardens in the city, 6,000 urban gardeners using them, and most of the recent gardens are for immigrants. I find the most creative solutions come out of the community, things the bureaucracy would never have done on its own. We had a neighborhood that had no street trees so the first thing somebody did was organize it block by

block, and they ended up planting 1,080 trees in one day. You can do that when you involve the whole neighborhood. Then they got so excited they went on and said, Now we need parks. So they built parks in the neighborhood. They built 12 parks over the past 12 years, all with volunteers.

Q: These are all working within the system.
A: They are. Because we've sort of opened up our system more and more.

Q: Do people in Seattle now have the sense that if they get a good idea the city is actually going to listen to them and make it work?
A: I think there's some of that, yeah. It's taken time with this program for what, 18 years now. When we started doing projects I met with the head of the Parks Department and said, We're creating this matching fund for projects that have a priority in neighborhoods but haven't been a priority for the government. It's a way to meet neighborhoods half-way: we'll match neighborhoods with equal cash, volunteer labor, donated goods and services or some combination of those. I said, I know there's a lot of interest at parks and people are going to want to create more parks so I just wanted to talk to you about how that's going to

When we plant new trees, we plant the seeds of peace.

— Wangari Maathai

Need a strategic hedge big and fast? The Leyland Cypress (*Cupressusocyparis leylandii*) is famous for vigorous growth. In fact, some consider planting it a potentially aggressive act against a neighboring site. Not that this should give you any ideas, but in England where they take their hedges seriously, putting in Leyland Cypress has led to arguments, court cases and even murder.

It's an attractive plant, as expected from the blend of two fine parents, the Monterey cypress (*Cupressus macrocarpa*) and the Nootka cypress (*Chamaecyparis nootkatensis*). But it really makes its name as a sprinter: this tall, pyramidic wonder can go from 0 to 20 feet in five years.

The downside of anything growing that fast is durability. The Leyland cypress can start to look scrappy in just 10 years and fail altogether in 20. But by then perhaps relations between you and the people next to you will be so good you'll agree on planting something else altogether.

work. And she said, Oh no, there aren't going to be any, we don't want anybody messing with our parks.

Q: I've heard that before.
A: Yeah. So it was a struggle to go from that point to where we are today. But what I did was listen. And she had some good concerns about liability, about ongoing maintenance, so we just worked to figure out those issues and stayed with the program, working with the departments but also in the neighborhoods and over time the departments really loosened up.

Q: That's all matching funds which means half the money comes from the city?
A: That's right.

Q: So you've been able to squeeze money out of places where the first reaction when someone asks for money is often, No.
A: Right. We started small, with a $150,000 fund. It was very controversial. It was a 5-4 vote of the city council. The city said, Why would we create a fund for projects that aren't the city's priority when we don't have enough money to fund all the things that *are* the city's priority? But those first projects were so successful, the next year city council voted to increase the fund and then it grew to $4.5 million for about 400 projects a year.

Q: And now it has a life of its own.
A: Yeah, it's very popular because it's a win-win. It's a way for people to work positively with the city government rather than always seeing government as the enemy. It's building partnerships between departments and the neighborhoods. It's a way to call the bluff of activists who have big mouths but no constituency.

Q: Or the gumption to do something.
A: That's right. And it really multiplies the city's resources. So the city's $35 million invested so far has leveraged about $50 million in community resources. It's just a real win. Because the conditions are made by neighborhood leaders, city officials don't have to say no to anything. Neighborhoods are very proud of the fund and are tougher than politicians would be in choosing projects. And yet the politicians can go out for photographs on ground breakings and so on. So yeah it's really successful. There are over 100 cities that have them now.

Q: Any advice on the non-official side?
A: A lot of it is getting inspired by stories of what people have

*Gardening is the
noblest of callings.*

— HORACE, Roman poet
and gardener/farmer

done. Then find your own way to do it. If it's public property being neglected by the city, go in at night and put in a park. Or, there's property that the city won't even come out and inspect, no one's going to care if you go out and fix it up. A lot of absentee landlords won't even know if a property's been changed. There are so many resources in a neighborhood. To me that's the major lesson. Do not just see neighborhoods as places with needs to be resolved by city government. That's true of both the city and the neighborhoods. People always look to governments for permission or the solution. But oftentimes the best solution comes right out of the community. Start thinking of the community not just as a place with needs but as a community with untapped resources. In every neighborhood you can find incredible people who know about plants, who know about landscaping, who know about architecture, who know planning, who know the history of the community, who have all this knowledge, who know all these places nobody else knows. You have all these resources that are just kind of sitting there untapped. The city government says, We don't have money to do that. But the community just has to do it. And it saves time. Instead of spending all your time going down to City Hall, just do it.

Nostalgia in gardening often surfaces as longing for that older, deeper relationship between person and place that we rarely achieve in modern life.

— MARY KEEN

IF I CAN DO IT...   Amy Twigge — Tree Lessons

"It's kind of fun to not ask permission. There's more of a bad ass element to it that way."

Amy Twigge was finishing a master's degree in urban planning at Montreal's McGill University when she decided to take a more hands-on approach to city-building. For an experienced tree planter, the strategy seemed obvious. But there's a difference between what you can do in the bush and what you can get away with in the city, guerrilla garden style.

Not every planting project is going to work. But every one should provide a lesson, even if it's only on what not to do the next time.

The problem with urban tree planting is you can't plant seedlings like you do on a clear-cut. They won't survive. They'll get run over by bicycles, or dogs will piss on them. The trees the city plants are probably ten years old and at that size might cost $300 or $500 per tree. Ours were taken from a subdivision being built on the West Island in a woodlot. The site was set to be cleared for housing so we were saving the trees from a certain death at that location.

We ended up taking six trees that were probably five years old. Initially we thought, when you've planted 3,000 trees a day for however many seasons, planting trees is easy. But in this context where we wanted to plant in public spaces, we needed something that would take up more space.

It wasn't that we planted the wrong trees. We planted the same species that was already on the street, maple. But the city's maples were really big and robust and ours weren't. And then the city killed them anyway when they took out what we'd done. Now we have one left that the city hasn't dug up or replaced. Pretty small scale, you'd have to say. It was all a humbling experience.

I suppose something could be worked out to partner with the city on this kind of thing. But I'm just not that organized. It's kind of fun to not ask permission. There's more of a bad ass element to it that way. I guess the moral to that story is if you're going to be a renegade tree planter, you've got to go big and really put trees where there weren't trees before. And where the city doesn't have plans for trees. We sort of hoped that at the very least we'd be adding to the total amount of trees on the island of Montreal, but in the end we didn't end up doing that because they took ours out and put others in their place. So there was no net gain.

Yes, I guess more planning would have helped. Be sure that when you do plant trees, people know that they're there and will help take care of them. It sounds ridiculous, but I was biking around with five gallons of water on my back trying to water these trees. The best way may have been to plant not six trees but two trees and spend more time doing educational material. If we had good signage saying, Listen, the city didn't plant these trees, concerned citizens did, and this is why, so if you want to plant a

Here's a tip for making your own anti-bug spray at home. Chop finely five garlic cloves and three hot peppers. Mix into a gallon of water and set aside, but not so far aside you forget the whole project for a few months. After 24 hours, strain the potion into a spray bottle and add two or three drops of dish soap. Use it on creepy crawly things of all kinds, spraying at will. If the garlic doesn't convince them, maybe the peppers or soap will. This should work to ward off aphids, ants, caterpillars and plenty more. Also pets, but that's another category.

renegade garden patch around this tree or plant symbiotic species around this tree, this is what they are so go for it. It would have been more effective to spend more energy doing that than the actual tree planting which is what gets people more excited.

You might even encourage people you don't know or aren't a part of your circle into helping with whatever you do.

Bibliography

Alexander, Christopher, Sara Ishikawa and Murray Silverstein. *A Pattern Language*. Oxford University Press, 1977.

Appleton, Jay. *The Experience of Landscape*. John Wiley, 1975.

Benton, Mike. *White Trash Gardening*. Taylor, 1996.

Biehl, Janet, ed. *The Murray Bookchin Reader*. Black Rose Books, 1999.

Brenzel, Kathleen, ed. *Sunset Western Garden Book*. Sunset Publishing Corporation, 1995.

Bridgman, Howard et al. *Urban Biophysical Environments*. Oxford University Press, 1995.

Briggs, Josie. *Creating Small Habitats for Wildlife in Your Garden*. Guild of Master Craftsman, 2000.

Campbell, Susan. *Naturescape British Columbia: The provincial guide*. British Columbia Ministry of Environment, Lands and Parks, 1995.

Clark, Janet, Mary Alice Collins and Gary Collins. *The Naturalist: Down to Earth*. Burgess, 1974.

Cleary, Thomas, trans. and ed. *Mastering the Art of War: Zhuge Liang and Liu Ji's commentaries on the classic by Sun Tzu*. Shambala, 1989.

Coon, Nelson. *The Dictionary of Useful Plants: The Use, History, and Folklore of More Than 500 Plant Species*. Rodale, 1974.

Creasy, Rosalind. *The Complete Book of Edible Landscaping*. Sierra Club, 1982.

Diers, Jim. *Neighbor Power: Building Community the Seattle Way*. University of Washington, 2004.

Engwicht, David. *Street Reclaiming: Creating Livable Streets and Vibrant Communities*. New Society, 1999.

Fisher, Sue. *Fast Plants: Choosing and Growing Plants for Gardens in a Hurry*. Fireside, 2002.

Fuhrman, Candice. *Publicity Stunt! Great Staged Events That Made the News*. Chronicle, 1989.

Gandy, Matthew. *Concrete and Clay: Reworking Nature in New York City*. MIT Press, 2002.

Hart, Rhonda Massingham. *Dirt Cheap Gardening: Hundreds of Ways to Save Money in Your Garden*. Garden Way, 1995.

Heinrich, Bernd. *The Trees in My Forest*. Cliff Street, 1997.

Hottes, Alfred Carl. *Garden Facts and Fancies.* Dodd Mead, 1949.

Hollingsworth, E. Buckner. *Flower Chronicles.* University of Chicago, 1958.

Hough, Michael. *City Form and Natural Process: Towards a New Urban Vernacular.* Routledge, 1984 (1991).

Jackson, John Brinckerhoff. *Landscape in Sight: Looking at America.* Yale University Press, 1997.

Jobb , Jamie. *The Complete Book of Community Gardening.* Morrow, 1979.

Kayden, Jerold. *Privately Owned Public Space: The New York City Experiment.* New York City Department of City Planning and the Municipal Art Society of New York, 2000.

Kunstler, James Howard. *The Geography of Nowhere: The Rise and Decline of America's Man-Made Landscape.* Touchstone, 1993.

Link, Russell. *Landscaping for Wildlife in the Pacific Northwest.* University of Washington Press, 1999.

Lipkis, Andy with TreePeople and Katie Lipkis. *The Simple Act of Planting a Tree: A Citizen Forester's Guide to Healing Your Neighborhood, Your City, and Your World.* J.P. Tarcher, 1990.

Low, Setha and Neil Smith, eds. *The Politics of Public Space.* Routledge, 2006.

Lynd, Mitch. "Great Moments in Apple History." Midwest Apple Improvement Society. [online]. [cited November 14, 2006]. hort.purdue.edu/newcrop/maia/history.html.

Martin, Laura C. *The Wildflower Meadow Book: A Gardener's Guide.* East Woods, 1986.

Merilees, Bill. *Attracting Backyard Wildlife: A Guide for Nature-Lovers.* Whitecap, 1989.

Nelson Mandela Foundation. *A Prisoner in the Garden: Opening Nelson Mandela's Prison Archive.* Penguin, 2005.

Olmsted, Frederick Law. "Public Parks and the Enlargement of Towns." 1871. In Donald Worster. *American Environmentalism: the formative period, 1860–1915* . John Wiley, 1973.

Orr, David. *Earth in Mind: On Education, Environment, and the Human Prospect.* Island Press, 2004.

Pfeiffer, E.E. *Weeds and what they tell.* Bio-dynamic Farming and Gardening Association, 1974.

Schaefer, Valentin, Hillary Rudd and Jamie Vala. *Urban Biodiversity: Exploring Natural Habitat and Its Value in Cities.* Captus, 2004.

Scott, Frank J. *The Art of Beautifying Suburban Home Grounds.* John Alden, 1886.

Shepard, Paul. *Traces of an Omnivore.* Island Press, 1996.

Simonds, John Ormsbee. *Landscape Architecture: The Shaping of Man's Natural Environment.* McGraw-Hill, 1961.

Sommers, Larry. *The Community Garden Book: New Directions for Creating and Managing Neighborhood Food Gardens in Your Town.* Gardens for All, 1984.

Snyder, Gary. *The Real Works: Interviews & Talks 1964–1979.* New Directions, 1980.

Snyder, Gary. *The Practice of the Wild.* North Point, 1990.

Teyssot, Georges, ed. *The American Lawn*. Princeton Architectural Press with
Canadian Centre for Architecture, 1999.

Tilgner, Linda. *Tips for the Lazy Gardener*. Storey, 1998.

Traeger, Tessa and Patrick Kinmonth. *A Gardener's Labyrinth: Portraits of
People, Plants & Places*. Booth-Clibborn Editions, 2003.

Tuan, Yi-Fu. *Space and Place: The perspective of experience*. University of
Minnesota Press, 1977.

Wilson, Alexander. *The Culture of Nature*. Blackwell, 1992.

Yepsen, Roger. *Apples*. W.W. Norton, 1994.

Notes

Introduction

1. Luke Harding and Andrew Culf, "The New World Cup rule: take off your trousers, they're offending our sponsor." [online]. [cited December 2, 2006]. UK Guardian, June 19, 2006. football.guardian.co.uk/worldcup 2006/story/0,,1800885,00.html.
2. UN-Habitat. "State of the World's Cities, 2006/07." [online]. [cited December 2, 2006]. csun.edu/~vasishth/State_of_the_World's_Cities_ 2006_07.pdf.
3. Woody Guthrie, "This Land is Your Land." [online]. [cited November 13, 2006]. woodyguthrie.org/Lyrics/This_Land.htm.
4. *Journal of Agricultural Food Chemistry*, June 2004. [online]. [cited November 20, 2006]. realfood.org.uk/index.php?option=com_content &task=view&id=114&Itemid=47.

Chapter One

1. P. Sabin Willett, "Wilting Dreams At Gitmo: A Detainee Is Denied A Garden, and Hope." [online]. [cited November 2, 2006]. *Washington Post*, April 27, 2006, Page A27. washingtonpost.com/wp-yn/content/ article/2006/04/26/AR2006042602390.html.
2. The Reclaim the Streets group in London appears to have moved on to greener pastures but it still maintains a spunky website with plenty of information on past campaigns and advice on how to throw a street party of your own. rts.gn.apc.org/.
3. Leif Utne, "Networking for the Earth." [online]. [cited November 2, 2006]. *Utne Reader*, November/December 2004. utne.com/issues/2004 _126/view/11426-1.html.
4. Lyrics taken directly from a cassette recording of the song. See earthwise.org.au/.
5. *Vancouver Sun*. May 31, 1971. P2.
6. Paul Rincon, "UK Wildlife 'heading into crisis'" [online]. [cited November 2, 2006]. BBC News Online, March 18, 2004. news.bbc.co.uk/2/hi/ science/nature/3520372.stm.

Chapter Two

1. Gary Snyder. *The Real Work. Interviews and Talks 1964–1979.* New Directions, 1980, p. 117.
2. Michael Hough. *City Form and Natural Process: Towards a New Urban Vernacular.* Routledge, 1991, page 118.
3. Hough, page 7.
4. Robert Klose. "The Secret Gardener." [online]. [cited November 6, 2006]. *Christian Science Monitor,* June 1, 2005. csmonitor.com/2005/0601/p18s03-hfes.html.

Chapter Three

1. Trees are priceless, as anyone living in the midst of a prize specimen knows, but there have been attempts to quantify their benefits. The American Forestry Association made a rough estimate in 1985, concluding that a 50-year-old urban tree would each year supply an average $73 worth of air conditioning, $75 worth of soil erosion and storm water control, wildlife shelter worth another $75 and air pollution control valued at $50. Total value in 1985 dollars: $273. Total value during the tree's lifetime, compounded at 5 percent for 50 years: $57,151. Quoted in Andy Lipkis with TreePeople and Katie Lipkis, *The Simple Act of Planting a Tree.* Tarcher, 1990, p. 28.
2. Jamie Jobb. *The Complete Book of Community Gardening.* Morrow, 1979, p. 156. This well-written book was also used extensively for general advice in the chapter on community gardening.

Chapter Four

1. "What on Earth Is Soil?" US Environmental Protection Agency Gulf of Mexico Program. [online] [cited November 14, 2006]. epa.gov/gmpo/ed resources/soil.html.
2. Linda Tilgner. *Tips for the Lazy Gardener.* Storey, 1998, p. 67.
3. If you had a burning curiosity about compost, a scientific bent and years to spend in the pursuit, you might do something like this too: researchers in New England have been piling up various concoctions of leaves and things and then studying how the decomposed results affect various crops. The verdict: "For most vegetables and cut flowers, recent research at The Connecticut Agricultural Experiment Station has shown that fertilizer can often be eliminated when the soil is amended annually with 1 inch of leaf compost." Other facts you can use from all their hard work: The best combination is one or two parts green (high nitrogen stuff like food scraps and cut grass) with three or four parts brown (high carbon stuff like leaves). The minimum size to hold heat is $3 \times 3 \times 3$ feet. If your compost pile never gets hot, it may be too small (the pile will still break down but will take more time), may be too dry (moisten while turning) or may lack nitrogen (add more table scraps, fresh grass or manure). If it smells bad, it needs air — turn the pile to aerate it. You may also need to check your materials to ensure a healthy mix of greens and browns, and reduce water. Reference: Abigail A. Maynard, "Compost: The Process and

Research." [online]. [cited November 20, 2006]. The Connecticut Agricultural Experiment Station, New Haven. Bulletin 966 (July 2000).
caes.state.ct.us/Bulletins/2000/b966.pdf

4. Personal interview — May 28, 2004, Yokohama, Japan.
5. Tessa Traeger and Patrick Kinmonth, *A Gardener's Labyrinth: Portraits of
People, Plants & Places.* Booth-Clibborn, 2003, p. 180.

Chapter Five

1. "Habitat Resources: Native Plants." National Wildlife Federation.
[online]. [cited November 14, 2006]. enature.com/articles/detail.asp?
storyID=647.
2. "Effective Control of Bats." Health Canada, Pest Management Regula-
tory Agency. [online]. [cited November 14, 2006]. pmra-arla.gc.ca/
english/consum/bats-e.html.
3. "Butterfly Questions and Answers." North American Butterfly Association. [online]. [cited November 14, 2006]. naba.org/qanda.html.
4. Quoted in Claire Hagen Dole, "Hibernation Boxes: Do They Work?"
Butterfly Gardeners' Quarterly #14 (Fall 1997). [online]. [cited November
14, 2006]. butterlywebsite.com/articles/showarticle.cfm?ID=27.
5. As quoted in Alan Stanley, "How to win: Saving wildlife sites." Friends of
the Earth UK, 2001. [online]. [cited November 14, 2006]. foe.co.uk/
resource/local/saving_wildlife_sites/getting_started/saving_wildlife
_sites_1.pdf.
6. Valentin Schaefer, Hillary Rudd and Jamie Vala, *Urban Biodiversity:
Exploring Natural Habitat and Its Value in Cities.* Captus Press, 2004,
p. 19.
7. *Arbor Age,* published by M2Media360. Vol. 26, # 8 (August 2006), p. 12.
8. Native Plant Society of British Columbia, "Code of Ethics." Adopted
1999. [online]. [cited November 14, 2006]. npsbc.org/Ethics/ethics.htm.

Chapter Six

1. National Coalition for Pesticide-Free Lawns website. [online]. [cited
November 15, 2006]. beyondpesticides.org/pesticidefreelawns/index.htm.
2. E-Times: The Electronic Newsletter of the Irrigation Association, February 2006. [online]. [cited November 15, 2006]. irrigation.org/news/
etimes/E-Times_February_2006.pdf.
3. Native Plant Conservation Campaign, "Endangered Species Acts Must
Protect Plants, Plant Conservation Fact Sheet" quoting USDA Forest
Service, Every Species Counts: Conserving Biological Diversity, Program
Aid 1499, 1993. [online]. [cited November 15, 2006]. cnps.org/programs/
conservation/files/WhyPlantsFinal2.pdf.
4. US Environmental Protection Agency, "Chapter 2, What are the Benefits
of Natural Landscaping, (subheading) Reduced Air Pollution" from
*Greenacres: Natural Landscaping for Public Officials. A Source Book on
Natural Landscaping for Public Officials.* [online]. [cited November 15,
2006]. epa.gov/greenacres/toolkit/chap2.html.
5. See primalseeds.org.

Chapter Seven

1. E.E. Pfeiffer, *Weeds and What They Tell*. Bio-dynamic Farming and Gardening Association, 1974.

Chapter Eight

1. Louisiana Department of Environmental Quality, "Did You Know… Earthworms." [online]. [cited November 17, 2006]. deq.louisiana.gov/ portal/Portals/0/assistance/educate/DYK-earthworms.pdf.
2. Cleary, Thomas, trans. and ed., *Mastering the Art of War: Zhuge Liang and Liu Ji's commentaries on the classic by Sun Tzu,* Shambala, 1989.
3. John Ormsbee Simonds, *Landscape Architecture: The Shaping of Man's Natural Environment,* McGraw-Hill, 1961, p. 150.

Chapter Nine

1. Candice Fuhrman, *Publicity Stunt! Great Staged Events That Made the News.* Chronicle, 1989.

Index

A

akebia vine, 51, 53
alfalfa, 70, 89
allotment garden, 151
All Seasons Park (Vancouver, BC), 24, 29, 57
alyssum, 51
antioxidants, in foods, 13
apple trees, 118–119, 194
The Art of War (Sun Tzu), 158
ash, European, 167
aster, 110
azalea, 71

B

back lanes, planting in, 53
balsam, 88
bats, 102
beans, pole, 41
beech, American, 167, 194
bells-of-Ireland, 163
Berkeley (CA), People's Park, 22–24, 57
bicycle use, promotion of, 27
biodiversity, 20, 89–90, 103–108
birch, Paper, 167
black-eyed Susan, 87
black medic, 113–114
bleeding heart, 163
blueberry, 71, 83, 196–197
boulevard planting, 164, 165, 168
buckwheat, 70, 89
butterflies, 31, 104–105
butterfly weed, 129

C

calendula, 98
Campbell, Tom, 29
car culture protest, 27, 199
carrots, 110
chamomile, 123
Chapman, John, 202–203
chives, 98
Christmas rose, 163
Christy, Liz, 24–25, 34
City Form and Natural Process (Hough), 48
clematis, 41, 51
clover, crimson, 70, 89
cold frames, 72–73
columbine, 163
community
    building, 7, 137–139, 200–201
    connection to place, 37–40
    gathering spots, 56
    signs and banners, 178
community gardens
    building community, 137–139
    core group, 143–144
    discouraging developers, 145–147
    Green Guerrillas, 24–25
    and municipal support, 147–149
    security, 140–141, 146
    site selection, 139–143
    Strathcona Community Garden, 149–153
    structure and planning, 144–147
    volunteers, 139
community orchard, 92

Community Supported Agriculture (CSA), 171–173
compost
  making, 71–72, 162
  obtaining, 70
  and water conservation, 91
consumerism, 29–30, 202
container planting, 96
  advantage of, 108–109
  potting mix, 76–77
  rooftop gardens, 54–55
  watering, 83
coreopsis, 88
corn cockle, 129, 163
cover crops (green manure), 70, 88–89
current, red-flowering, 92

D

daisy, 110, 129
Dalai Lama, 6–7, 21
design tips
  discouraging developers, 42, 145–147
  entrances, 192
  experiments, 72, 74
  footpaths, 113, 152
  from Japanese gardening terms, 183
  local conditions, 179
  long term, 4, 133
  placement of rocks, 63, 126
  plant groupings, 24, 92, 126
  for the senses, 34
  use of objects, 50, 55
  use of space, 10, 86, 116
  use of structures, 14
  vertical design, 31
  visual appeal, 90, 161, 168
  water distribution, 140
  willow fencing, 105
Devonian Park (Vancouver, BC), 22–24
Diers, Jim, on self-help projects in Seattle, 204–207
dill, 110
Duncan, Alan, on working with city officials, 166–171

E

earthworms, 71, 160
echinacea, 88
ecosystems. *see also* naturescaping
  and biodiversity, 20, 89–90, 103–108
  and weeds, 113–114
elm, 194
elm, American, 167
elm, English, 167
engaged ecology, 20
environmental issues
  extinction, 13, 31, 132
  public awareness of, 20, 175–176
  water conservation, 43, 74–75, 91
equipment and tools
  for concrete removal, 54
  gloves, 64–65
  list of, 62
  to look like city worker, 11
  obtaining, 61–62, 64, 67
  shovels, 63–64, 65
  trowels, 65–66
ethical issues, 6–7, 31–32
events
  fund-raising, 67–69, 73
  newsworthy stories, 180

F

farming, history of, 19–20
fences
  plants for, 41, 125, 174, 193
  willow fencing, 105
fennel, 98, 110
fertilizer, 86–89
feverfew, 110
fir, Douglas, 194
flowers, 126–127, 163
foxglove, 88, 132
Francis, Robyn, 27
Fruit Tree Project (Vancouver, BC), 150
fruit trees, 41, 92–93, 118–119, 150
fund-raising, 67–69, 73

G

gardening. *see also* naturescaping; plants; topsoil
  basics, 41–44, 81–85

block planting tip, 92
in captivity, 21–22
cleaning hands tip, 6
containers, 54–55, 76–77, 83, 96, 108–109
fertilizer, 86–89
hybrid seeds, 67
keeping a journal tip, 169
organic, 33, 152
pest control, 68–69, 90–91, 109–112, 208
plant hardiness zone, 42
plant identification tip, 34
planting bulbs tip, 88
raised beds, 147
rooting hormone tip, 105
seed saving, 74–75
starting seeds, 62, 72–73, 75
use of botanical names, 87
use of transplants tip, 82
watering plants, 83, 140, 152
genetically modified plants, 73–74
Gibson, Peter, interview with street artist, 186–193
gillyflower, 163
global warming, 30
governments. *see* municipal governments
grapes, 41
grass, 121–122. *see also* lawns
Green, Matthew, on project with at-risk youth, 194–196
Green Guerrillas (New York), 24–25, 34–35, 93–95
Green Streets (Vancouver, BC), 97, 166
groundcovers, 51
guerrilla tactics. *see also* planning stage
concrete removal, 54
definition, 4
ethical issues, 31–32
history of, 22–26
impact, 6, 101–103, 199–200
justification for, 28–33, 200–203
legal implications, 3–4, 6, 158, 182–183
non-violence, 6–7
participation, 1–4, 30–31, 101, 199
planting in existing beds, 55–56
public lawns, 124, 126–127
seed bombs, 93–95
sites for, 40, 47–56, 139–143
tactics by night or by day, 11
Urban Explorers, 48–49
website on, 48
Guthrie, Woody, 4

H
habitat, 102, 103–104, 107–108, 114, 147
hawthorne, 41, 51
hazelnut, 53
hemlock, Western, 167
herbal lawns, 123
hickory, 194
holly, 41
hollyhock, 163
Hough, Michael, 48
hydrangea, climbing, 51

I
insects
attracting beneficial, 110
pest control, 68–69, 90–91, 109–112, 208
intersections as public squares, 56
Inuvik Community Greenhouse, (NT), 145
invasive species, 31, 110
ivy, Boston, 51

J
Jacob's Well garden (Vancouver, BC), 171–173
Japanese gardening, 86, 183
Jerusalem artichoke, 193–194
Johnny Appleseed, 202–203

K
Kayden, Jerold, 190
King, Les, on his rose garden, 153–154
Klose, Robert, on garden by a cement plant, 58–59
Kurbis, Susan, on projects in Vancouver, 116–118

L

lady's-mantle, 163
land developers, 42, 145–147
Landscaping for Wildlife in the Pacific Northwest (Link), 102
larch, European, 167
lavender, 55, 134–135
lawns
    alternative plants, 123
    and guerrilla gardening, 124, 126–127
    lawn lounge construction, 130–131
    removal of, 125–126
    suburban, 121–124, 133
legal implications
    acting without permission, 3–4, 6, 158
    getting arrested, 182–183
lettuce, 125
liability insurance, 173
lilac, wild, 103
linden, 167
Link, Russell, 102
Loggins, Donald, 34
London (England), Reclaim the Streets, 25–26
London (ON), Old East Guerrilla Garden Posse, 78–80
love-in-a-mist, 129
lungwort, 163
lupin, 88, 89

M

mallow, 88
Mandela, Nelson, 21
manure, obtaining, 70
maple, 194
Marcuzzi, Liberia, 138
marigold, 110
meadow, creation, 125–129
mint, Corsican, 123
monoculture, 89–90
Monsanto, 29, 33, 74
morning glory, 34, 41
municipal governments
    advice from Alan Duncan, 166–171
    funding of projects, 205–206
    maintenance contract, 147

    proposal documents, 162–163
    support by, 147–149
    working with city officials, 159–164

N

nasturtium, 35, 98
native plants
    advantage of, 91–92
    in meadow creation, 127
    in naturescaping, 104–107
    obtaining, 106–107
naturescaping. *see also* gardening
    biodiversity, 103–108
    meadows, 125–129
    park spaces, 104–107
    project goals, 101–103
    urban environment, 14–15, 37–40, 45–50
    and wildlife, 102, 103–104, 107–108, 114
neighborhood. *see* community
Neighbor Power: Building Community the Seattle Way (Diers), 204
New York City
    Green Guerrillas, 24–25, 34–35, 93–95
    privatized public space, 190
nicotiana, 163

O

oak, Tanbark, 194
oats, 70, 89
Old East Guerrilla Garden Posse (London, ON), 78–80
oregano, 51
organic gardening, 33, 152

P

Paris, car culture protest, 199
parking lots, planting in, 53–54
parsley, 110
Pasternak, Al, planting advise, 97–98
peas, bush, 83
pennyroyal, 123
People's Park (Berkeley, CA), 22–24, 57
permission
    acting without, 3–4, 6, 158, 207

after the fact, 116–117, 172–173
from city officials, 159–164
from land owners, 157–158
personal narratives
    on California poppy use, 132–134
    on community gardens, 150–153,
        172–173
    empty lot cleanup, 7
    on foxglove use, 129, 132
    on garden by a cement plant, 58–
        59
    on gardening, 95–97
    on growth in an empty lot, 112–115
    on guerrilla gardening tactics, 57–
        58, 78–80, 88
    interview with street artist, 186–
        193
    on planting advise, 97–98
    on projects in Vancouver, 116–118
    on project with at-risk youth,
        194–196
    on a rose garden, 153–154
    on self-help projects in Seattle,
        204–207
    on sunflower research, 76–78
    on tree planting, 8–13, 207–209
    on working with city officials,
        166–171
pest control
    aphids, 68–69
    bug spray recipe, 208
    natural methods, 90–91, 109–111
    slugs, 111–112
pesticides, misuse of, 33, 122–123
pH balance, 85, 196–197
pine, 194
planning stage. see also guerrilla tac-
    tics
    city property use, 159–164
    events, 67–69, 73, 180
    forming a group, 22, 54, 68
    how to begin, 57, 203–204, 207
    private property use, 157–158
    site selection, 40, 47–56, 139–143
plants. see also gardening
    and antioxidants, 13
    for cover crops, 70, 88–89
    easy of grow, 70

exchange of, 73
for on fences, 41, 125, 174
for flowers, 163
glossary of terms, 124
heirloom seeds, 67, 74
hybrid, 67
to improve the soil, 70
invasive species, 31, 110
light requirement of, 40, 83, 144
native, 91–92, 104–107, 127
for in shade, 69, 144
starting seeds, 62, 72–73, 75
terminator, 73–74
use of botanical names, 87
for on walls, 51
website on, 98
wildflower seed mixes, 126–127
Plants for a Future database, 98
poles, plants for, 173–174
politics
    and guerrilla gardening, 32, 96
    help from politicians, 163
poppy, 59–60, 129, 132–134
Portland (OR), City Repair website,
    56
potato, 95, 98–99
potato, caribou, 116
Primal Seeds website, 126
primrose, 163
Privately Owned Public Space: The
    New York City Experiment (Kay-
    den), 190
private property
    getting permission to use, 157–158
    and public space, 5–6, 190
project ideas. see also community
    gardens; personal narratives
    lawn lounge construction, 130–131
    message in a lawn, 126–127
    project examples, 102, 108
    signs and banners, 178
    websites about, 26, 56
publicity
    controversy, 182–184
    interviews, 181–182
    mass media, 176–179
    newsworthy stories, 179–181
    print media, 177–179

public speaking, 184–185
signs, 185–186
stunt examples, 25, 176–177
public space
aesthetics, 31–32
in community, 14–15, 191
definition, 5–6
privatized, 190
pulmonaria, 163

Q

quince, 93

R

rain water collection, 74–75, 140
Reagan, Ronald, 23
Reclaim the Streets (London, England), 25–26
redwood, Dawn, 167
Rieseberg, Loren, on sunflower research, 76–78
rooftop gardens, 54–55
rose, climbing, 41
rose garden narrative, 58–59
rosemary, 98
rugosa rose, 163
rye, 70, 89

S

Sarti, Robert, on guerrilla gardening, 57–58
scarlet runner bean, 173–174
school gardens, 117–118, 181
Seattle (WA), self-help projects, 204–207
sedum, 55
seed bombs, 93–95
seed grenades, 34
sewer system, 42, 44
shade plants, 69, 144
Shepard, Paul, 46
signs and banners, 178, 185–186
Sigurgeirson, Muggs, on community gardens, 150–153
site selection
for community gardens, 139–143
sites to avoid, 40
where to start, 47–56

slug control, 111–112
Snetsinger, Robert (quotation), 105
Snyder, Gary (quotation), 38
soil. *see* topsoil
"Songs of a Green Guerrilla" (Francis), 27
soybeans, 89
spruce, 194
Stephen, Bill, on foxglove use, 129, 132
stonecrop, 51
Strathcona Community Garden (Vancouver, BC), 149–153
street art, 186–193
street signs, 178
sumac, smooth, 54
sunflower, 77–78, 80, 110
Sun Tzu (quotation), 158
sweet pea, 154–155

T

Tarrant, David, on gardening, 95–97
Taylor, Terry, on growth in an empty lot, 112–115
"This Land Is Your Land" (Guthrie), 4
thyme, 51, 113, 123
Tilgner, Linda, 83
Tips for the Lazy Gardener (Tilgner), 83
tomato, 96, 148
tools. *see* equipment and tools
topsoil
characteristics, 84, 85–86
compacted soil, 40, 83
condition of, 43–44, 142
improving of, 70–72, 85–89
obtaining, 69–70, 128
pH balance, 85, 196–197
potting mix, 76–77
website of free materials, 69
traffic circle planting, 164–166, 168
tree planting
apple trees, 118–119
fruit trees, 41, 92–93
Johnny Appleseed, 202–203
need for, 50–51, 111
personal narratives, 8–13, 207–209

recommended types, 54, 167, 194
from seed, 76
tulip tree, 167
Twigge, Amy, on urban tree planting, 207–209

U
urban environment, 14–15, 37–40, 45–50
Urban Explorers website, 48–49
urban planning, history of, 10

V
Vancouver (BC)
    All Seasons Park protest, 24, 29, 57
    Fruit Tree Project, 149–153
    Green Streets, 97
    Jacob's Well garden, 171–173
    promoting bicycle use, 27
    school gardens, 117–118
    Strathcona Community Garden, 149–153
    urban planning, 10
    Windsor Castle playground, 168–169, 171
    Youth Garden, 116–117
vegetables, for shady conditions, 144
vermiculture. *see* worm composting
vetch, summer, 89
vines, 51

Virginia creeper, 51
volunteers, 139

W
Wagar, Bev, on guerrilla gardening, 78–80, 88
walls, plants for, 51
water conservation, 43
 and composting, 91
 and rain water collection, 74–75, 140
watering plants, 83, 140, 152
watershed, 41, 44–45
weather patterns, 42
weeds, 113–114, 142
wildlife habitat, 102, 103–104, 107–108, 114, 147
willow fencing, 105
Windsor Castle playground (Vancouver, BC), 168–169, 171
wine cups, 88
worm composting, 71, 160
Wuest, Tom, on Jacob's Well community garden, 171–173

Y
Yardas, Mark, on California poppy use, 132–134
Youth Garden (Vancouver, BC), 116–117

About the Author

David Tracey is a journalist and environmental designer based in Vancouver.

His reports on politics, the environment and culture have appeared in the *International Herald Tribune,* the *Economist,* the *South China Morning Post,* the *Globe and Mail,* CBC Radio, and many other places.

His company, EcoUrbanist, specializes in ecological landscape design and tree care. He also serves as Executive Director of Tree City, an engaged ecology group helping citizens plant and care for the urban forest.

If you have enjoyed *Guerrilla Gardening* you might also enjoy other

BOOKS TO BUILD A NEW SOCIETY

Our books provide positive solutions for people
who want to make a difference. We specialize in:

Environment and Justice • Conscientious Commerce • Sustainable Living
Ecological Design and Planning • Natural Building & Appropriate Technology
New Forestry • Educational and Parenting Resources • Nonviolence
Progressive Leadership • Resistance and Community

New Society Publishers

ENVIRONMENTAL BENEFITS STATEMENT

New Society Publishers has chosen to produce this book on Enviro 100, recycled paper made with **100% post consumer waste**, processed chlorine free, and old growth free.

For every 5,000 books printed, New Society saves the following resources:[1]

33	Trees
2,971	Pounds of Solid Waste
3,269	Gallons of Water
4,264	Kilowatt Hours of Electricity
5,401	Pounds of Greenhouse Gases
23	Pounds of HAPs, VOCs, and AOX Combined
8	Cubic Yards of Landfill Space

[1]Environmental benefits are calculated based on research done by the Environmental Defense Fund and other members of the Paper Task Force who study the environmental impacts of the paper industry.

For a full list of NSP's titles, please call **1-800-567-6772** *or check out our website at:*

www.newsociety.com

NEW SOCIETY PUBLISHERS